THE
SOUTHERN
FOODWAYS
ALLIANCE
COMMUNITY
COOKBOOK

THE SOUTHERN FOODWAYS ALLIANCE COMMUNITY COOKBOOK

EDITED BY SARA ROAHEN AND JOHN T. EDGE

Published in association with
The Southern Foodways Alliance
at the Center for the Study of Southern Culture
at the University of Mississippi

THE UNIVERSITY OF GEORGIA PRESS Athens & London

Publication of this work was made possible, in part, by a generous gift from the University of Georgia Press Friends Fund.

Images are by Devin Cox.

Published by the University of Georgia Press
Athens, Georgia 30602
www.ugapress.org

Designed by Erin Kirk New
Set in Adobe Garamond Pro
Printed and bound by Kings Time Printing Press

The paper in this book meets the guidelines for
permanence and durability of the Committee on
Production Guidelines for Book Longevity of the
Council on Library Resources.

Printed in China

14   13   12   11   10   C   5   4   3   2   1

Library of Congress Cataloging-in-Publication Data
Roahen, Sara.
    The Southern Foodways Alliance community cookbook /
edited by Sara Roahen and John T. Edge.
        p.   cm.
    "Published in association with The Southern Foodways
Alliance at the Center for the Study of Southern Culture at
the University of Mississippi."
    Includes index.
    ISBN-13: 978-0-8203-3275-8 (hardcover : alk. paper)
    ISBN-10: 0-8203-3275-5 (hardcover : alk. paper)
    1. Cookery, American—Southern style. I. Edge, John T.
II. Southern Foodways Alliance. III. Title.
    TX715.2.S68R62 2010
    641.5975—dc22   2010011415

British Library Cataloging-in-Publication Data available

I daresay any fine recipe used in Jackson could be attributed to a local lady, or her mother—Mrs. Cabell's Pecans, Mrs. Wright's Cocoons, Mrs. Lyell's Lemon Dessert. Recipes, in the first place, had to be imparted—there was something oracular in the transaction—and however often they were made after that by others, they kept their right names. I make Mrs. Mosal's White Fruitcake every Christmas, having got it from my mother, who got it from Mrs. Mosal, and I often think to make a friend's recipe is to celebrate her once more, and in that cheeriest, most aromatic of places to celebrate in, the home kitchen.

EUDORA WELTY OF JACKSON, MISSISSIPPI

CONTENTS

Meet the Southern Foodways Alliance   ix

Foreword by Alton Brown   xi

Preface by John T. Edge   xiii

Acknowledgments   xvii

A TASTE   *What We Eat While We Cook*   1

1 GRAVY   *Where We Begin*   13

2 GARDEN GOODS   *Straight from the Dirt*   27

3 ROOTS   *A Sweet Potato Is Not a Yam*   51

4 GREENS   *From Collards to Mustards*   65

5 RICE   *Limpin', Hoppin', and Every Which Way*   81

6 GRIST   *Biscuits, Breads, and Other Grindstone Goods*   97

7 YARDBIRD   *Chickens and Eggs*   121

8 PIG   *From Snoot to Tail*   139

9 THE HOOK   *Pulled from Our Waters*   169

10 THE HUNT   *Deer Camp and Quail Lodge Cookery*   193

11 PUT UP   *Pickled, Brined, Jarred, and Canned*   207

12 CANE   *Sweet Stuff from the Banana Pudding Republic*   227

More about the Southern Foodways Alliance   259

Contributors   261

Index of Names   273

Index of Food   277

MEET THE SOUTHERN FOODWAYS ALLIANCE

The Southern Foodways Alliance, founded in 1999, is an institute of the Center for the Study of Southern Culture at the University of Mississippi. We document, study, and celebrate the diverse food cultures of the changing American South. We've recorded more than five hundred oral histories, from row-crop farmers to artisan ham curers. We've made more than twenty-five short films, documenting the lives of fried chicken cooks, bartenders, and cattlemen who raise grass-fed beef. We also publish books and magazines, mentor students, and stage six to eight events each year—symposiums and field trips and film festivals—that function as camp meetings for true believers in the cultural import of regional cookery and culture.

The SFA works to pay down debts of pleasure, earned over generations. In doing so, we set a common table where black and white, rich and poor— all who gather—may consider our history and our future in a spirit of reconciliation. Membership in the SFA is open to anyone. Regardless of his geographical status. No matter her biscuit technique. Even if—bless your heart—you put sugar in your grits.

FOREWORD   Alton Brown

Community cookbooks are a passion of mine. I've gathered a couple hundred prize specimens over the years, from all over the country. But I especially appreciate those published in the South, where I live, and where at some time or another every church, social club, utility, school, charity, and trade association, at least those trying to raise a buck, has published one.

In my experience, four attributes indicate authenticity:

First, such books must be spiral-bound or they are not to be trusted.

Second, all the recipes must be directly attributed to a member of the community. Food is mighty personal, and the sharing of a recipe, especially one that may have been polished and perfected through years of practice, is powerful medicine.

Third, community cookbooks must be truly democratic. Rarely do you feel the heavy hand of an editor on such tomes, which means they're honest if nothing else.

Fourth, community cookbooks convey a strong sense of place. That's no small feat in this age of global-international-world-pan-planet-fusion cuisine.

The book you now hold is a community cookbook. A very good one.

I have no idea how the folks at the Southern Foodways Alliance pulled it off. To come up with such culinary gold, they must have dug through countless shoe boxes, lock boxes, notebooks, and kitchen drawers. They must have sifted through piles of scraps, napkins, store receipts, and post cards. They must have tested recipe after scribbled recipe.

For all I know, they queried every cook in the South. What I am sure of is that each page herein delivers a strong sense of community; the contributions are from real people with real names; the collection is democratic, but with nary a sign of culinary chaos; and the food is just plain good.

And here's the best part, as far as I'm concerned: Regardless of whether it looks back into the past or ahead into the future, this book looks ever Southward.

PREFACE John T. Edge

Recently, a friend-of-a-friend dropped off two pasteboard boxes overstuffed with cookbooks. (One box, it seems important to note, was originally manufactured for a lettuce wholesaler.) The total haul was fifty books, maybe more.

Most were Southern in origin and published in the 1950s and 1960s. A few, heavy on brie and onion soup mix, were published in the 1970s and 1980s. All were, pursuant to Alton Brown's edict, spiral-bound. (Okay, some of those books were plastic tooth–bound, but that's philosophically the same thing. With that idea in mind, please note that the book you now hold in your hands is bound in a manner that is a tribute to, but not a direct replication of, those spiraled cookbooks of yore.)

Dog-eared and gravy-splattered, their margins scribbled with notes, their spines bulging with yellowed newspaper clippings and pastel index cards, those books were homely, in the best sense of that word. Which is why, of course, my colleagues and I descended on that box like so many locusts. We were somehow hungry. As if we had been waiting, all along, for the arrival of such a trove.

In a way, we had. At the Southern Foodways Alliance, we swear allegiance to community cookbooks. Such allegiance might as well be a job requirement for an organization like ours, dedicated to sharing tales of our region's vernacular culinary culture.

We read community cookbooks as informal histories of people and place told through recipes. And we read those recipes like short stories, as nuanced and economical slices of community life. By way of this book, we share a series of stories told on the farm, at the stove, at the table.

We hope that you recognize this compendium as a truly democratic effort. The idea was to assemble a book that is reflective of our broad membership in particular and the South we know and love in general.

Not all of these recipes come from born-and-bred Southerners. While the geographical South is traditionally defined as a swath of land running from east-central Texas up through Virginia, the region we know and love is unbound by geography.

We're not ones to define the South by race or ethnicity, either. Recent immigrants get their due in these pages and, in exchange, we get refried black-eyed peas. Situational Southerners belong here too, the sort of folks who come to New Orleans one year for Jazz Fest and never truly leave.

Our South reflects contradictions and contains multitudes. Our take on Southern food culture embraces the region's ongoing evolution. With that idea in mind, the goal here is straightforward: to publish a cookbook that reflects this large family of cooks and eaters, artisans and farmers, writers and thinkers.

Herein, we showcase complex recipes from home cooks and simple recipes from chefs. We recognize that community cookbooks, as published in years past, were never perfect. And we know that the same is true of our modern-day effort. We don't seek to showcase perfection. Instead, by way of this community endeavor, we celebrate everyday life.

Join us at the welcome table. As we pass bowls of collards, as we butter second biscuits, as we cadge pan-fried drumsticks, as we tell stories of the farmers who sustain us and the cooks who taught us how, we pay homage to the possibilities of time spent in the field, in the kitchen, and at the table.

This cookbook was a true collaboration. I had the pleasure of working with six colleagues:

Sheri Castle of Chapel Hill, North Carolina

Timothy C. Davis of Nashville, Tennessee

April McGreger of Chapel Hill, North Carolina

Angie Mosier of Atlanta, Georgia

Sara Roahen of New Orleans, Louisiana

Fred Sauceman of Johnson City, Tennessee

All work in the broad world of food. Sheri tested the recipes for the SFA, offering edits and converting weight and liquid-ingredient measures. She was indefatigable. Sara Roahen, a New Orleanian, served as the lead editor. She fretted over the regional distribution of contributors and the attribution of their recipes. Each of the others listed above led the compilation of three to four chapters of content.

Brett Anderson, a New Orleanian who laughs like a goose and cusses with real talent, warned us early in the process of developing this book that it wouldn't be easy. He said that we might better fix our sights on solving world hunger. He was right. It wasn't easy. But just try the stuffed pork chops on pages 155–56 or the creamed greens on page 70, and you'll know that our effort was worthwhile.

ACKNOWLEDGMENTS

The following folk also were indispensable collaborators:

ANN ABADIE, the longtime associate director of the Center for the Study of Southern Culture, earmarked funds for a center cookbook ten years back.

ALTON BROWN, an author and television personality, hipped America to culinary science by way of his show *Good Eats*.

GEORGEANNA MILAM CHAPMAN compiled many of the recipes that eventually made their way into this cookbook while a graduate student in the master's program in Southern studies at the Center for the Study of Southern Culture.

DEVIN COX began his career with the SFA as an undergraduate intern, honed the look of SFA materials over the past few years, and crafted the engravings herein.

MARCIE FERRIS, onetime president of the SFA board of directors, is recognized as the board member who catalyzed the book.

MELISSA BOOTH HALL grew up in Middlesboro, Kentucky, just a few hundred yards from the Cumberland Gap. She once made one thousand deviled eggs for an SFA event. She now serves as the SFA events maven.

BROOKS HAMAKER, a friend of the SFA, offered sage advice during early discussions of the cookbook and steered the collaborative toward some great recipes.

MARY BETH LASSETER, a south Georgia native, wrote a thesis on Elvis for her Southern studies master's degree from the University of Mississippi. She now serves as the SFA's associate director.

NICOLE MITCHELL, the University of Georgia Press director, has had the foresight to publish not only the *Southern Foodways Alliance Community Cookbook* but also the biannual Cornbread Nation series.

JULIE PICKETT, the SFA's newest employee, is a South Carolina native who came to us by way of a recommendation from oysterman Robert Barber of Bowen's Island, just outside of Charleston. She worked wonders as copyeditor and content juggler.

ERIKA STEVENS is the University of Georgia Press editor who whipped the manuscript (and at least one of the authors) into shape, doing Herculean work while maintaining a sense of humor.

AMY EVANS STREETER, the SFA's oral historian, has stood in pig lots in Cajun Country and on oyster skiffs in the Apalachicola Bay, collecting the stories behind the food.

A TASTE
WHAT WE EAT WHILE WE COOK

Nothing is so musical as the sound of
pouring bourbon for the first drink on a
Sunday morning. Not Bach or Schubert or
any of those masters.
—Carson McCullers, *Clock without Hands*

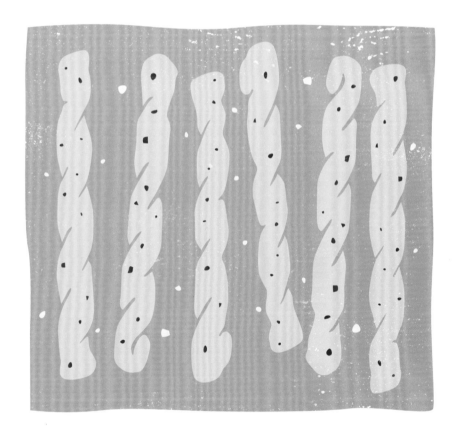

JUSTIN WILSON taught us that serious home cooks develop a thirst best quenched with a nip from the Burgundy bottle. We'd be as likely to sip a Sazerac, a julep, or homemade lemonade. Whether it's a cramped galley-style space in the city or an open affair with space for multiple generations, the kitchen is always the favorite place to entertain when company comes for dinner.

A lagniappe before the main event helps the cook maintain his or her momentum and keeps guests' fingers out of the cooking pots.

While you could simply crack open a can of boiled peanuts, we recommend whipping up a batch of Vance and Julie Vaucresson's super-easy hot sausage balls or frying up some peanuts à la Sean Brock. It may add some extra cooking time to your dinner party itinerary, but a hard-working cook deserves some quality sustenance, and guests will notice the difference.

Blue Ribbon Pimento Cheese

Red velvet cake, fried chicken, barbecue pork ribs, pimento cheese—these are among the iconic Southern dishes for which including just one recipe would be ridiculous, begging for controversy. Yet here we present the pimento cheese that won Nan Davis first place in our pimento cheese contest some years back—and the story of how she acquired her aunt's recipe: "I grew up in Coffeeville, just down the road from Oxford," says Nan Davis.

> My very special aunt Ella lived there her entire life and had a deep impact on the community until her untimely death in 1996. My brother, Hilly, could not say Aunt Ella when he started to talk and so he called her "Lella." It stuck, and eventually even people outside the family called her by that name. Lella was famous, and I do mean famous, for her pimento cheese. While other people prepared casseroles as a preferred "funeral" food, Lella would arrive with a huge platter of delicious pimento cheese sandwiches. One time I called Lella and asked how she made her sandwiches. She started with, "Well, first you make the mayonnaise." I interrupted her and said that I was not going to make homemade mayonnaise, just to give me the proportions on the cheese, pimentos, and spices. There was a long pause, and then she said, "Well, you might as well not bother."

Makes about 3 cups

20 ounces Cheddar cheese, grated (5 cups)
1 (4-ounce) jar whole pimentos, drained
½ to 1 cup Lella's mayonnaise, divided (recipe follows)

¼ teaspoon onion powder
¼ teaspoon ground cayenne pepper
¼ teaspoon Worcestershire sauce
Pinch of sugar

Place the cheese and pimentos in the bowl of a food processor fitted with a metal blade. Pulse to finely chop the pimentos. Add ½ cup of the mayonnaise and pulse to combine. Add the onion powder, cayenne, Worcestershire, and sugar and pulse to mix until smooth. The pimento cheese should be a solid color; the pimentos don't show. It should be the consistency of thick paste, but if it is too dry, add more mayonnaise and pulse to combine.

LELLA'S MAYONNAISE

Makes 1 cup

1 large egg
1 cup vegetable oil, divided
½ teaspoon dry mustard
¼ teaspoon onion powder

Pinch of ground cayenne pepper
½ teaspoon salt
1 tablespoon fresh lemon juice

Place the egg, ¼ cup of the oil, mustard, onion powder, cayenne, salt, and lemon juice in the bowl of a food processor fitted with a metal blade and process to blend. With the machine running, add the remaining ¾ cup of oil in a very slow, steady stream until the mayonnaise is thick. My processor is old, but the pusher in the food tube has a tiny hole in the bottom. (I don't know if they all do.) My sister-in-law, Libby Griffin, discovered this trick while learning to make Lella's mayonnaise. If you pour the oil into the pusher, oil dribbles into the mayonnaise while you are process-ing. Using this method, we never had the mayonnaise separate.

Nan Davis of Oxford, Mississippi

Benedictine: The Spread (Not the Liqueur)

Ari Weinzweig loves to unearth little-known recipes, so when he heard about Benedictine spread from Louisville, Kentucky, he immediately set to digging up the history, tracing it back to a caterer called Jennie Benedict, who wrote *The Blue Ribbon Cook Book*. "Over the last hundred years it's become to Louisville what pâté is to Paris or baked beans are to Boston," Ari says. "Benedictine is omnipresent at Louisville parties, where it's often served in the form of little finger sandwiches. It's great on bigger sandwiches too, often paired up with crisp slices of bacon."

Makes about 2 cups

1 large cucumber, peeled, seeded,
   and grated
10 ounces cream cheese, at room
   temperature

2 tablespoons grated onion
Coarse sea salt
Ground black pepper

Place the cucumber in a fine sieve set over a bowl. Place in the refrigerator to drain for 2 hours. Transfer the cucumber into the bowl of a food processor and discard the collected liquid. Add the cream cheese and onion; pulse to combine. Season with salt and pepper. Cover and refrigerate for at least 1 hour before serving lightly chilled.

Ari Weinzweig of Ann Arbor, Michigan

Cheese Boxes

Blair Hobbs adapted the recipe for these "greasy little appetizers" that taste like a baked version of cheese straws from a Chi Omega cookbook she dug out of her mother's closet. "These are great right out of the oven when the topping puffs up and would be great little trashy treats with tomato soup or a Bloody Mary," she says.

Makes about 24

8 ounces extra sharp Cheddar cheese, grated (2 cups)
4 tablespoons (½ stick) butter, at room temperature
2 tablespoons mayonnaise
1 tablespoon lemon juice
¼ teaspoon salt
¼ teaspoon ground black pepper
¼ teaspoon ground cayenne pepper
½ teaspoon dry mustard
Dash of hot sauce
1 large egg white, beaten to stiff peaks
1 loaf unsliced good white sandwich bread, crusts trimmed off, cut into 1½-inch cubes

Stir together the grated cheese, butter, mayonnaise, lemon juice, salt, pepper, cayenne, dry mustard, and hot sauce in a bowl until well mixed. Fold in the egg white. Coat the top and sides of each bread cube with the mixture, like frosting a little cake. Arrange the cubes about 1 inch apart on a baking sheet and refrigerate until the cheese is firm. Preheat the oven to 400°F. Bake until the cubes are puffed and browned, about 10 minutes. Serve hot.

Blair Hobbs of Oxford, Mississippi

Cheese Straws

"This venerable Southern classic is a standard for any hostess worth her iced tea," Damon Lee Fowler asserts with such confidence that we had to try his. While a traditional Southern cook would only use super-sharp orange Cheddar, for color and for flavor, sharp white Cheddar produces equally tasty straws. Extra grated Parmesan ups the sharpness quotient when only mild Cheddar is available.

Makes about 10 dozen

12 ounces well-aged, extra-sharp orange Cheddar, finely grated (3 cups)
4 ounces Parmigiano-Reggiano, finely grated (1 cup)
¼ pound (1 stick) unsalted butter, at room temperature

1 teaspoon ground cayenne pepper, or to taste
½ teaspoon salt
10 ounces (about 2 cups) Southern soft wheat flour or all-purpose flour

Put the Cheddar and Parmigiano-Reggiano into a large bowl. Add the butter and beat with an electric mixer until the mixture is fluffy. Whisk together the cayenne, salt, and flour in a bowl. Add the flour mixture to the cheese mixture and mix on low speed to form smooth dough. Wrap the dough well in plastic wrap and refrigerate until the dough is chilled but still pliable.

Position a rack in the center of the oven and preheat the oven to 325°F. To extrude the straws, put the dough in a cookie press fitted with a star die or in a pastry bag fitted with an open star tip. Squeeze out the dough into narrow 2½-inch straws on an ungreased baking sheet, leaving about a ½ inch of space between the straws. To roll and cut the straws, roll out the dough to a ¼-inch thickness on a lightly floured work surface. Use a sharp knife or a pastry wheel to cut the dough into ½-by-2½-inch strips. Transfer the strips to an ungreased baking sheet and gently twist each straw into a spiral. Alternatively, use small cookie cutters to cut the dough into seasonal or holiday shapes, such as autumn leaves, Christmas stars, Valentine hearts, and in Savannah, of course, St. Patrick's Day shamrocks.

Bake until the straws are firm and golden on the bottoms, but do not let them brown, 16 to 18 minutes. Carefully transfer to wire racks to cool to room temperature. Store in an airtight container.

Damon Lee Fowler of Savannah, Georgia

Blue Cheese Straws

Making cheese straws with anything but the sharpest of sharp Cheddars is risky. The flavor goes wrong, or the texture veers off, or the color tends too pale. But this recipe works. Steven Satterfield found inspiration for it in his love for fine Southern cheeses—not just Cheddar but also Georgia's Sweet Grass Dairy Asher Blue and the Clemson Blue made at Clemson University in South Carolina. He molds these in the shape of little shortbreads.

Makes about 6 dozen

1½ cups all-purpose flour
1 teaspoon kosher or sea salt, plus more
   for sprinkling
1 teaspoon ground black pepper

4 tablespoons (½ stick) unsalted butter
8 ounces blue cheese, crumbled
1 cup finely chopped pecans or walnuts
2 large egg yolks, slightly beaten

Stir together the flour, salt, and pepper in a medium bowl. Use a pastry blender or your fingertips to cut in the butter and cheese until the mixture resembles coarse crumbs. Stir in the nuts and egg yolks until the mixture forms large clumps. Press and knead the clumps until the dough is well mixed. (It will stay crumbly.) Divide the dough in half and shape each piece into a 9-inch log with round or flat sides. Wrap the logs tightly in plastic wrap and refrigerate for at least 2 hours and up to overnight.

When ready to bake, preheat the oven to 425°F. Line a baking sheet with parchment paper or a silicone baking mat. Cut the logs into ¼-inch-thick slices. Arrange the slices about 1 inch apart on the prepared baking sheet. Bake until golden brown, 8 to 10 minutes. Sprinkle the tops with salt. Place the pan on a wire rack and let the shortbreads cool to room temperature. They will firm up as they cool.

Steven Satterfield of Atlanta, Georgia

Spiced Pecans

Jessica Harris serves these spicy pecans to friends on her porch on Martha's Vineyard and in New Orleans, where she lives part-time. "They've got just enough heat to entice folks into another glass of champagne," she says. "The pinch of pimentón gives them a smoky flavor while a dash of cinnamon adds an exotic touch."

Makes about 2 cups

4 tablespoons (½ stick) unsalted butter
2 cups pecan halves
2 tablespoons packed light brown sugar
2 tablespoons coarsely chopped rosemary
  leaves
2 teaspoons Worcestershire sauce

2 teaspoons pimentón (smoked paprika)
1 teaspoon chili powder
1 teaspoon kosher salt
½ teaspoon hot sauce
¼ teaspoon ground black pepper
¼ teaspoon ground cinnamon

Line a rimmed baking sheet with parchment paper and set it aside. Heat the butter in a large skillet over medium heat. Stir in the pecans and cook, stirring constantly, until they are toasted, about 5 minutes. Add the brown sugar, rosemary, Worcestershire, pimentón, chili powder, salt, hot sauce, black pepper, and cinnamon and cook, stirring constantly, until the pecans are well-coated and fragrant, 1 to 2 minutes. Pour the pecans onto the prepared baking sheet and let cool to room temperature, stirring occasionally to break up any clumps. Store the pecans in an airtight container.

Jessica Harris of Brooklyn, New York

Boiled Peanuts

South Louisianans boil peanuts with Tabasco mash; others throw in crab boil. Some fans prefer them warm; others demand that they be chilled. John Martin Taylor uses only freshly dug "green" Valencia peanuts in season (July to September) and prepares them as simply as possible. You may start with dried peanuts, he says, but their magic is lost.

Makes 8 servings

3 quarts water
3 tablespoons salt

3 pounds (8 cups) freshly dug green
  peanuts in the shell, preferably
  Valencia

Bring the water and salt to a low boil in a large pot over medium heat. Add the peanuts and cook to your liking, 1 to 2 hours. I like the shell to become soft enough almost to be edible. Let the peanuts sit in the water off the heat until the desired degree of saltiness is reached.

John Martin Taylor of Washington, D.C.

Deep-Fried Peanuts

McCrady's Restaurant in Charleston, South Carolina, is old and full of dark wood and decanters of brown liquor. A bowl of peanuts sits on the bar, and the bartender instructs his customers to eat them whole, shell and all. They are crunchy and salty and spicy—perfect drinking food. And they are deep-fried—perfectly Southern.

Makes 8 to 12 servings

2 cups lard
2 cups peanut oil
1 pound green peanuts in the shells
1 to 2 tablespoons spice blend (recipe follows)

Heat the lard and oil in a deep pot or deep fryer to 350°F. Place the peanuts in a colander or frying basket and submerge in the hot oil until the peanut shells are crispy, 2 to 5 minutes. Drain well and toss the hot peanuts with spice blend to taste. Serve warm.

SPICE BLEND

Makes about ¾ cup

¼ cup chili powder
2 tablespoons hickory-flavored salt
1½ tablespoons onion powder
1 tablespoon ground cumin

1½ teaspoons paprika
1½ teaspoons garlic powder
1½ teaspoons packed light brown sugar
½ teaspoon ground cayenne pepper
¼ teaspoon dry mustard

Stir all ingredients together and store in an airtight container.

Sean Brock of Charleston, South Carolina

Hot Sausage Balls

Sausage was Vance Vaucresson's destiny. His grandfather was a butcher and his father, Sonny Vaucresson, turned to sausage-making as a specialty, supplying the first ever New Orleans Jazz and Heritage Festival with hot sausage po-boys. Vance describes his hot sausage–making technique as putting "more emphasis on seasoning rather than pepper." It's the overall seasoning of the product—a balance common to all Creole cooking—that's important. Home cooks may add more red pepper to taste to these New Orleans party staples.

Makes about 4 dozen

1 pound hot bulk pork sausage
8 ounces sharp Cheddar cheese, grated (2 cups), at room temperature
3 cups biscuit mix

Preheat the oven to 350°F. Place the sausage, cheese, and biscuit mix in a large bowl and mix by hand until well combined. Shape into 1-inch balls. Arrange the balls about 1 inch apart on ungreased baking sheets. Bake until cooked through and well browned, 12 to 15 minutes. Serve hot.

Vance and Julie Vaucresson of New Orleans, Louisiana

1

GRAVY
WHERE WE BEGIN

The most nourishing liquid in the world
is the gravy that fried ham gives up.
—Allan M. Trout, *Louisville Courier-Journal*

GRAVY implies a certain excess. And a certain economy.

Spread butter or jam on a biscuit and you better it. But ladle sawmill gravy on a biscuit, until the crown of that biscuit can barely be seen amid a pool of sausage-pocked gravy, and you transform that quick bread into a feed suited for plow hands (and plow-hand pretenders).

You could, of course, make the same transformative argument for a bowl of rice or mashed potatoes or grits or cornbread dressing. No matter. The addition of gravy, while appearing to be ancillary, is, in fact, defining.

The Southern way with gravies was born of privation. For the longest time, we were the poorest region of the United States. President Franklin D. Roosevelt dubbed the South "this country's number one economic problem." Owing to the South's antebellum adoption of unjust chattel slavery, not to mention our postbellum devotion to an unsustainable cotton monoculture, we have, until recently, sucked economic hind teat.

And when folks are poor, folks make do. Which means folks make gravy. The recipes that follow, by and large, are dishes born of privation. More to the point of a recipe book, they are dishes born of the marriage of fat and flour and liquid, of skillet stirring and innovation.

Gravy has many fans, but the best sermonizer is, without a doubt, Roy Blount Jr., a Georgia native now living in Massachusetts. As evidence of the meaning burbling beneath the surface of a skillet full of gravy, he cites the Memphis Minnie song "Selling My Pork Chops." The refrain is, "I'm selling my pork chops but I'm giving my gravy away." Says Roy, "Gravy is a personal expression of the soul. You can't sell gravy."

As you might expect, while Memphis Minnie provides the soundtrack for Roy's recollection, his mother did the work in his family kitchen:

My mother tended to make thinnish gravy, thin in terms of physical bulk and globbiness. Her gravy was never globby. You had no notion you were getting fat from it. But I guess you were. She also made wonderful beef stew with onions and potatoes and carrots. When she finished cooking it, little glistening, round grease circles floated on top of the gravy. Now that might sound off-putting, but I remember those glistening gravy circles as if they were little halos. The gravy somehow managed to be greasy yet light.

But there's a sad side to gravy. The terrible thing about gravy is it's so hard to get at all of it. It slips off into the corners. You can't get it with a spoon or a fork, so you've got to have something to sop it with. That's what white bread and cornbread were made for—sopping. But even then you can't quite get it all.

Breakfast Shrimp Gravy

In *Charleston Receipts*, that spiral-bound standard-bearer of the Lowcountry culinary scene, the Junior League ladies call this dish "Breakfast Shrimp." As offered by Mrs. Ben Scott Whaley (née Emily Fishburne), their receipt begins with bacon grease and gains color by way of a tablespoon of ketchup. Mrs. Whaley and friends serve their breakfast shrimp over grits. You should too. It's a simple coupling. Far simpler than the shrimp-and-grits dishes that now dot the menus of every third restaurant in the South. This recipe returns us to the days when shrimp and grits was a fisherman's dish, composed on the fly, with whatever happened to be on hand. So feel free to eliminate and substitute ingredients at will.

Makes 4 to 6 servings

1½ pounds small shrimp,
    peeled and deveined
Juice of 1 lemon
Hot pepper sauce
6 slices bacon, coarsely chopped
2 tablespoons finely chopped onion

½ cup chopped green onions
    (white and tender green parts)
2 tablespoons all-purpose flour
1 cup chicken stock, shrimp stock,
    or water
½ teaspoon salt

Toss the shrimp with the lemon juice and a few shakes of hot pepper sauce in a bowl. Let it sit while you start the gravy.

Fry the bacon in a large skillet over medium heat until browned but not crispy or hard. Stir in the onion and cook, stirring often, until softened, about 5 minutes. Stir in the green onions. Sprinkle the flour over the onion mixture and cook, stirring and scraping from the bottom of the pan until the flour lightly browns, about 5 minutes. Stir in the stock and salt and cook, stirring, until the gravy thickens, about 5 minutes. Stir in the shrimp and the accumulated liquid and cook until they are opaque, 3 to 5 minutes. Serve at once over hot, buttered grits.

Mary Beverly Evans Edge of Bowman, South Carolina

Butterbean Gravy

Consider that pot of butterbeans on the stove, the one that's been on the back burner for the better part of an afternoon. Take note of how those beans are turning creamy as they cook. See the ham hock bobbing in the pot? That hunk of pork is infusing those butterbeans with porky goodness, giving the beans, and the sauce soon to be made from them, a meaty base note that one usually associates with the introduction of demi-glace.

Jim Shirley is the man who divined butterbean gravy. He suggests serving it with pan-fried redfish.

Makes 4 to 6 servings

2 tablespoons extra-virgin olive oil
1 tablespoon chopped garlic
1 tablespoon chopped shallots
3 cups cooked butterbeans

4 cups clam broth or chicken stock
Salt and ground black pepper
3 fresh basil leaves, thinly sliced

Heat the oil in a large saucepan over medium-high heat. Stir in the garlic and shallots and cook, stirring often, until they soften, about 5 minutes. Stir in the butterbeans and heat through. Puree the butterbean mixture in a food processor fitted with a metal blade. Return the puree to the saucepan. Stir in the broth and cook over low heat until the gravy thickens, about 15 minutes. Season with salt and pepper. Stir in the basil. Serve hot.

Jim Shirley of Pensacola, Florida

Creole Red Gravy

Semantics. That's what we're talking here, for one person's tomato sauce is another's tomato gravy. And both taste great on pasta or meatballs, or on meatloaf, for that matter.

This recipe comes from Liz Williams, a New Orleans native of Italian extraction. Specifically, she's Sicilian, like many of the Italians who began arriving in New Orleans in the latter half of the nineteenth century in search of economic opportunity. Some came to work the sugar plantations west of New Orleans. Others made their way as peddlers who dominated the city's fruit and vegetable trade. Among the legacies of their arrival are totemic New Orleans eats like olive salads, muffalettas, and, yes, a New Orleans adaptation of Italian red gravy, which is built on a base of roux.

Makes 6 servings

¼ cup bacon grease
¼ cup all-purpose flour
1 medium onion, finely chopped
    (about 1½ cups)
1 garlic clove, minced
2 stalks celery, finely chopped
    (about ½ cup)

1 green bell pepper, finely chopped
    (about 1 cup)
1 teaspoon dried thyme
3 (15-ounce) cans tomato sauce
¼ cup finely chopped parsley
1 teaspoon hot sauce
Salt and ground black pepper

Heat the bacon grease in a large pot over medium-high heat. Whisk in the flour and cook, whisking constantly, until the flour is the color of café au lait, 5 to 7 minutes. Stir in the onion and cook, stirring often, until it begins to soften, about 5 minutes. Stir in the garlic, celery, bell pepper, and thyme. Cook, stirring occasionally, until softened, about 10 minutes. Stir in the tomato sauce. Reduce the heat, partially cover the pot, and simmer until thickened, about 1 hour. Stir in the parsley. Season with hot sauce, salt, and pepper. Serve hot.

Liz Williams of New Orleans, Louisiana

Tomato Gravy

Pervasive in Appalachia, where frugal cookery is foundational, this gravy is chunkier and more countrified than a New Orleans red gravy. It's also more likely to be poured atop biscuits or fried chicken than pasta.

Leftovers of tomato gravy make the beginnings of tomato soup, says Ronni Lundy, a native of Corbin, Kentucky, "created simply by adding ¾ cup milk and ¼ cup half-and-half. . . . Make sure you heat the milk and half-and-half mixture before adding them to the tomato mixture. If you heat them all together, you risk curdling the milk. That won't affect the taste, but it's less appetizing in appearance."

Makes 2 to 4 servings

4 thick slices bacon, chopped
½ cup finely chopped sweet white onion
2 cups peeled and chopped ripe tomatoes
   with their juice

1 teaspoon dried thyme (optional)
½ teaspoon salt
¼ teaspoon ground black pepper

Fry the bacon until crisp in a large skillet over medium-high heat. Transfer with a slotted spoon to drain on paper towels. Pour off all but 1 tablespoon of the bacon grease from the skillet. Stir in the onion and cook, stirring often, until it softens, about 5 minutes. Stir in the tomatoes and juice; cook, stirring frequently, until the tomatoes begin to bubble and the gravy thickens, about 5 minutes. Remove from the heat. Stir in the thyme. Season with salt and pepper. Serve hot over biscuits, meat, or vegetables, and top with the cooked bacon.

Ronni Lundy of Albuquerque, New Mexico

Country Ham with Redeye Gravy

Among the more spurious and entertaining stories about how this dish came to get its curious name is this myth: On a military campaign in the early 1800s, Andrew Jackson beckoned his camp cook and ordered breakfast. Evidently, just the night before, the cook had drunk deeply from a jug of corn whiskey. His breath was toxic, and his eyes were as red as fire. Jackson, who was known to take a nip, too, told the cook to bring country ham with gravy as red as the cook's eyes. Jackson's men adopted the descriptive coinage as their own.

   Tall tales aside, this gravy likely owes its name to the look of the quick-to-separate emulsion, a gravy that, when properly prepared, exhibits a telltale "red eye" at its center. Allan Benton, a ham and bacon curer of great acclaim, swears by the addition of brown sugar. That makes sense when you know that Allan cures his hams with salt, black pepper, cayenne pepper, and brown sugar, before aging them a year and a half or so.

Makes 2 servings

2 slices country ham, about ¼-inch thick
1 teaspoon vegetable oil, as needed

½ cup fresh, hot coffee, divided
1 tablespoon packed light brown sugar

Trim the fat from the ham slices. Put the fat in a large cast-iron skillet and set the ham aside. Cook the fat over medium heat until it renders, about 3 minutes. (If there isn't much rendered fat, add the vegetable oil.) Pour ¼ cup of the coffee into the skillet.

Add the brown sugar and stir until melted. Place the ham slices on top and cover the skillet with a lid. Cook over medium heat until wisps of steam come out from under the lid, then uncover and cook the ham until it is lightly browned.

Transfer the ham to a warm plate and keep warm. Discard any remaining pieces of fat. Add the remaining ¼ cup of coffee. Increase the heat to medium-high, and cook, stirring up from the bottom, until the gravy comes together and cooks down a little, about 2 minutes. Serve hot with the ham slices, as well as biscuits for sopping.

Allan Benton of Madisonville, Tennessee

Mississippi Madras Okra Gravy

Many Southerners believe that a love of okra begins and ends in the South. The truth is more complicated. Vishwesh Bhatt, a native of India, hails from a land where okra is revered. In the recipe that follows, he offers a taste of the emerging global South, fusing his birthplace and his adopted home of Mississippi, revealing that okra, the most totemic of Southern vegetables, travels well.

Makes 4 to 6 servings

3 tablespoons vegetable oil
1 pound okra pods, trimmed and halved
  lengthwise
1 teaspoon mustard seeds
1 small onion, finely chopped
  (about 1 cup)
1 teaspoon Madras curry powder

1 teaspoon ground turmeric
1 teaspoon ground cayenne pepper
1 teaspoon salt
1 garlic clove, slivered
1 large tomato, chopped
  (about 2 cups)
1½ to 2 cups chicken or shrimp stock

Heat the oil in a large, deep skillet over medium-high heat. Cook the okra, stirring often until nearly tender, about 5 minutes. Transfer to a plate and set aside. Add the mustard seeds to the skillet and cook, stirring constantly, until they toast. A few seeds might pop. Add the onion and cook, stirring often, until it softens, scraping up the browned glaze from the bottom of the pan. If the onion begins to scorch, add 1 or 2 tablespoons of water. Stir in the curry powder, turmeric, cayenne, and salt; cook for 1 minute. Stir in the garlic and tomato and cook for 2 minutes. Stir in the okra and enough stock to make the mixture the consistency of thin gravy. Cook until the gravy thickens slightly, stirring often, about 10 minutes. Serve at once over hot cooked rice.

Vishwesh Bhatt of Oxford, Mississippi

Oyster Gravy

Think oyster stew, reduced down until it doesn't coat the back of a spoon but clings there, and you've got an idea of what oyster gravy is like. Alex Young, a native of Great Britain and the chef at Zingerman's Roadhouse in Ann Arbor, Michigan, is an unlikely proponent of Southern cooking.

Yet the Zingerman's crew has been importing Apalachicola oysters to Ann Arbor since 2006. (Apalachicola Bay, home to one of the world's healthiest estuaries, is the source point for some of the nation's best oysters.) The recipe below approximates Alex's original. We say approximates because, in compiling the recipe, we appropriated a traditional ham-chocked oyster stew recipe, mixing it with Alex's simpler and more elegant oyster gravy. The reason? When we served the stew over biscuits, we served those biscuits alongside rashers of bacon and slices of ham, and we noticed that one out of three eaters crumbled in bacon or tore in ham.

Makes 4 to 6 servings

1 tablespoon butter
2 ounces country ham, coarsely chopped
¼ cup chopped leeks, white parts only
½ teaspoon minced garlic
1 cup heavy cream

1 pint shucked oysters with their liquor
¼ teaspoon salt
¼ teaspoon ground black pepper
2 tablespoons finely chopped flat-leaf
   parsley

Melt the butter in a large skillet over medium heat. Add the ham and cook, stirring often, until lightly browned, about 2 minutes. Add the leeks and garlic and cook, stirring often, until the leeks soften, about 8 minutes. Stir in the cream and cook until it reduces and thickens slightly, about 1 minute. Add the oysters with their liquor and cook only until the edges of the oysters begin to curl, 1 to 2 minutes. Remove from the heat. Season with salt and pepper. Stir in the parsley. Serve hot, ladled over hot biscuits or toast points.

Alex Young of Ann Arbor, Michigan

Roan Mountain Corn Gravy

This recipe can be traced to Carter County, Tennessee. That's where, in the early years of the twentieth century, the late Florence Graybeal perfected it.

More recently, her daughter, Margaret Propst, was the cook with her hand on the skillet full of corn gravy. In 2005, she passed away. Mrs. Propst worked as a teacher most of her life, instructing high school students, alternately, in chemistry and home economics. She reportedly served corn gravy for breakfast, lunch, and dinner, and she preferred white corn such as Silver Queen, although she occasionally fell back on yellow or even canned.

Makes 4 to 6 servings

4 large, fresh ears of white corn,
    preferably Silver Queen
½ cup tepid water
2 tablespoons sugar
½ teaspoon salt
¼ teaspoon ground black or white pepper
2 tablespoons butter
3 cups whole milk
4 tablespoons all-purpose flour
½ cup cold water

Cut the top halves of the corn kernels from the cobs into a large saucepan. Use the back of a knife or a small spoon to scrape the remaining corn and milk into the saucepan. If the cobs are juicy, squeeze the remaining milk into the pan as well. Stir in the tepid water, sugar, salt, pepper, and butter. Cook over medium heat until the corn is tender, about 5 minutes. Stir in the milk. In a small bowl, stir together the flour and cold water, mixing until smooth. Bring the corn mixture to a boil and gradually stir in the flour slurry. Cook, stirring, until the raw flour taste is gone and the gravy thickens, about 10 minutes. The gravy should be slightly thick, but not as thick as cream-style corn. Serve hot on top of homemade biscuits.

Margaret Propst of Roan Mountain, Tennessee

Sawmill Gravy

In Appalachia, you may hear this gravy called poor-do. As in, here's a dish by which the poor made do. This is a frugal gravy, no doubt about it. And it's found, in various iterations, throughout the South.

Although some theorize about how the black pepper and sausage crumbles resemble sawdust, it's more likely that gravies like this got their names in the lumber camps. It's a dish defined by and perfected for working-class Southerners, the sort of folks who earn their wages muscling logs into planers at sawmills.

This version, born of a more prosperous South, does not get all its flavor from the requisite scrape of the skillet. Perfectly good patties get crumbled in, too. But the heart and soul—and a goodly measure of the flavor—still come from those gnarled bits of meat and fat that cling tenaciously to the skillet surface and, upon being loosed by a fork or spatula, infuse this gravy with a caramely, almost ferrous resonance.

Makes 4 servings

8 ounces smoked breakfast sausage,
    either patties or bulk
4 tablespoons all-purpose flour

1 cup whole milk
½ teaspoon salt
¼ teaspoon ground black pepper

Brown the sausage in a large cast-iron skillet, breaking it into large clumps with the side of the spoon. Transfer with a slotted spoon to drain on paper towels. Pour off all but 3 or 4 tablespoons of the grease from the skillet. Stir in the flour, scraping up the browned bits from the bottom of the skillet. Cook, stirring constantly, until the flour is chestnut colored. Slowly stir in the milk and cook, stirring constantly, until the gravy thickens. Stir in the cooked sausage. Season with salt and pepper. Pour into a gravy boat or spoon directly over split and toasted biscuits.

Clinton Robinson of Gray, Georgia

Sopping Chocolate (a.k.a. Chocolate Gravy)

Southern cooking owes a deep debt to the farm. But it owes a debt to the country store too. That's where we bought white bread and hoop cheese and canned pimentos for pimento-cheese sandwiches. That's where this biscuit gravy was likely born, in the use of everyday indulgences, like soft white winter wheat trucked in from the Midwest and processed and powdered chocolate shipped in from the Northeast.

One taste of this gravy and you'll be inclined to compare it to the moles of Mexico. But that's not the place to look. Better to ponder the inventiveness of the cooks of the Appalachian South. After all, breakfast biscuits have always soaked up sweetness. Southerners have sopped sorghum syrup and cane syrup for generations.

One thing to know: While bacon grease would have been the traditional starter for a roux, most cooks now use butter or oil. We think the smoky punch of bacon grease adds a depth to the dish, one that butter or peanut oil can't quite claim.

Makes 4 to 6 servings

4 slices bacon, chopped
Butter, as needed
3 tablespoons self-rising flour

¼ cup cocoa powder
1 cup sugar
2 cups whole milk

Fry the bacon until crisp in a large cast-iron skillet over medium heat. Transfer with a slotted spoon to drain on paper towels. Pour off all but 6 tablespoons of bacon grease from the skillet. (If there are less than 6 tablespoons, make up the difference with butter.) Whisk together the flour, cocoa, and sugar in a small bowl. Sprinkle the flour mixture over the bacon drippings and whisk until the dry ingredients are moist. Slowly whisk in the milk. Increase the heat to medium-high and cook, stirring constantly, until the gravy thickens to the consistency of thin pudding, 5 to 8 minutes. Serve warm over buttered and toasted biscuits, topped with the cooked bacon.

John T. Edge of Oxford, Mississippi

GARDEN GOODS
STRAIGHT FROM THE DIRT

It may be poor for eating chips with,
It may be hard to come to grips with,
But okra's such a wholesome food
It straightens out your attitude.
—Roy Blount Jr., "Song to Okra"

EVEN WHEN COTTON was called "king" and the idea was to plant that cash crop on every slip of arable land, black and white people alike didn't—and wouldn't—stop growing vegetables. Southerners kept gardens, growing sweet potatoes, collards, corn. Some of the crops from cabin patches fed families who would have had, otherwise, to subsist on a rationed diet of side meat, cornmeal, and molasses. Other farmers raised a vegetable crop with an eye toward entrepreneurship.

Regardless of race, class, and economics, Southern food culture can't be separated from its agrarian heritage. It prizes connectedness to the land, hoping, always, to keep the distance from farm to fork a short one.

Take purple-hull peas, a humble relative of more fabled legumes, such as black-eyed and crowder peas. Buying preshelled purple-hull peas is a luxury. But it's a loss as well. Perhaps the greater luxury, in this day, is having the time to grow and shell your own. Nothing broadcasts the vital connectivity between the farm and the table like purple-stained thumbs. One bushel into a shelling session, we see our grand-parents' hands in ours. We are inspired by that connection. We believe that the peas that we harvested and shelled taste better than peas pulled from a plastic bag stored on a grocery shelf.

This isn't mere nostalgia. Homegrown vegetables from heirloom seeds in well-tended gardens enriched with manure from animals raised on the farm and with ashes from the woodstove are tastier and more nutritious than synthetic fertilizer–pumped vegetables. Today's hybrid seed varieties are chosen primarily on the basis of disease resistance, yield, ability to withstand transport, visual appeal, and shelf life.

Today, although many cherished vegetable varieties have been lost because they did not adapt well to commercialization or large-scale farming, things are changing for the better. A revival of interest in locally grown, regional goods is well underway.

We now remember that the harvest at our back door is the source of the richest, most pleasurable foods on earth.

Heirloom seed–saving organizations and small-scale, grower-only farmers' markets are on the rise: they provide the raw ingredients we need. What better way to retrieve the wealth of our grandparents' and great-grandparents' generations than by paying them homage through a pot of hand-shelled field peas?

Creamy Corn Pudding

Corn pudding is one of summer's great delicacies. Wrenched from the stalk, milked of its liquid, enriched with butter and eggs, a summer-picked ear of corn is worthy of a soufflé, which, of course, is where this recipe finds its inspiration. Sara Foster's version owes a debt to French technique, but like most good Southern cooks, she knows the real work is done in the fields, by farmers who know how to wrest the most sugar per kernel from Silver Queen and other beloved varieties.

Makes 6 to 8 servings

1 tablespoon unsalted butter, at room temperature
1½ cups fresh corn kernels (about 3 ears)
2 green onions, trimmed and finely chopped
½ cup diced red bell pepper
1 jalapeño chile, seeded and minced
1 tablespoon yellow cornmeal
2 tablespoons sugar

2 teaspoons chopped fresh marjoram or basil
2 teaspoons salt
1 teaspoon ground black pepper
1 cup half-and-half
5 large eggs, beaten
4 ounces sharp Cheddar cheese, grated (1 cup)

Preheat the oven to 350°F. Butter a 3-quart soufflé dish or deep casserole dish and set it aside.

Stir together the corn, green onions, bell pepper, jalapeño, cornmeal, sugar, marjoram, salt, and pepper in a large bowl. In another bowl, whisk together the half-and-half, eggs, and cheese. Stir the egg mixture into the corn mixture. Pour into the prepared dish and bake until puffy and light golden brown, about 1 hour. The pudding should be very moist and soft in the center. Let stand at room temperature for 5 to 10 minutes before serving warm.

Sara Foster of Durham, North Carolina

CREAMED CORN, as told by Jennie Sue Murphree of Batesville, Mississippi

Makes 6 servings

To make a skillet full, I am guessing at about 10 ears of corn. Shuck and silk the corn. Over a large bowl cut the corn off the cob by cutting a little off the top of the kernels and then scraping the remainder of the kernels and their milk off the cob with the back of your knife. Add a little water to the bowl to make the kernels and milk mixture soupy. Add about a tablespoon of sugar as well as salt and pepper and bacon drippings to taste. Pour in a skillet and cook down low. When corn is cooked, add a little butter. Sometimes I use yellow sweet corn, but most of the time I use what we grew, mostly white field corn.

Country Cooked Green Beans with New Potatoes

Buy green beans from the regular grocery store and you will likely find them to be of the stringless variety. (They're probably going to beanless as well, as far as flavor is concerned.) Speaking of the days when beans and strings were intertwined, Kentucky native Ronni Lundy said, "Ask anybody from the hills, and they'll tell you that a bean with strings beats a bean without on flavor anytime."

In the Appalachia of which Lundy speaks, localized seed-saving reflected idiosyncratic preferences in flavor and texture, and hundreds of varieties of beans resulted. But the story goes deeper than flavor and diversity. Grown in mountain soil, strung on back porches while workers indulged in iced tea and conversation, and canned around a community kettle, the string bean was the centerpiece in a network of connections to land, family, and community.

Makes 6 to 8 servings

8 cups (2 pounds) strung and broken green beans, such as Mountain White Half-Runner or Kentucky Wonder
4-ounce piece of salt pork, streak-o-lean, or white bacon

1 to 2 tablespoons salt
8 medium (2 pounds) new potatoes, scrubbed well, but not peeled

Place the beans in a large, heavy pot with a lid. Push the salt pork down into the center and cover the beans with cold water. Bring to a boil over high heat. Reduce the heat to medium-low, cover the pot, and simmer rapidly until the beans are tender, about 1 hour.

Check the pot occasionally and add water if the beans start to cook dry. Taste the bean broth and add salt accordingly, depending on how salty the seasoning meat is. Lay the new potatoes on top of the beans. Cover and simmer until the potatoes are tender, 20 to 30 minutes. Serve hot.

Ronni Lundy of Albuquerque, New Mexico

Crowder Peas with Potlikker

Crowder peas are legumes, also known as field peas and cowpeas. It seems likely that they get their name from how they're crowded in the pod. Crowder peas generally tend to be fatter than most peas and darker in color. Some are speckled. They produce a rich, dark potlikker, for which they are prized. Kathy Starr, a Mississippi-born cook, cooks her crowder peas with a handful of fresh okra, plenty of seasoning meat, and a touch of sugar.

Although this recipe is straight out of the Delta, crowder pea potlikker is beloved elsewhere. In eastern North Carolina, cooks use the broth to make cornmeal dumpling batter—and also as a dumpling cooking medium. (See page 112 for Flavius B. Hall Jr.'s cornmeal dumplings.)

Makes 8 servings

2 smoked ham hocks
14 cups water, divided
2 quarts hulled crowder peas or other
   similar field peas

Salt and ground black
   pepper
½ teaspoon sugar
6 fresh okra pods

Bring the hocks and 6 cups of the water to a boil in a large pot over high heat. Reduce the heat to medium-low and simmer for 90 minutes. Add the remaining 8 cups of water and the field peas. Simmer until the peas are tender, about 1 hour. Season with salt, pepper, and sugar. Lay the okra pods on top of the peas, but don't stir them in. Partially cover the pot and simmer until the okra is tender, about 15 minutes. Transfer the peas and okra with a slotted spoon into a serving dish and keep warm while the dumplings cook, if you choose to include dumplings.

Kathy Starr of Snellville, Georgia

Refried Black-Eyed Peas

As the Latino population in the South grows, it becomes more and more obvious that Southern cookery and Mexican cookery have much in common, including a reverence for corn, legumes, and all things porcine. In Atlanta, Mexico-born restaurateur Eddie Hernandez lets this synergy speak for itself through cross-cultural dishes such as these chorizo-spiked refried black-eyed peas.

Makes 6 to 8 servings

1 large tomato
1 jalapeño chile
½ cup plus 2 teaspoons vegetable oil, divided
½ cup diced onion

2 garlic cloves
8 ounces dry chorizo, finely chopped
6 cups cooked and drained black-eyed peas
Salt

Preheat the broiler. Rub the tomato and jalapeño with 2 teaspoons of the oil and place them on a baking sheet. Broil the vegetables, turning with tongs, until they are lightly charred all over. Cover with a towel and set aside until cool enough to handle. Core and coarsely chop the tomato, collecting the juices in a bowl. Scrape off the stem and charred jalapeño skin with the tip of a paring knife. Coarsely chop the jalapeño, discarding the seeds to reduce the heat, if desired. Puree the tomato, its juice, and the jalapeño in the bowl of a food processor fitted with a metal blade. Set aside.

Heat the remaining ½ cup of oil in a large, heavy skillet over medium-high heat. Add the onion and cook until it softens, about 8 minutes. Stir in the garlic and chorizo and cook until the chorizo renders its fat, about 5 minutes. Stir in the black-eyed peas and pureed tomato mixture. Cook until the peas start to break down, about 30 minutes, then mash some or all of the peas with the back of the spoon. Season with salt. Serve hot.

Eddie Hernandez of Atlanta, Georgia

Eggplant, Oyster, and Tasso Gratin

You are, no doubt, familiar with the so-called trinity of Louisiana cookery: onions, celery, and bell pepper. Susan Spicer of New Orleans, a self-described eggplant freak who cooks in an internationally inflected Creole style, has honed a new sort of trinity: eggplant, oysters, and tasso.

Here, tasso, an intensely flavored smoked pork of Cajun origin, serves as a seasoning, in the same way that a smoked pig trotter flavors a pot of greens. Although Spicer recommends that you serve scoops of this gratin as an appetizer, consider yourself warned: We have done the same. And no matter what we served to follow, it paled in comparison. Your guests might be happier with a large helping of this Creolized casserole and a salad.

Makes 4 to 6 servings

1 pint shucked oysters with their liquor
2 tablespoons butter
2 tablespoons flour
½ cup chicken stock or milk
½ cup cream
Salt and ground black pepper
Hot sauce
Pinch of freshly grated nutmeg
½ cup extra-virgin olive oil
1 small eggplant, peeled and diced
　(about 2 cups)
1 medium onion, chopped

2 ounces finely chopped tasso
　(about 3 tablespoons)
1 garlic clove, minced
1 teaspoon chopped fresh sage
1 teaspoon chopped fresh rosemary
½ cup dry bread crumbs
2 tablespoons chopped parsley
1 tablespoon butter, melted
2 tablespoons olive oil
2 ounces Grana Padano or Parmesan
　cheese, grated (¼ cup)

Preheat the oven to 400°F. Butter a 2-quart baking dish and set aside.

Pour the oysters into a bowl and check for bits of shell. Strain the oyster liquor through a fine sieve into a small bowl and set aside. Set drained oysters aside in a small bowl.

Melt the butter in a small saucepan over low heat and whisk in the flour. Whisk in the reserved oyster liquor and stock. Increase the heat to medium-high and bring the mixture to a boil, whisking constantly. Whisk in the cream. Reduce the heat to medium-low and simmer gently, stirring from time to time, until the sauce thickens, about 10 minutes. Season the sauce with salt, pepper, hot sauce, and nutmeg. Remove the pan from the heat and cover to keep the sauce warm.

Heat the extra-virgin olive oil in a medium skillet over medium-high heat. Add the eggplant and cook, stirring often, until lightly browned, about 5 minutes. Stir in the onion, tasso, garlic, sage, and rosemary. Cook until the eggplant is tender, 5 to 7 minutes. Season with salt and pepper. Transfer the eggplant mixture into a colander to drain for 5 minutes.

Stir together the crumbs, parsley, melted butter, oil, and cheese in a small bowl and set aside.

To assemble the gratin, spread about one-third of the oyster liquor sauce in the bottom of the prepared baking dish. Spoon the eggplant mixture into the dish. Arrange the oysters in a single layer over the eggplant mixture and drizzle with the remaining sauce. Sprinkle the crumb topping over the entire dish. Bake until golden brown and bubbly, 10 to 15 minutes. Serve hot.

Susan Spicer of New Orleans, Louisiana

Okra and Butterbean Succotash

There is no separate botanical classification for butterbeans. Some Southerners have always thought of them as the huge, mushy white beans rehydrated from the dried form and sometimes called limas. Poor darlings. They have never had the pleasure of facing down a bowl full of tiny, fresh, green butterbeans. Nor have they known the joy of standing at the stove before a simmering pot of darker, meatier speckled butterbeans, trailing plumes of pork-scented steam.

Jessica Harris, whose recipe follows, knows beans. Butter and otherwise. She's not a native of the South, but like so many African Americans, she has family that claims deep roots in this place, which shows in her knowledge of Southern gardening, cookery practices, and the natural interplay of beans and corn, okra and tomatoes.

Makes 8 to 10 servings

1 tablespoon bacon drippings or
    vegetable oil
3 cups chopped onion
2 cups fresh corn kernels
3 cups peeled, seeded, and coarsely
    chopped ripe tomatoes

1 cup shelled fresh butterbeans
4 cups ½-inch rounds of okra
Salt and ground black pepper
Pinch of sugar

Heat the drippings in a large heavy saucepan over medium-high heat. Add the onion and cook, stirring often, until it softens, about 8 minutes. Stir in the corn, tomatoes, butterbeans, and okra. Cover with water. Season with salt, pepper, and sugar. Bring to a boil, reduce the heat, and simmer until the vegetables are tender, about 30 minutes, stirring from time to time. Serve hot.

Jessica Harris of Brooklyn, New York

Stuffed Mirliton

Mirlitons are pale green members of the gourd family. They resemble pears and have puckered bottoms. Outside of Louisiana, you'll likely find them marketed by their Spanish name, chayote. Mirliton flesh is distinctively refreshing, like a cross between a cucumber and summer squash with a hint of apple. Mirlitons play well with seafood.

Here, we stuff mirlitons in the Creole-soul style of Austin Leslie, renowned fry cook and restaurateur, who died of a heart attack on September 27, 2005, at age seventy-one, during the grueling aftermath of the levee failures that followed Hurricane Katrina.

Makes 6 to 12 servings

6 medium mirlitons
½ pound (2 sticks) butter, divided
2 cups finely chopped onion
⅓ cup finely chopped parsley
⅓ cup finely chopped green bell pepper
3 garlic cloves, finely chopped
1 teaspoon fresh thyme leaves
2 bay leaves

1½ pounds fresh shrimp, peeled, deveined, and cut into bite-sized pieces
5 ounces ham, diced
8 ounces crabmeat, picked over
Salt and ground black pepper
Hot sauce
2 large eggs, lightly beaten
2 cups coarse fresh bread crumbs, divided

Preheat the oven to 375°F. Bring a large saucepan of generously salted water to a boil. Add the mirlitons and cook until they are tender enough to pierce with the tip of a sharp knife, about 25 minutes. Drain well. When cool enough to handle, cut the mirlitons in half lengthwise and discard the pits. Use a small spoon to scoop out the flesh, leaving a ¼-inch-thick shell. Arrange the shells in a baking dish just large enough to hold them upright and set aside. Dice the flesh, transfer it into a large bowl, and set aside.

Melt ¼ pound plus 4 tablespoons (1½ sticks) of the butter in a large skillet over medium heat. Add the onion, parsley, bell pepper, garlic, thyme, and bay leaves and cook, stirring often, until the vegetables soften, about 10 minutes. Stir in the shrimp, ham, and crabmeat; cook over low heat, stirring often, until the shrimp are barely opaque, about 5 minutes, then pour into the bowl of diced mirlitons. Mix well and season with salt, pepper, and hot sauce. Add the beaten eggs and stir vigorously to mix well. Stir in 1½ cups of the bread crumbs.

Spoon the stuffing into the mirliton shells, mounding it high. Sprinkle with the remaining ½ cup of bread crumbs and dot with the remaining 4 tablespoons (½ stick) of butter. Bake until the stuffing is golden brown, 20 to 25 minutes. Serve hot, although they are insanely good when eaten cold standing in front of an open refrigerator late at night.

Austin Leslie of New Orleans, Louisiana

Summer Squash Soufflé

At the height of summer, squash is omnipresent in the South. Farmers often have a hard time selling crooknecks, because everyone seems to be growing their own. No family reunion or church supper table is complete without squash casserole. Some versions rely heavily on binders of canned cream soups. And sour cream. Too bad. Too many fillers and you mask the delicate flavor of the squash. This recipe keeps it simple, allowing the squash flavor to shine. The texture is light. And puffy. As it sits, the casserole deflates, becoming denser and more custardy, which, in the grand scheme of things, is not at all a bad development.

Makes 6 to 8 servings

3 pounds yellow summer squash, trimmed and roughly chopped
1 medium onion, chopped (about 1½ cups)
Salt and freshly ground pepper

4 saltine crackers, crushed
4 tablespoons (½ stick) butter, melted
2 large eggs, separated
1¼ ounces Cheddar cheese, grated (⅓ cup)

Preheat the oven to 350°F. Butter a 2-quart baking dish and set it aside.

Using a steamer or a pasta pot with a built-in strainer, steam the squash and onion until completely tender but not waterlogged. Drain well and transfer into a large bowl. Mash to a coarse puree with a handheld potato masher or a fork. Season with salt and pepper. Stir in the cracker crumbs, butter, egg yolks, and cheese.

Whip the egg whites to stiff peaks in a bowl. Gently fold the whites into the squash mixture with a rubber spatula. Scrape the batter into the prepared baking dish. Bake until set and lightly browned on top, about 30 minutes. Serve hot.

Grace Riley of Decatur, Alabama, by way of Amy Evans Streeter of Oxford, Mississippi

Cushaw Griddle Cakes

John Coykendall, of Blackberry Farm in the foothills of the Great Smoky Mountains, grows cushaw using the Cherokee Three Sisters method of intercropping corn, pole beans, and squash. The cornstalks support the bean vines; the beans fix nitrogen into the soil, fertilizing the corn; and the squash sprawl underneath, shading the corn roots, trapping moisture, and keeping weeds to a minimum. This recipe, he says, "is an old-time winter favorite, cooked on a wood-burning stove and eaten by the light of coal oil lamps and a hot fire in the fireplace." He recommends serving the griddle cakes with fried pork chops and tomato gravy.

Makes 6 to 8 servings

4 cups cushaw puree (recipe follows)
4 tablespoons (½ stick) butter, at room
    temperature
Salt and ground black pepper

2 teaspoons baking powder
¼ to ½ cup all-purpose flour
Pan drippings, butter, or oil,
    for frying

Stir together the cushaw and butter in a bowl. Season with salt and pepper. Stir in the baking powder and enough flour to make dough stiff enough to form into small cakes, about like biscuit dough. Shape the dough into cakes about 3 inches across and ½-inch thick. If they don't hold together, dust the outsides with a little more flour, but use no more than necessary so that they won't get gummy.

Heat the drippings in a large cast-iron skillet over medium-high heat. Working in batches to avoid crowding the pan, cook the cakes until golden brown, about 3 minutes per side. Serve hot.

ROASTED CUSHAW PUREE

Each pound of cushaw yields about ½ cup of puree

8 to 10 pounds cushaw
Vegetable oil, for brushing

Preheat the oven to 375°F. Cut the cushaw into large wedges and scrape away the seeds and fibers. Place the wedges cut side up on a rimmed baking sheet or inside a roasting pan. Brush the cut surfaces with oil. Roast until the flesh is very soft, about 1 hour. When the cushaw is cool enough to handle, use a spoon to scrape the roasted flesh away from the skin. Working in batches, puree the pulp with a food mill or in a food processor.

To be suitable for recipes, the finished puree must have the smooth, thick consistency of canned pumpkin. Most fresh pulp needs to be drained, so transfer it into a large sieve lined with a double thickness of white paper towels or overlapping large paper coffee filters set over a large bowl. Press a piece of plastic wrap directly onto the surface of the puree to keep it from drying out and refrigerate at least 8 hours. Discard the accumulated liquid. Use the puree within 3 days or freeze in airtight containers for up to 3 months.

John Coykendall of Walland, Tennessee

Macaroni and Cheese

Walk into just about any meat-and-three in the South and macaroni and cheese is one of the three. Without irony, without a wink and a nod, it's considered, by meat-and-three operators, to be a vegetable. Thus its presence in this chapter.

Ari Weinzweig, a Midwesterner who, by way of his work, has fallen hard for the South, offers this childhood favorite, modified. "Although I grew up on Kraft macaroni and cheese, this stuff is about eighteen thousand times better," he says. "It's amazing what happens when you use artisanally made macaroni and marvelously good farmhouse Cheddar instead of industrial noodles and cheese. I use an American farmhouse Cheddar that's at least a year old. The older the cheese, the better the dish."

Makes 6 servings

1 tablespoon sea salt
1 pound uncooked macaroni
2 tablespoons butter
1 small onion, coarsely chopped (about 1 cup)
1 garlic clove, peeled and bruised with the side of a knife
1 four-inch sprig fresh thyme

1 four-inch sprig fresh rosemary
¼ cup dry white wine
2 tablespoons all-purpose flour
3½ cups whole milk
2 tablespoons Dijon mustard
Salt and ground black pepper
1½ pounds farmstead white American Cheddar cheese, grated (4½ cups)

Preheat the oven to 400°F.

Bring a large pot of water to a boil. Stir in the salt and the macaroni. Cook the pasta for about 10 minutes, until it is 3 minutes short of being done so that it won't get mushy in the oven. Drain and set it aside.

Melt the butter in a large heavy saucepan over medium-high heat. Add the onion, garlic, thyme, and rosemary and cook until the onion softens, about 5 minutes. Add the wine and cook until the liquid is nearly gone, about 3 minutes. Discard the garlic, thyme, and rosemary. Sprinkle the flour over the onion and cook, stirring constantly, for 2 minutes. Slowly add the milk, stirring constantly to avoid lumping. Stir in the mustard and season with salt and pepper. Simmer the sauce over medium heat, stirring constantly, until it thickens, about 3 minutes. Stir in 3 cups of the cheese, one handful at a time, letting each addition melt before adding more. Remove the pan from the heat. Taste and adjust the seasonings if necessary.

Stir the macaroni into the cheese sauce and mix well. Transfer into a 9-by-13-inch baking dish and top with the remaining 1½ cups of the cheese. Bake until the cheese is golden, about 25 minutes. Serve hot.

Ari Weinzweig of Ann Arbor, Michigan

MACARONI PUDDING, as recounted by Mary Randolph

Mary Randolph offers this recipe in the first edition of *The Virginia House-wife* cookbook, published in 1824. It must be one of the South's first for macaroni and cheese. Not incidentally, Randolph was a distant relative of the founding father and gourmet Thomas Jefferson, who is credited for bringing pasta to America. In her cookbook she includes general—and somewhat philosophical—tips for cooking puddings of all kinds. Here's one:

Promptitude is necessary in all our actions, but never more so than when engaged in making cakes and puddings.

Simmer half a pound of maccaroni in a plenty of water, with a table-spoonful of salt, till tender, but not broke—strain it, beat five yelks, two whites of eggs, half a pint of cream—mince white meat and boiled ham very fine, add three spoonsful of grated cheese, pepper, and salt; mix these with the maccaroni, butter the mould, put it in and steam it in a pan of boiling water for an hour—serve with rich gravy.

Fried Green Tomatoes and Shrimp Rémoulade

It's a simple dish, really, this combination of two iconic and exalted Southern foods. The taste relies on contrasts: Hot, crunchy, cornmeal-dredged fried green tomatoes, born of the rural and resourceful farming tradition. Cool, creamy, spicy, luxuriant New Orleans shrimp rémoulade, born of Uptown, New Orleans. When JoAnn Clevenger first put it on the menu at her Upperline Restaurant in New Orleans, she codified a modern classic. This version comes from Ken Smith, who spent summers on his grandparents' Natchitoches, Louisiana, farm.

Makes 6 servings

SHRIMP

4 quarts water
2 tablespoons seafood seasoning blend
Dash of hot sauce
Juice of 1 lemon

Salt and ground black pepper
36 large shrimp in their shells
  (about 2 pounds)

RÉMOULADE

½ cup Creole or other coarse mustard
⅓ cup ketchup
1 tablespoon prepared horseradish
1½ teaspoons fresh lemon juice
1½ teaspoons paprika
½ teaspoon ground white pepper

¼ teaspoon ground cayenne pepper
⅓ cup extra-virgin olive oil
Salt
¼ cup chopped celery
1½ teaspoons chopped green onions

TOMATOES

4 large green tomatoes
1½ cups buttermilk
2 cups corn flour or fine cornmeal

2 tablespoons kosher salt
2 teaspoons ground black pepper
Vegetable oil, for frying

6 small handfuls of mesclun salad greens

To make the shrimp: Pour the water into a large pot. Add the seasoning blend, hot sauce, lemon juice, salt, and pepper and bring to a boil. Remove the pot from the heat, add the shrimp, and stir gently until the shrimp are opaque, 1 to 2 minutes. Drain the shrimp, rinse under cool running water to stop the cooking, and drain again. Peel and devein the shrimp. Transfer into a bowl, cover, and refrigerate until chilled, at least 30 minutes.

To make the rémoulade: Stir together the mustard, ketchup, horseradish, lemon juice, paprika, white pepper, and cayenne in a bowl. While whisking vigorously, add the oil in a slow, steady stream. Season with salt and additional cayenne pepper, if needed. Stir in the celery and green onions. Cover and refrigerate until chilled, at least 30 minutes.

To make the tomatoes: Cut three ½-inch thick slices from the center of each tomato, for a total of 12 slices. (Discard the rest of the tomatoes or save for another use.) Put the slices in a large bowl, add the buttermilk, and turn the slices to make sure they are well coated. Set aside for 5 minutes. Mix the corn flour, salt, and pepper in a wide, shallow bowl.

Pour oil into a large, heavy skillet to a depth of 2 inches. Heat the oil to 325°F. Working in batches, remove the tomatoes from the buttermilk and let the excess drip off. Coat the tomatoes in the corn flour mixture and gently shake off the excess. Slip the coated tomatoes into the hot oil and fry until golden brown, turning once, about 2 minutes per side. Drain on paper towels.

To assemble the dish: Divide the greens among 6 serving plates. Top with the tomatoes, shrimp, and rémoulade. Serve at once.

Ken Smith of New Orleans, Louisiana

Tomato and Watermelon Salad

In the steamy heat of a Southern summer, it may be impossible to improve on thick, juicy slabs of homegrown tomatoes and ice-cold wedges of sweet, crisp watermelon. But we're hell-bent on trying. Truth be told, this refreshing salad is the perfect solution for what to do when—early in the season—you crack open a rattlesnake melon and find that the flesh is somewhere short of ethereal.

Makes 4 to 6 servings

5 cups ripe, bite-sized chunks of
   watermelon, mostly seeded
1½ pounds very ripe tomatoes, seeded
   and cut into ½-inch dice
3 teaspoons sugar
½ teaspoon salt

1 small red onion, quartered
   and thinly sliced
½ cup red wine vinegar
½ cup strongly flavored extra-virgin
   olive oil

Toss the melon and tomatoes with the sugar and salt in a large bowl. Let sit at room temperature for 15 minutes. Gently fold in the onion, vinegar, and oil. Cover and refrigerate until very cold. Serve chilled.

Bill Smith Jr. of Chapel Hill, North Carolina

Tomato Pie

Store-bought mayonnaise, sharp Cheddar sold in shrink-wrapped sleeves, and Ritz crackers straight from the box. Depending on your perspective, these are either beloved Southern ingredients or totems of what's gone wrong with home cooking, of compromises made in the name of serving home-cooked meals to busy modern families.

In the recipe that follows, Billy Reid, a native of Amite, Louisiana, reclaims the tomato pie, layering on homegrown tomatoes and using good-quality Cheddar cheese.

Makes 1 nine-inch pie, or 6 to 8 servings

1½ pounds fresh vine-ripened tomatoes, cut into ¼-inch-thick slices
½ teaspoon salt
2 tablespoons fresh thyme leaves or 12 fresh basil leaves
8 slices bacon, cooked crisp and crumbled
1 nine-inch pie shell, prebaked until golden and cooled to room temperature

2 tablespoons extra-virgin olive oil
Salt and ground black pepper
3 ounces sharp Cheddar cheese, grated (¾ cup)
¾ cup mayonnaise
⅓ cup of ¾-inch crumbles of buttery crackers (such as Ritz)

Preheat the oven to 350°F.

Arrange the tomato slices in a single layer on a wire rack lined with paper towels. Sprinkle the tomatoes with salt and let drain for at least 10 minutes. Layer the drained tomatoes, thyme, and bacon in the pie shell. Drizzle with oil and season with salt and pepper. Stir together the cheese and mayonnaise in a small bowl and spread evenly over the filling. Sprinkle the crushed crackers over the top.

Bake until the top of the pie is nicely browned, about 30 minutes. Let cool for at least 10 minutes before slicing and serving warm or at room temperature.

Billy Reid of Florence, Alabama

Skillet-Fried Okra

Thickly sliced, battered, and deep-fried has become the okra norm. Tasty it may be, but even the best fry-basket okra cannot hold a candle to this simple home version, which you'll find slow-frying (or sautéing) in well-seasoned cast-iron skillets across the South. Some Southerners so love this style of fried okra that they freeze bags of sliced okra tossed in seasoned cornmeal, so that all winter the soulful taste of perfect summer remains at hand.

One quick note: When cooking, be patient. You want the okra to brown over moderate heat. Don't worry about the burned pieces: Folks will fight over them.

Makes 1 to 4 servings

1 pound small, tender okra pods, stem
   ends trimmed
½ cup cornmeal
1 teaspoon kosher salt

½ teaspoon ground black pepper
½ cup bacon drippings, peanut oil,
   shortening, or extra-virgin olive oil

Cut the okra into thin rounds about ¼-inch thick. Transfer into a colander and rinse well under cool running water and set aside to drain. Stir together the cornmeal, salt, and pepper in a large bowl. Heat your chosen fat in a 12-inch cast-iron skillet over medium-high heat. Add the wet slices of okra to the cornmeal mixture and toss to coat evenly. Add the okra to the hot fat and cook, stirring gently every minute or so, until the okra is tender and dark brown, about 10 minutes. Reduce the heat if the okra is getting brown too quickly. A few pieces will burn, but they turn out to taste the best. The cornmeal will fall off a good deal of the okra. Transfer the okra with a slotted spoon to drain on a plate lined with a brown paper bag or paper towels. Taste and add more salt or pepper if needed. Try not to make a pig of yourself.

Walter Murphree of Batesville, Mississippi

Okra Tempura

Edward Lee, a Brooklyn native of Korean ancestry, fell for Louisville, Kentucky, when visiting a friend on Derby Day. As a staunch supporter of the farm-to-table agricultural movement, Lee was impressed by Kentucky's rich array of growers and soon found himself there permanently. Here, he swaddles tiny baby okra in a light and crunchy batter for a worldly twist on an old favorite. You can also use the batter to experiment with other vegetables, such as tiny crookneck squash, spring onions, green beans, and asparagus.

Makes 4 servings

1 cup all-purpose flour	2 cups soda water or club soda
⅔ cup cornstarch	Corn oil, for frying
1 teaspoon baking powder	1 pound tender okra pods, trimmed and
¼ teaspoon salt	halved lengthwise
2 large egg yolks	

Sift together the flour, cornstarch, baking powder, and salt into a bowl. Whisk in the egg yolks. Slowly add the soda water, whisking vigorously to make batter the consistency of pancake batter. Set aside.

Pour oil into a large, heavy pot to a depth of 2 inches. Heat the oil to 350°F. Working in batches, coat the okra in the batter and let the excess drip off. Gently lower the okra into the hot oil. Fry until golden, about 2 minutes. Transfer with a slotted spoon to drain on paper towels. Fry the remaining okra, letting the oil return to 350°F between batches. Serve hot.

Edward Lee of Louisville, Kentucky

Vegetable Soup

Every day Hal White makes a soup from scratch at his neighborhood restaurant and bar in downtown Jackson, Mississippi. His waitstaff tries to guess the ingredients of his flavorful and intricate soups. That is quite a challenge because Hal's soup theory is from the everything-but-the-kitchen-sink school. What's so Southern about vegetable soup? Just check Hal's ingredient list for that most favored of Atlanta, Georgia, products: Coca-Cola.

Feel free to throw in a ham bone or some stew meat if you want a richer, meatier soup, but no matter how you tweak it, be sure to serve it with some hot, crispy cornbread.

Makes 2 quarts, or 8 servings

4 tablespoons (½ stick) butter
½ cup chopped onion
½ cup chopped celery
1 teaspoon seasoned salt
1 teaspoon dried basil
¼ teaspoon dried oregano
¼ teaspoon dried marjoram
¼ teaspoon dried dill
Pinch of crushed red pepper flakes
¼ teaspoon ground allspice
¼ teaspoon paprika
3 cups chicken stock
½ cup Chablis or other dry white wine

2 cups v8 juice
1 or 2 good glugs of Coca-Cola (about
    1/3 cup)
2 tablespoons chopped parsley
1 (15-ounce) can diced tomatoes
3 cups chopped cabbage
1 cup chopped potatoes
½ cup sliced mushrooms
4 cups assorted chopped vegetables (such
    as snap beans, corn, peas, butterbeans,
    carrots, okra)
Salt and ground black pepper

Melt the butter in a large, heavy pot over medium-high heat. Add the onion and celery and cook, stirring often, until they soften, about 8 minutes. Stir in the seasoned salt, basil, oregano, marjoram, dill, red pepper flakes, allspice, and paprika; cook, stirring constantly, for 1 minute. Stir in the stock, wine, juice, and Coke and cook for 1 minute, stirring up any bits from the bottom of the pot. Stir in the parsley, tomatoes, cabbage, potatoes, mushrooms, and assorted vegetables. Bring just to a boil, reduce the heat to low, and simmer, partially covered, until all of the vegetables are tender, 30 to 40 minutes. Season with salt and pepper. Serve hot.

Hal White of Jackson, Mississippi

Peanut Soup

The tenured clientele at the Jefferson Hotel in Richmond, Virginia, expect there always to be peanut soup on the menu. It's part of the hotel's history. This recipe is a decades-long collaboration of the hotel's many chefs. One of them, James Schroeder, grew up in a family of eight that dined together. "Soup frequently made its way to the table. Any time we prepare a regional soup at the hotel it takes me right back to our family dinners."

Makes about 2 quarts, or 8 servings

4 tablespoons (½ stick) butter
½ cup finely chopped Vidalia onion
½ cup finely chopped celery
½ cup finely chopped carrot
2 tablespoons all-purpose flour
1 cup hazelnut liqueur, such as Frangelico

1½ cups chicken stock
1 cup creamy peanut butter
¼ cup roasted Virginia peanuts, shelled
2 cups heavy cream
Salt and ground white pepper

Melt the butter in a large saucepan over medium heat. Stir in the onion, celery, and carrot and cook, stirring occasionally, until the vegetables soften, about 5 minutes. Sprinkle the flour over the vegetables and cook, stirring, for 2 minutes. Add the liqueur and cook, stirring, until the mixture is smooth and thick, about 5 minutes. Add the stock, peanut butter, and peanuts and stir, until smooth and hot. Stir in the cream and heat through, but do not let the soup boil. Working in batches, puree the soup in a blender and strain through a fine mesh sieve. Season with salt and white pepper. Serve warm.

Walter Bundy and James Schroeder of Richmond, Virginia

Cranberry Congealed Salad with Poppy Seed Dressing

Sheri Castle protested when she saw that this cookbook might go to press with nary a mention of Jell-O. Downright un-Southern, she said, and we agreed. "I was raised to expect congealed salad on the holiday table," she said. "My husband was raised to expect a can of sauce extruded onto a plate. This combines both."

The dollop of poppy seed mayonnaise makes the dish and should never be skipped.

Makes 9 servings

2 (3-ounce) boxes lemon Jell-O
2 (3-ounce) boxes cranberry or
   cherry Jell-O
2 cups boiling water
1 cup crushed pineapple, well drained

1 (16-ounce) can whole-berry
   cranberry sauce
1 cup real mayonnaise (preferably
   homemade)
1 tablespoon poppy seeds

Dissolve the Jell-O in the boiling water in a large bowl. Stir in the pineapple and cranberry sauce and mix well, making sure the cranberry sauce dissolves. Pour the mixture into a pretty 9-inch-square glass or ceramic dish and refrigerate until set, at least 4 hours.

Meanwhile, make the dressing by stirring together the mayonnaise and poppy seeds in a small bowl. Cover and refrigerate.

To serve, cut the salad into squares and top each serving with a dollop of the poppy seed dressing.

Sheri Castle of Chapel Hill, North Carolina

3 ROOTS
A SWEET POTATO IS NOT A YAM

Draw over and dig
The loose ash soil
Hoe handles are short,
The sun's course long
Fingers deep in the earth search
Roots, pull them out; feel through;
Roots are strong.
—Gary Snyder, "Roots,"
 from *Regarding Wave*

WE SOUTHERNERS take comfort in our roots. This is especially true in tough times, when the economy fluctuates in synch with ever-inconsistent rain cycles. In tough times, of which the South has seen its fair share, we seek comfort where we can find it. We seek comfort in food.

Few foods offer as much comfort as roots—those tubers and such that incubate in the loam: potatoes, rutabagas, turnips, sweet potatoes, beets, parsnips, radishes, onions, garlic, and shallots, to name but a few.

Booker T. Jones, the Memphis musician famous for leading the Stax house band, dubbed his most recent album *Potato Hole*, a reference to slaves' practice of stowing away homegrown sweet potatoes—beneath the floorboards of a cabin, say—in an effort to lay by for the future, supplementing their diets and, maybe, earning a little money by peddling their produce to friends and neighbors. With every parsnip we pick, with every turnip we spade from the earth, with every sweet potato we pull from beneath the floorboard, we pull memories from below, roots from which the bright green shoots of the season grow.

Root vegetables aren't exactly glamorous. They're often best prepared simply: roasted, baked, pan fried, mashed, or pureed into soups. Lately, however, they're showing up on china plates, both Southern and otherwise, prepared by white-toqued chefs—as well as by home cooks, who, as we all know, are the beating heart of Southern cuisine.

Roots speak to an admittedly romantic idea: By planting a seed, we guard against our own obsolescence, making sure—by our hand, and by our god's will—that there will be something left for the next week, the next year, the next generation. Whether Germanic, Irish, or African in origin, these roots recipes speak to the cycle that sustains both the plants themselves and us, the lucky cusses who get to wolf them down.

Carrot Soup with Bourbon and Ginger

Live long enough in Louisville and the stereotypes take on a veracity of their own. Live long enough in Louisville and you start putting bourbon in everything. When Todd Richards took his turn in a hotel dining room there, he began spiking his carrot soup with two to three fingers of Kentucky's finest.

That might scare off the teetotaler, but the effect isn't much different than a splash of sherry in she-crab soup. That brown whiskey makes the soup sing without leaving the lucky diner soused.

Makes 2 quarts, or 8 servings

2 tablespoons extra-virgin olive oil
1½ pounds carrots, peeled and coarsely
    chopped (about 4 cups)
1 medium onion, coarsely chopped
2 teaspoons kosher or sea salt
¾ teaspoon ground white pepper
2 garlic cloves, minced
2 tablespoons freshly grated ginger

1½ cups plus 2 tablespoons Kentucky
    bourbon, divided
3 cups carrot juice
1 cup chicken or vegetable stock
1 bay leaf
2 teaspoons fresh thyme leaves
1 cup whipping cream

Heat the oil in a large heavy pot over medium-high heat. Add the carrots and onion and stir to coat. Season with salt and white pepper. Cook, stirring often, until the vegetables are completely soft and starting to caramelize, 15 to 20 minutes. Add the garlic and ginger and cook, stirring constantly, for 1 minute. Remove the pan from the heat and carefully pour in 1½ cups of the bourbon. Return the pot to the stove and cook, scraping up the browned glaze from the bottom of the pot, until the bourbon reduces to ¾ cup, about 10 minutes. Stir in the carrot juice, stock, and bay leaf and simmer for 20 minutes. Add the thyme and discard the bay leaf. Working in batches, puree the soup in a blender. Strain through a fine sieve back into the pot; discard the solids. Keep the soup warm over low heat.

Whip the cream and remaining 2 tablespoons of bourbon to soft peaks in a chilled bowl.

To serve, ladle the warm soup into serving bowls and garnish with a dollop of cream.

Todd Richards of Atlanta, Georgia

Drippings-Cooked Potatoes, Onions, Turnips, and Carrots

The use of bacon and bacon drippings may well be something of the food-obsessed's equivalent of a video-gamer's cheat code: an easy way to move forward to the next level. In this case, we're talking flavor.

But there's a reason it works: Bacon tastes good. And, in a region like ours, where pigs have long been the primary source of meat protein, bacon grease is prominent—even among Southerners of Jewish ancestry, like the author of this recipe.

Makes 6 to 8 servings

1 to 1½ pounds potatoes
1 to 1½ pounds carrots
1 to 1½ pounds turnips
1 to 1½ pounds onions

4 to 8 tablespoons bacon drippings
Salt and ground black pepper
1 tablespoon chopped fresh rosemary

Preheat the oven to 350°F. Peel the potatoes, carrots, turnips, and onions and cut them into bite-sized wedges or chunks. Leave a little of the onion root in place to hold the wedges together. Heat the drippings in a large, heavy, oven-proof skillet. Add the vegetables and stir to coat. Season with salt and pepper. Roast the vegetables, turning every 15 minutes, until they are tender and nicely browned with a few crispy edges. Taste for seasoning, sprinkle with rosemary, and serve hot.

Nathalie Dupree of Charleston, South Carolina

Root Cellar Gratin

Let's say it's January and, hungering for something cozy and comforting, you've procured yourself some potatoes. You look around your farmers' market or local grocer: what else? You pick up a rutabaga, some parsnips, some turnips. Having tubers in your root cellar, or, in this case, your shopping cart, is tantamount to reassurance that you'll make it through winter.

The following catch-all casserole is all you could ask for in a hot supper for a cold, cold day: soulful, seasonal, simple to prepare, and—thanks to the twang of the herbed salt, pepper, and garlic—a gentle reminder that all that ice will soon give way to the sun showers of spring.

Makes 6 to 8 servings

5 tablespoons unsalted butter, melted, divided
1 large garlic clove, smashed
1¼ teaspoons herbed salt, divided (recipe follows)
8 ounces fingerling potatoes, unpeeled and cut lengthwise into ⅛-inch slices
8 ounces rutabaga, peeled and cut into ⅛-inch slices

8 ounces parsnips, peeled and cut lengthwise into ⅛-inch slices
8 ounces turnips, peeled and cut into ⅛-inch slices
2 teaspoons chopped fresh thyme, divided
1½ cups heavy cream

Preheat the oven to 350°F.

Pour 1 tablespoon of the melted butter into an 8-inch square baking dish and use the garlic clove to spread it over the bottom and sides of the dish; discard the garlic. Sprinkle ¼ teaspoon of the herbed salt over the butter. Arrange about one-fourth of the potatoes, rutabaga, parsnips, and turnips evenly over the bottom of the dish, slightly overlapping their edges. Drizzle with 1 tablespoon of the melted butter and sprinkle with ½ teaspoon of the thyme and ¼ teaspoon of the herbed salt. Repeat to make three more layers, ending with a layer of round turnip slices arranged in a concentric pattern on the top of the gratin.

Pour the cream over the vegetables, gently pressing them down into the liquid. Cover the dish tightly with aluminum foil and bake for 30 minutes. Uncover and continue baking until the vegetables are tender and the gratin is bubbling and golden brown on top, another 30 to 45 minutes. Let cool for 10 to 15 minutes before serving.

HERBED SALT

Makes about ½ cup

1 large garlic clove
1 small Thai chile or chile de arbol
1 tablespoon chopped flat-leaf parsley
1½ teaspoons chopped fresh rosemary leaves

1 tablespoon chopped fresh sage leaves
1 teaspoon chopped fresh thyme leaves
½ cup kosher salt

Pulse all of the ingredients in a food processor until the herbs are minced and blended with the salt, stopping to scrape down the sides of the bowl with a rubber spatula as needed. The herbs will turn the salt a light green color. Store frozen in an airtight container for up to 6 months.

Chris Hastings of Birmingham, Alabama

Ginger Ale–Spiked Sweet Potatoes

The recipe below isn't what you'd call complicated in construction. But the flavors (buttery and sweet and hot, all at once) are.

The use of three-sneeze-fit hot Blenheim Ginger Ale ups the ante. Call it a lazy man's cheat if you like. Decry the presence of soda pop in what should be a relatively healthy dish. But for John T. Edge, whose family has roots in South Carolina, where Blenheim is bottled, the drink has resonance, both on the palate and in his family's collective memory.

To keep his son in ginger ale–spiked sweet potatoes and sate a taste for highballs of bourbon and Blenheim, Edge's father ships a case of Blenheim to Mississippi every year.

Makes 4 to 6 servings

1 tablespoon butter, at room temperature
2 pounds slender sweet potatoes,
   peeled and cut crosswise into ¼-inch-
   thick slices

Salt and ground black pepper
1 (12-ounce) bottle Blenheim Ginger Ale
   (either regular or hot)

Preheat the oven to 350°F.

Butter the bottom of a shallow 2-quart casserole or gratin dish. Arrange the sweet potato slices in rows with their edges overlapping. Season with a bit of salt and a grind or three of pepper. Pour the ginger ale over the top. Bake until the potatoes are tender and glazed with syrupy sauce, about 30 minutes. Serve hot.

John T. Edge of Oxford, Mississippi

CHICKEN AND ROOT VEGETABLE HOT POT,
from Nikki Giovanni of Christiansburg, Virginia

When I was on special leave to my alma mater, Fisk University in Nashville, I taught two evening courses on Mondays and Tuesdays from six until nine. Since I really do enjoy my own cooking, I was looking for a way to have a good meal that wasn't just steak on the grill all the time. I had taken my Crock-Pot with me, which turned out to be the smartest thing I did. My favorite dish became root vegetables with chicken (although once I had a guinea fowl, which was stupendous).

This dish works from a frozen state as well as fresh. When you get your small chicken—whole definitely works best—clean and rinse it. You can freeze several and use them straight from the freezer. I start with sweet potatoes, a couple of small ones or a medium-sized one. Peel and cut into pieces slightly larger than bite-sized. Then add a small rutabaga, peeled and cut into similarly sized pieces. I like to add a chopped medium white onion because it adds a bit of a bitter taste to the pot. Toss in a parsnip, peeled and cut; a couple of carrots, peeled and cut; 3 or 4 little baby red or white potatoes (you don't have to peel them); and a bulb of garlic (I really love garlic)—not garlic salt or any other form of garlic—peeled.

I then add fresh fennel, bok choy, and the chicken on top. I then pour in an 8-ounce jar of beef broth, a 12-ounce can of chicken broth, and enough beer to cover the vegetables. I sprinkle some sea salt and fresh ground pepper to taste. The chicken doesn't have to be covered. I put my Crock-Pot on adjustable heat; it will change automatically. It takes about 10 hours to cook. If you want it faster, then after 5 hours, put everything into an oven-proof dish and put it in a 350°F oven. Don't worry about preheating it. Check the chicken every 30 minutes or so until it reaches your own perfect tenderness.

Then go change your clothes. Come back, make a wonderful green salad with whatever green things are in season, and toss with olive oil and very little balsamic vinegar. If you're really hungry, make some drop biscuits or cold-water cornbread. (I know some folk think this dish needs couscous, but it doesn't.) A really good cold beer and the last half of a football game make this perfect.

Jerusalem Artichoke Relish

Thanks to its irregular shape, the Jerusalem artichoke can hold more grit and dirt than a mill house. Also known as a sunchoke, this hardy delicacy has been savored in the South since at least the mid-nineteenth century. A slave in a WPA-era narrative recalls scouring the woods for "hickory nuts, acorns, cane roots, and artichokes," by which he likely meant the tubers we know as Jerusalem artichokes.

Peeling and grating the choke makes it easier to avoid all the grime, and canning it allows you to enjoy it year-round, anytime you want to spoon a little piquant flavor atop a hunk of meat. Bill Smith Jr.'s recipe is a simple way to sample this delicacy.

Makes 4 pints

2½ pounds Jerusalem artichokes, washed and trimmed of blemishes
2 cups apple cider vinegar
1 cup sugar
1 teaspoon salt
1 tablespoon turmeric
2 teaspoons dry mustard

1 medium onion, peeled, halved, and thinly sliced
1 small bell pepper (any color), thinly sliced
¾ teaspoon whole mustard seeds
¾ teaspoon whole celery seeds
2 small bay leaves

Grate the Jerusalem artichokes in a food processor using the coarsest disk. Bring the vinegar, sugar, salt, turmeric, and mustard to a rolling boil in a large nonreactive pot that is big enough to comfortably hold all the vegetables. Stir occasionally to help dissolve the sugar. Add the onion and bell pepper and return to a boil. Add the artichokes. Bring this back to a boil once again and cook it exactly 10 minutes more. You want the relish to retain some crunch. Remove from the heat and add the mustard seeds, celery seeds, and bay leaves.

The relish keeps well in the refrigerator for a few weeks and can also be canned in pint jars processed in a hot-water bath for 10 minutes.

Bill Smith Jr. of Chapel Hill, North Carolina

Shout Hallelujah Potato Salad

This is a kitchen-sink kind of recipe, an endeavor that sprung from the mind of a mother who wanted to introduce her young son to a potato salad that, upon first taste, would compel said son to hug her neck and shout hallelujah.

There's a furious balance in this modernized version of the classic salad. This amalgam of potatoes and eggs and pickles and such is salty and sweet, hot and cool, creamy and crunchy. Blair Hobbs insists that to exact the most pleasure from preparation you must mix it with your own mitts.

Makes 15 servings

5 pounds petite yellow-fleshed potatoes
  (such as Yukon Gold)
4 hard-cooked eggs, peeled
1 (4-ounce) jar diced pimentos, drained
4 fat drops of hot sauce
2 teaspoons celery salt
2 tablespoons seasoned rice wine vinegar
2 tablespoons fresh lemon juice
1 cup sweet salad cube pickles, drained
1 tablespoon extra-virgin olive oil

1 cup plus 2 tablespoons mayonnaise
¼ cup yellow ballpark mustard
1 or 2 seeded and minced jalapeño chiles
½ cup chopped red onion
½ cup chopped green bell pepper
½ cup chopped celery
¼ cup chopped flat-leaf parsley
Salt and ground black pepper
2 teaspoons smoked hot paprika

Cook the whole, unpeeled potatoes in a large pot of boiling salted water until they are easily pierced with the tip of a sharp knife, about 20 minutes. Drain and peel, with your fingers, under cool running water (as if peeling hard-cooked eggs). Transfer to a large chilled bowl. Add the eggs and chop into large, bite-sized chunks. Plop on the pimentos, hot sauce, celery salt, vinegar, lemon juice, pickles, oil, mayonnaise, mustard, jalapeños, onion, bell pepper, celery, and parsley. Don't stir; dive in with your hands and mix well, mashing some of the potatoes to bond the intact golden chunks. Season with salt and pepper. Transfer to a serving bowl or platter and shape into a pretty mound with a spoon or spatula. Dust the top with paprika. Cover and refrigerate until chilled. Serve cold.

Blair Hobbs of Oxford, Mississippi

Caramelized Onion Pudding

Kathy Cary's pudding isn't the smooth, creamy kind Bill Cosby famously slurped but rather a close cousin to corn pudding—a light, eggy, savory-sweet concoction that gains its complexity from caramelized onions.

Served with a broiled haunch of pork roast or a baked ham, the pudding plays the role of both accompaniment and sauce, amplifying the natural sweetness of the meat.

Makes 8 servings

¼ pound (1 stick) butter
6 cups halved and thinly sliced yellow
   onions (about 4 medium onions)
6 large eggs
4 tablespoons sugar

2 teaspoons salt
2 teaspoons baking powder
3 tablespoons all-purpose flour
2 cups heavy cream

Melt the butter in a large skillet over medium heat. Add the onions and stir to coat. Cook, stirring often, until the onions are completely soft and the color of caramel, 30 to 40 minutes. Remove the skillet from the heat and set aside.

Preheat the oven to 350°F. Butter a glass or ceramic 9-by-13-inch baking dish. Whisk together the eggs, sugar, salt, baking powder, and flour in a bowl. Slowly whisk in the cream. Stir in the caramelized onions. Pour into the prepared baking dish. Bake until the pudding is set and golden brown on top, about 45 minutes. Serve hot.

Kathy Cary of Louisville, Kentucky

Spring Onion Puree

This is among the simplest recipes in our cookbook. But then again, good honest cooking requires nothing more than fresh ingredients. We'd say fresh, *local* ingredients, but unless you live within a twenty-county region of southern Georgia, your Vidalias will arrive on a long-haul truck. Since 1986, the state of Georgia has legislated that hypersweet Vidalia onions may be sold under that name only if they are grown in the sandy soil of that region, the economic and culinary capital of which is the town of Vidalia. In doing so, the state of Georgia proved an early U.S. adopter of the same rules that have long dictated the marketing of various European foodstuffs, from hams to melons to grapes.

Makes 4 servings

2 to 2½ pounds spring Vidalia onion
   bulbs (tough green tops removed)
4 tablespoons (½ stick) unsalted butter
   or duck fat

4 to 5 hearty sprigs of fresh thyme
Salt and ground black pepper

Cut the onions crosswise into ¼-inch-thick slices. Melt the butter in a large skillet over medium heat. Add the onions and stir to coat. Add the thyme sprigs and season lightly with salt and pepper. Cook the onions, stirring occasionally, until they are completely tender but not browned at all, about 20 minutes. Discard the thyme sprigs. Puree the onions and any liquid in a food processor or pass them through a food mill into a bowl. Season with salt and pepper. Serve warm with just about anything.

Robby Melvin of Birmingham, Alabama

4 GREENS
FROM COLLARDS TO MUSTARDS

Published: February 23, 1982

POT LIQUOR OR POTLIKKER?

Dear Sir: I always thought the *New York Times* knew everything, but obviously your editor knows as little about spelling as he or she does about Appalachian cooking and soul food. Only a culinarily-illiterate damnyankee (one word) who can't tell the difference between beans and greens would call the liquid left in the pot after cooking greens "pot liquor" (two words) instead of "potlikker" (one word) as yours did. And don't cite Webster as a defense because he didn't know any better either.

Sincerely,
ZELL MILLER, Lieutenant Governor, State of Georgia

COLLARD, turnip, creasy, kale, cabbage, rape, dandelion, sorrel, and mustard greens, to name a few—greens have long been integral to, if not the centerpiece of, Southern meals. Simple, nutritious food that transcends race and class, greens are as likely to appear on a plastic folding table as they are a polished mahogany sideboard. Of late, white-tablecloth chefs have taken up these crucifers and their kin. They've cut greens into a chiffonade. They've creamed greens. They've stewed them with artisan bacon. And so on.

Such fillips aside, we know, first and foremost, that you can't go wrong with washing greens, drowning them in ham-hock stock, boiling the whole down, and ladling them and their potlikker atop a square of cornbread.

As a general rule, turnip greens are more popular in the upper South, collard greens in the Deep South. There are pockets of cabbage proponents, especially in Louisiana, where the Irish immigrants to New Orleans hold sway in the choice of greens. (On Saint Patrick's Day, they toss cabbages to celebrants from atop floats.) But historically, many Southerners preferred collard greens because they withstand greater extremes of heat and cold and require less intensive cultivation—or hands-on cooking—than most other vegetables. For slaves, sharecroppers, and factory workers, such economies were essential.

Popular culture reflects the wide adoption of collards. Jazz great Thelonious Monk, a native of North Carolina, wore a collard leaf in his lapel when playing New York clubs. Archibald Leigh, a black American expatriate living in Paris, penned a poem for the 1984 collection *Leaves of Greens: The Collard Poems*, a compendium commissioned on behalf of the Ayden, North Carolina, Collard Festival. Leigh claimed collard greens' blackness:

FROM *Leaves of Green*

Rednecks
(with their hoots and hollers)
can try and claim 'em
New Southerners
(with their nouveau dollars)
may defame them
But
anyone who knows from beans
knows
they's color'd people's greens

Eat 'em
steamin' wit' chunks of pork
or
never let them stain your fork
still
collard greens is color'd greens
even in New York.

The fact is, no one is ambivalent about greens. Zell Miller, the onetime governor of Georgia, knew the import. So did Huey Long, the longtime governor of Louisiana, who engaged in an extended argument, in 1931, publicized in newspapers and movie reels, about the proper way to consume potlikker, the distilled essence of greens. Long was a dunker. His combatant, Julian Harris, son of Joel Chandler Harris of Uncle Remus fame, was a crumbler.

Their Depression-era argument might seem frivolous now, but it was more than a mere goof. We think it can be boiled down thusly: Few folks had much green in their wallets at the time, but edible greens, prepared with a little seasoning meat and a lot of love, still allowed most any man to, as Long famously put it, be a king, if only for supper.

Braised Collard Greens with Ham-Hock Broth

Ham broth is to greens as a mother sauce is to all manner of French dishes. It's the beginning and the end, the crutch and the crux. Beef, chicken, and vegetable broths, of both the canned and powdered varieties, are readily available in grocery stores. (Granted, they're rarely very good.) But ham-hock broth has not won wide acceptance among our nation's grocers. Ham-hock broth is a product of the home kitchen. So get some hocks and get to it.

Makes 6 to 8 servings

1 teaspoon vegetable oil
2 slices bacon, diced
2 cups diced onions
1 cup ham-hock broth (recipe follows)

2 pounds stemmed collard greens,
   roughly chopped
1 teaspoon salt
Ground black pepper

Heat the oil in a large, heavy stockpot over medium-high heat. Add the bacon and cook until the fat is rendered and the bacon is crispy, about 8 minutes. Add the onion and cook until softened, about 5 minutes. Add the ham-hock broth and bring the mixture to a boil.

Add the collards, stirring until they begin to wilt. Stir in the salt. Reduce the heat to medium-low. Cover the pot and cook, stirring occasionally, until the greens are tender, about 40 to 45 minutes. Season with additional salt and pepper. Serve warm.

HAM HOCK BROTH

Makes about 2 cups

3 smoked ham hocks
8 cups water
2 sprigs fresh thyme
1 bay leaf

3 black peppercorns
3 garlic cloves
2 medium onions, peeled and quartered

Lightly brown the ham hocks in a large pot over medium-high heat, about 2 minutes on each side. Add the water, thyme, bay leaf, peppercorns, garlic, and onions. Bring to a boil, reduce the heat, and simmer until the stock reduces to 2 cups, about 3 hours, skimming the surface occasionally. Strain the stock through a fine sieve into a clean bowl and cool to room temperature in an ice bath. Cover and refrigerate for up to 3 days or keep frozen in an airtight container for up to 2 months.

Chris Hastings of Birmingham, Alabama

Brown Butter Creamed Winter Greens

Linton Hopkins does not consider the vegetable plate to be a compromise crafted for calorie parsers. His take on the vegetable plate is a lusty casserole, a buttery jumble of—depending on the season—turnips, new potatoes, beets, and asparagus tips.

Linton especially loves root vegetables and winter greens, lavishing them with attention and, in this case, brown butter and béchamel.

Makes 6 to 8 servings

BÉCHAMEL SAUCE

2 tablespoons unsalted butter
2 tablespoons all-purpose flour
2 cups whole milk

2 tablespoons minced shallot
1 Turkish or ½ California bay leaf
6 black peppercorns

GREENS

6 ounces slab bacon, rind trimmed
4 tablespoons (½ stick) unsalted butter
1 cup finely chopped onion
3½ pounds mixed baby winter greens
   (such as collards, mustard greens, and
   kale), stemmed and coarsely chopped
Béchamel sauce

½ cup heavy cream
2 garlic cloves, minced
1 teaspoon dried hot red pepper flakes
¾ teaspoon salt
½ teaspoon ground black pepper
1 tablespoon apple cider vinegar,
   or to taste

To make the béchamel: Melt the butter in a heavy medium saucepan over medium heat. Whisk in the flour and cook, whisking constantly, for 1 minute. Slowly whisk in the milk. Add the shallot, bay leaf, and peppercorns and bring to a boil, whisking constantly. Reduce the heat to medium and cook, whisking constantly, until the sauce thickens enough to coat the back of a spoon, about 5 minutes. Strain the sauce through a fine sieve into a bowl. Press parchment paper or plastic wrap directly onto the surface of the sauce and set aside.

To make the greens: Cut the bacon into ¼-inch-thick slices. Cut the slices crosswise into ¼-inch-wide sticks. Cook these lardoons in a Dutch oven or heavy pot over medium heat, stirring occasionally, until golden brown but not crisp, about 8 minutes. Transfer the bacon to paper towels to drain, then pour off the fat from the pot and wipe it clean. Heat the butter in the pot over medium-low heat until browned and fragrant, about 2 minutes. Add the onion and cook, stirring constantly, until softened, about 5 minutes.

Increase the heat to medium-high and stir in the greens one handful at a time, letting each handful wilt before adding the next. Stir in the béchamel sauce, cream, garlic, pepper flakes, salt, and pepper. Cook stirring, until the greens are tender and coated with sauce, about 10 minutes. Stir in the lardoons and vinegar. Season with salt and pepper and serve hot.

Linton Hopkins of Atlanta, Georgia

Cream of Sorrel Soup

Sorrel grows well in iron-rich soil, which provides mature sorrel with its slightly acidic lemony flavor. That tang makes all the difference. "It depends greatly on the quality of the ingredients," says scientist and avid cook Kenneth Ford, explaining the key to his soup. "Sorrel grows like a weed—that is, fast—in our garden." He also cites farm-fresh eggs. And ground-to-order nutmeg.

Makes 6 to 8 servings

1 tablespoon butter
1 pound fresh sorrel, stemmed and
    shredded into chiffonade ribbons
    (about 3 loosely packed cups)
Salt and ground black pepper

3 cups chicken stock
5 large egg yolks, lightly beaten
1 cup heavy cream
⅛ teaspoon freshly grated
    nutmeg

Melt the butter in a large skillet over medium-high heat. Add the sorrel and cook only until wilted, about 45 seconds. The sorrel will darken. Remove from the heat and season with salt and pepper. Set aside.

Bring the chicken stock to a bare simmer in a saucepan over medium-low heat. In another saucepan, whisk together the yolks, cream, and nutmeg. Whisk the warm stock into the egg yolk mixture. Cook over medium-low heat, stirring constantly, until the soup thickens to the consistency of light custard, 8 to 10 minutes; don't let the soup boil or the yolks will curdle. Stir in the wilted sorrel and heat though. Serve piping hot.

Kenneth Ford of Pensacola, Florida

POKE SALLET

Plucked from fields, pastures, and backyards across the South, pokeweed, a perennial, is employed as a folk remedy to treat a wide variety of ailments, including rheumatism. Its roots and berries, however, are toxic. Pokeweed leaves must be boiled for safety—we recommend three times, changing the water for each boil. Jason Edwards of Johnson City, Tennessee, shares his recipe.

Makes 4 servings

To prepare poke sallet, you pick the medium-sized leaves. The big ones are bitter, and it takes too many of the small ones to fill a sack. A large brown paper grocery bag full will make about four servings, since the poke greens cook down considerably. Rinse your poke leaves well. Boil the leaves three times, discard the water each time, and rinse the leaves each time. Melt some lard or bacon grease in a cast-iron skillet. Add your poke. Cook it until almost all of the water is gone. Crack 2 eggs into the poke and stir. Mix the eggs and poke together well. Cook until the eggs are done.

Gumbo z'Herbes

Much was lost in the wake of the levee failures that followed Hurricane Katrina. Armed with a sense of collective responsibility to avoid further losses, many work to preserve what remains. We do that, in part, by recovering imperiled culinary traditions. Gumbo z'Herbes is an example of a dish that, at least to outlanders, was little known before the storm and is now better known. Leah Chase, who cooked this gumbo for innumerable post-Katrina events, is largely responsible for that.

Leah grew up eating green gumbo every Holy Thursday in Madisonville, Louisiana. The idea then, and now, was to feast on the hearty, meat-heavy soup before fasting on Good Friday. This recipe is an expansion of Leah's original, amended after she and Sara Roahen shopped and cooked together. Leah says that Creoles always add filé to their gumbo z'herbes, even though few cookbook recipes call for it.

Makes 12 to 15 servings

2 ham shanks

1 gallon water

Between 7 and 11 of the following greens to total 6 to 8 pounds: collard greens, mustard greens, turnip greens, spinach, cabbage, carrot tops, beet tops, arugula, parsley, green onions, watercress, romaine or other lettuce, curly endive, kale, radish tops, and/or pepper grass

3 medium yellow onions, roughly chopped

8 whole garlic cloves, peeled

2 pounds fresh hot sausage

1 pound chicken drumettes

1 pound andouille sausage, cut into ½-inch slices

1 pound smoked pork sausage, cut into ½-inch slices

1 pound beef stew meat, cut into ½-inch pieces

8 ounces ham, cut into ½-inch pieces

1 cup all-purpose flour

Vegetable oil

3 teaspoons dried thyme

2 teaspoons ground cayenne pepper

3 bay leaves

2 teaspoons salt

½ teaspoon filé powder (optional)

Hot, cooked white rice, for serving

Place the ham shanks and water in a large pot. Bring to a boil over high heat; reduce the heat to medium-low and let simmer until needed.

Wash all of the greens thoroughly in salt water, being sure to remove any grit, discolored outer leaves, and tough stems. Rinse in a bath of plain water. (A clean double sink works well for this.) Drain the greens in a colander. Place the greens, onions, and garlic in a very large stockpot and cover with water. (If all of the vegetables won't fit in the pot, cook them in batches, using the same cooking liquid for each batch.) Bring to a boil, reduce the heat, and simmer until the greens are very tender, about 45 minutes. Use a slotted spoon to transfer the cooked vegetables into a large bowl to cool for a few minutes. Pour the cooking liquid into a large bowl and set it aside. Working in batches, puree the vegetables in a food processor or by running them through a meat grinder. Use a little cooking liquid to loosen the puree, if needed. Transfer the puree into a large bowl and set aside.

Cook the fresh sausage in a large skillet over medium heat until it renders its fat and moisture, breaking up the sausage with the side of a spoon. Transfer with a slotted spoon into a large bowl and set aside. Brown the chicken in the rendered sausage fat over medium-high heat and then transfer with a slotted spoon to the bowl with the cooked sausage. (The chicken will cook more later, so it does not need to cook through at this point.) Set the skillet and drippings aside.

Remove the ham shanks from their cooking liquid, reserving the liquid to use as stock. When cool enough to handle, pull the meat from the bones. Chop the meat into bite-sized pieces and add it to the bowl with the sausage and chicken. Discard the bones and the fat. Pour the ham stock into a large bowl and set it aside.

Return the vegetable puree to the large stock pot. Add the hot sausage, chicken, andouille, smoked pork sausage, stew beef, ham-shank meat, and chopped ham. (If it will not fit into one pot, divide it between two pots.) Cover with equal parts ham stock and greens cooking liquid and bring to a simmer over medium-high heat.

To make the roux, place the skillet containing the hot sausage pan drippings over medium-high heat. Sprinkle the flour over the drippings and stir well with a wooden spoon. If the mixture is dry and crumbly, stir in enough vegetable oil to make a smooth, thick paste. Cook, stirring constantly, slowly, and intently until the roux turns light brown. (This isn't a dark roux, but the flour should be cooked.) Drop tablespoons of roux into the simmering gumbo, stirring well after each addition. Stir in the thyme, cayenne, bay leaves, and salt. Simmer the gumbo until the stew meat is tender and the chicken is cooked through, about 1 hour. Stir often to prevent scorching. If the gumbo gets too thick to stir, add more stock or water.

If desired, slowly add the filé at the end of cooking. (It will lump if you're not careful.) Serve hot over cooked white rice.

Leah Chase and Sara Roahen of New Orleans, Louisiana

Killed Lettuce

Killed lettuce takes best advantage of the first, tender leaves of lettuce that emerge in spring (along with native ramps, which are often harvested at the same time). Dressed—wilted, basically—in a hot bacon grease and vinegar concoction, the greens hold their own.

Although some people include bacon in the recipe, it was more or less the grease alone in meager times. The vinegar helps cut the fat of the grease, which adds a wonderfully intense, layered flavoring to the tender lettuce shoots and salty-sweet onion.

Makes 4 servings

12 cups freshly picked baby leaf lettuce
4 spring bulb onions or ramps, trimmed
  and sliced thinly
4 slices bacon, cut crosswise into ½-inch-
  wide pieces

¼ cup apple cider vinegar
2 teaspoons sugar
1 teaspoon salt
½ teaspoon ground black pepper

Dry the lettuce thoroughly. Place the lettuce and onions in a large serving bowl and set aside. Fry the bacon in a large cast-iron skillet over medium heat, stirring often, until it renders its fat and is very crispy, about 15 minutes. Transfer with a slotted spoon to drain on paper towels. Add the vinegar, sugar, salt, and pepper to the drippings and stir until the sugar dissolves. Cook until the mixture is shimmering hot and carefully pour it over the lettuce and onions, tossing with tongs to coat and wilt the greens. Sprinkle the bacon over the top and serve immediately—this won't keep.

Madge Castle of Boone, North Carolina

Skillet Greens

The marriage of salted pork and leafy greens is a natural. So is the presence of chile peppers preserved in vinegar. In this recipe, Mike Lata takes regional favorites like kale, collard, mustard, and turnip greens and gives them a twist via a quick wilt in a hot pan with a few fishy and acidic accompaniments.

While most Southerners tend to impart salt to their greens via a dousing of ham broth, Lata goes Mediterranean and opts for anchovies. He also adds red pepper flakes, which, one might argue, are a tip of the hat to omnipresent pepper vinegar.

Makes 2 servings

8 ounces extremely tender baby greens
(such as kale, collard, turnip, and/or
mustard greens)
2 tablespoons extra-virgin olive oil, plus
more for drizzling

2 garlic cloves, thinly sliced
1 teaspoon crushed red pepper flakes
1 to 2 anchovy fillets, mashed coarsely
with a fork
Salt and ground black pepper

Tear the greens into bite-sized pieces. Wash in cool water. Lift from the water, but do not spin dry. Set aside. Heat the oil in a large, heavy skillet over medium heat. Add the garlic, crushed red pepper, and anchovies and cook, stirring constantly, until the garlic releases its aroma, about 30 seconds. Add the greens and toss to coat. The water clinging to the greens will keep the garlic from burning. Cook, tossing with tongs, until the greens are barely wilted, no more than 2 minutes. Season with salt and pepper. Serve at once, drizzled with a little more oil.

Mike Lata of Charleston, South Carolina

Spicy Turnip Greens

Eddie Hernandez was born in Monterrey, Mexico. That's where he learned to cook. He arrived in the States with a taste for pork and corn and an affinity for cooking both. In the process of adapting to his new home, Eddie has made turnip greens his own, adding chile de arbol, creating the taste of a true New South.

Makes 8 to 10 servings

¾ pound (1½ sticks) butter or margarine
1 cup chopped onion
½ cup chopped garlic
1 tablespoon ground chile de arbol or
   cayenne pepper

1½ cups diced tomatoes
6 cups cooked turnip greens
3 cups chicken stock
2 teaspoons salt

Melt the butter in a large, heavy pot over medium-high heat. Stir in the onions and cook until softened, stirring often, about 8 minutes. Stir in the garlic and chile de arbol and cook, stirring constantly, for 1 minute. Stir in the tomatoes, greens, and chicken stock. Bring to a boil, reduce the heat, and simmer, partially covered, until the flavors are blended and the greens are heated through, about 15 minutes. Season with salt. Serve hot.

Eddie Hernandez of Atlanta, Georgia

Collard Green and White Bean Gratin

Each fall, Frank Stitt and his friends spend a long weekend traipsing through the south Georgia woods, kicking the underbrush in search of bobwhite quail. One year, his hosts asked Frank to bring a side dish to accompany grilled quail, served at the lodge where the hunters gather. This gratin recipe is a vestige of that trip.

Use this recipe as a guide, not a rule, says Frank. You can always incorporate other ingredients on hand.

Makes 8 to 10 servings

1 pound collard greens, stems and tough ribs removed
5 garlic cloves, divided, 1 crushed and 4 chopped
¼ cup extra-virgin olive oil, divided
1 medium onion, chopped
1 small red bell pepper, cut into ½-inch pieces
3 cups cooked white beans, ½ cup cooking liquid reserved

½ cup diced or chopped cooked ham-hock meat, sausage, chorizo, or bacon
¼ cup freshly grated Parmigiano-Reggiano, divided
1 tablespoon finely chopped fresh rosemary leaves
Kosher salt and ground black pepper
¼ cup medium-coarse fresh bread crumbs

In a large pot, cover the collards with salted water, then heat and boil until tender, about 30 minutes. Drain well and chop into small pieces. Set aside.

Preheat the oven to 475°F. Vigorously rub the inside of a 10- or 12-inch gratin dish with the crushed garlic. Discard the crushed garlic and set the dish aside.

Heat 2 tablespoons of the oil in a large sauté pan over medium-high heat. Add the onion and bell pepper and cook, stirring often, until tender, about 10 minutes. Add the chopped garlic and cook, stirring, for 1 minute. Add the collard greens, stir to coat, and cook for 1 minute. Transfer into a large bowl.

Stir in the beans, meat, 2 tablespoons of the Parmigiano-Reggiano, 1 tablespoon of the oil, and rosemary. Season with salt and pepper. Add enough of the reserved bean cooking liquid to moisten, then spread the mixture in the prepared dish. Top with the bread crumbs and the remaining Parmigiano-Reggiano. Drizzle with the remaining oil.

Cover the dish with aluminum foil and bake until the filling is hot and bubbly, 30 to 35 minutes. Remove the foil and bake until the top of the gratin is golden and crusty, about another 10 minutes. Serve hot.

Frank Stitt of Birmingham, Alabama

Smothered Cabbage

Eula Mae Doré cooked on Louisiana's Avery Island for more than fifty years. She passed in 2008, leaving a legacy of recipes composed and meals shared. She was a traditional Cajun cook who honed her talent while cooking for the McIlhenny Company commissary.

Smothered cooking, a time-honored tradition, might sound almost violent. It's actually quite gentle. To smother a meat such as chicken, pork chops, steaks, or wild game is to tenderize and fix flavors. It's not just a technique for meats, either—onions, peppers, garlic, potatoes, cabbage, and okra are smothered, softened by way of judicious heat and a little moisture.

Makes 4 to 6 servings

12 ounces salt meat, cut into 1-inch cubes
¼ cup vegetable oil
1 small head (about 2 pounds) white
   cabbage, coarsely chopped
1 small yellow onion, chopped
   (about 1 cup)

1 cup water
1 tablespoon sugar
¼ teaspoon salt
¼ teaspoon ground black pepper
¼ teaspoon ground cayenne
   pepper

Place the salt meat in a small saucepan and cover with cold water. Bring to a boil over high heat. Reduce the heat to medium and simmer for 30 minutes. Drain and set the meat aside.

Heat the oil in a large, heavy pot or Dutch oven over medium heat. Add the drained salt meat and cook, stirring constantly, for 2 minutes. Stir in the cabbage, onion, and water. Cover and simmer over medium-low heat, stirring occasionally, until the cabbage begins to soften, about 30 minutes. Stir in the sugar, salt, pepper, and cayenne. Cover and cook until the cabbage is completely tender, about another 30 minutes. Serve hot.

Eula Mae Doré of Avery Island, Louisiana

Carolina Coleslaw

North Carolina takes its coleslaw as seriously as it does its barbecue. There are slaw factions. They are defined by variations both familial and geographical. Vinegar versus mayonnaise. Shredded versus chopped. With barbecue sauce or without.

All kinds of sandwiches are worthy of a cap of coleslaw, including the slaw burgers that Tom Sasser makes. Spiked with Worcestershire and ketchup, Tom's recipe is a take on a regional red slaw.

Makes 10 to 12 servings

1½ teaspoons red wine vinegar
2 tablespoons sugar
2 teaspoons lemon juice
2 teaspoons Worcestershire sauce
2 tablespoons spicy brown mustard
¼ cup mayonnaise
¼ teaspoon hot sauce

2 teaspoons ketchup
2 teaspoons salt
1½ cups vegetable oil
7 cups shredded green cabbage
1 cup shredded red cabbage
¼ cup finely diced red onion
½ cup shredded carrots

Beat the vinegar and sugar in a large bowl with an electric mixer on low speed to dissolve the sugar. Add the lemon juice and Worcestershire sauce; beat to mix well. Add the mustard, mayonnaise, hot sauce, ketchup, and salt; beat to mix well. With the mixer running, slowly add the oil; beat only until the dressing is thick and creamy. Cover and refrigerate until ready to use.

Toss together the green cabbage, red cabbage, onion, and carrots in a large bowl. Blot with a clean towel to make sure the vegetables are completely dry. Refrigerate until the vegetables are chilled.

Just before serving, pour the dressing over the vegetables and stir to mix well. Serve at once.

Tom Sasser of Charlotte, North Carolina

5 RICE
LIMPIN', HOPPIN', AND EVERY WHICH WAY

I was sixteen years old before I knew that everyone didn't eat rice everyday. Us being Geechees, we had rice everyday. When you said what you were eating for dinner, you always assumed that rice was there. That was one of my jobs, too. To cook the rice. . . . I could cook it till every grain stood by itself.

—Vertamae Grosvenor, *Vibration Cooking*

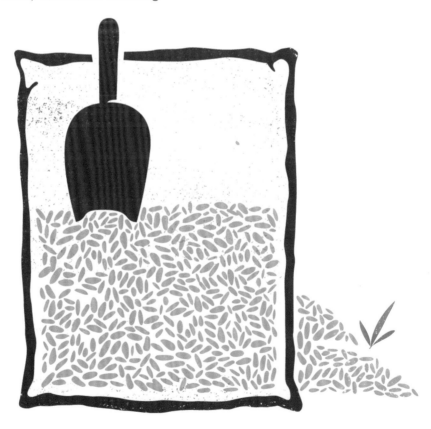

SOUTHERNERS have been eating rice since seeds of the plants first made the circuitous trip to Charleston, South Carolina, in the 1600s. Rice cultivation, powered by slave labor and nurtured by the abundant moisture and warm temperatures of the region's marshlands, flourished in the Lowcountry of South Carolina and Georgia.

Within just a few years of its introduction, rice became the primary source of wealth in South Carolina. Composed rice dishes—rice that is cooked or combined with other ingredients—such as tomato pilau became centerpieces of the cuisine.

Throughout the region, cooks still stir beans and peas into pots of rice. Think of hoppin' John, likely born in the Carolinas but widely adopted elsewhere. Think of the black-bean-and-rice combination called Moors and Christians, fetishized in the Spanish settlements of Florida. Think of red beans and rice, traditionally prepared on Monday, wash day, in Louisiana.

Aided by modern irrigation methods, Arkansas, Louisiana, Mississippi, and Texas are now important rice-growing states, and the heirloom variety known as Carolina Gold is making a resurgence in South Carolina.

Rice was introduced into south Louisiana in the late nineteenth century, becoming a basis for much of the state's Cajun and Creole cooking. In rural Louisiana, rice is a bed for smothered or stewed shrimp or crawfish, a medium for soaking up a bowl of gumbo, and the matrix for countless versions of jambalaya—one-pot amalgams of African, Spanish, French, and New World influences. In New Orleans, rice fritters called calas, once on the brink of extinction, are reappearing.

Rice puddings have been eaten as desserts since at least the early nineteenth century. In the schoolrooms of the South, especially in the upland South, plain boiled rice was often served as a side dish along with a bowl of sugar for sweetening.

Immigration has further enriched the rice-based cuisine of the South. At one barbecue restaurant in Virginia, jasmine rice from Thailand is served as an accompaniment to pork ribs. In New Orleans, fried rice is a staple in corner stores that also tend to serve egg rolls and po-boys. Served with fried chicken, rice is a home-cooked comfort food that knows no ethnic bounds.

Chicken Purloo

When John Egerton was researching his book *Southern Food*, he found sixteen alternate spellings of pilau—purloo being one of them. In *The Carolina Rice Kitchen*, Karen Hess wrote, "Word and dish come from Persia; the Persian word pilau took various forms in the countries to which the dish spread, such as pullau in India, pilaf in Turkey, and pelau in Provence."

Robert Stehling, who is more concerned with cookery than nomenclature, adds eggplant to this version of chicken purloo, which connects the dish back to the Near East, which, of course, would have pleased Hess.

Makes 4 to 6 servings

1 four-pound chicken, cut into serving
    pieces
Kosher salt
3 tablespoons peanut oil, divided
2 cups diced yellow onion
1 cup diced celery
2 tablespoons chopped garlic
½ cup diced green bell pepper
⅛ teaspoon crushed red pepper flakes
⅛ teaspoon dried basil
⅛ teaspoon dried thyme

2 bay leaves
1 cup peeled and diced eggplant
2 cups raw long-grain white rice
¼ teaspoon freshly ground black pepper
½ cup diced tasso or other smoked ham
2 cups sliced okra
¼ cup red wine
2½ cups canned whole peeled tomatoes,
    chopped
2 cups chicken stock
Hot sauce (optional)

Preheat the oven to 375°F.

Season the chicken with salt. Heat 1 tablespoon of the oil in a large sauté pan or skillet over medium-high heat. Brown the chicken pieces on both sides. Transfer to a medium bowl and set aside.

Add the onion (and 1 teaspoon of the oil if needed) to the pan and sauté until golden brown, about 6 minutes. Add the celery (and 1 teaspoon of the oil if needed) and sauté until slightly softened, about 4 minutes. Add the garlic, bell pepper, red pepper flakes, basil, thyme, and bay leaves and sauté for 2 minutes. Add the eggplant (and 1 teaspoon of the oil if needed) and sauté until it is tender, about 4 minutes. Spread the vegetables and pan juices evenly in a shallow 3- to 4-quart ovenproof casserole dish.

Heat 2 teaspoons of the oil in the sauté pan. Add the rice and sauté until it is light golden, 2 to 3 minutes. Spread the rice in an even layer over the vegetables in the casserole. Sprinkle with 1 teaspoon of salt and with pepper.

Heat 1 teaspoon of the oil in the sauté pan. Add the ham and sauté until it is fragrant, about 2 minutes. Add the okra and sauté until lightly browned, about 6 to 8 minutes. Add the wine and cook until the pan is almost dry. Add the tomatoes and simmer vigorously until the mixture thickens, about 6 minutes. Spread the okra mixture over the rice in the casserole.

Bring the chicken stock to a boil in a small saucepan, remove the pan from the heat, and set it aside. Arrange the chicken pieces over the rice, placing the thigh and leg portions around the edge of the pan and the breast pieces in the center. Top with any juices from the bowl of chicken. Pour the hot stock into the casserole. Cover the dish tightly with a lid or foil. Bake until the rice has absorbed all of the liquid, about 1 hour.

Transfer the chicken pieces to a platter. Gently stir the rice and vegetables together. Season with salt, pepper, and hot sauce. Place a portion of the chicken and a serving of rice and vegetables on each plate and serve hot.

Robert Stehling of Charleston, South Carolina

Dirty Rice

Dirty rice, beloved in southwestern Louisiana, gets its name and color from chopped organ meats, typically livers and gizzards. Celeste Uzee also uses pork breakfast sausage, browned and crumbled.

Some south Louisiana cooks call the dish rice dressing. Uzee's father, Donald Uzee of Larose, Louisiana, differentiates between the two. Says his daughter, "My father calls it rice dressing when the sautéed meat mixture is added to the rice before it is cooked."

Makes 4 to 6 servings

½ cup water
½ teaspoon salt, plus more for taste
1 cup raw long-grain white rice
3 to 4 slices good-quality bacon, chopped
½ cup chicken livers, cleaned of all fat and connective tissue and roughly chopped

8 ounces hot bulk pork breakfast sausage, ground pork, or ground beef
½ cup finely chopped celery
½ cup finely chopped green bell pepper
2 garlic cloves, chopped
Ground black pepper
Ground cayenne pepper
1 bunch green onions, chopped

Bring the water and salt to a boil in a heavy saucepan over high heat. Stir in the rice. Cover the pan tightly and reduce the heat to the lowest possible setting. Cook the rice undisturbed until it absorbs the liquid, about 20 minutes. Remove the pan from the heat and set aside.

Fry the bacon in a large skillet over medium-high heat until crisp. Transfer with a slotted spoon to drain on paper towels. Add the chicken livers to the skillet. Cook, stirring constantly, until the livers are cooked through, breaking them up into small pieces with the side of the spoon. Transfer with a slotted spoon into a bowl and set aside. Add the sausage to the skillet and brown well, crumbling the sausage into very small pieces with the side of the spoon. Add the celery, green pepper, and garlic; cook, stirring often, until the vegetables soften, about 5 minutes. Return the livers and bacon to the skillet and stir well. Season with salt, black pepper, and cayenne. Stir in the cooked rice and green onions. Serve hot.

Celeste Uzee of Luling, Louisiana

Mushroom Dirty Rice

Corbin Evans created this alternative dirty rice as an homage to Leah Chase, the grande doyenne of New Orleans chefs. He knew that her dirty rice would be impossible to replicate, so he didn't try.

He chucked pork in favor of chicken and honored the earthy funk of liver by way of mushrooms and giblets. Corbin originally served it with smothered chicken, but this dish is dirty (and flavorful) enough to stand on its own.

Makes 6 to 8 servings

1 pound chicken giblets (including livers and a couple of necks), trimmed and washed
4½ cups water, divided
2 cups chicken stock
½ cup chopped shallot
3 to 4 sprigs flat-leaf parsley
8 to 10 black peppercorns
Kosher salt
3½ tablespoons vegetable oil
¼ cup all-purpose flour
1 medium onion, minced (about ½ cup)

1 pound cremini mushrooms, chopped
1 green bell pepper, finely diced (about 1 cup)
1 red bell pepper, finely diced (about 1 cup)
1 celery stalk, finely diced (about ½ cup)
5 garlic cloves, thinly sliced
1 tablespoon fresh thyme leaves
½ cup raw short-grain rice
Ground black pepper
1 bay leaf
½ cup thinly sliced green onion tops

Bring the giblets, 2 cups of the water, stock, shallot, parsley, peppercorns, and a pinch of salt to a boil in a medium saucepan. Reduce the heat to medium-low and simmer just until the livers are cooked through, about 10 minutes. Use a slotted spoon to transfer the livers into a bowl and set aside. Simmer the remaining ingredients for another 30 minutes. Transfer the rest of the giblets to the bowl with the livers and let cool. Trim the kidneys, pull the meat from the neck, and discard the skin and bones. Chop the giblets and set aside. Strain the giblet stock through a mesh sieve into a bowl and set aside.

Make a roux by stirring the oil and flour together in a large cast-iron skillet until smooth. Cook over medium heat, stirring constantly, until the roux is the color of milk chocolate, about 30 minutes. Stir in the onion; continue cooking and stirring until the roux is the color of mahogany, about another 15 minutes. Stir in the mushrooms, green pepper, red pepper, celery, and garlic and cook, stirring constantly, until the vegetables soften, about 8 minutes. Stir in the giblet stock and thyme. Reduce the heat to low and simmer for 30 minutes, stirring occasionally and skimming off any fat or foam that bubbles to the surface.

Meanwhile, stir together the rice and the remaining 2½ cups of water in a large saucepan. Toss in the bay leaf and season with salt and pepper. Bring to a boil, reduce the heat to low, cover the pan, and simmer until the rice is tender and absorbs the water, about 15 minutes. Remove the pan from the heat and let sit for 5 minutes.

Just before serving, stir the giblets and green onion tops into the gravy. Stir the gravy into the cooked rice. Serve hot.

Corbin Evans of Philadelphia, Pennsylvania

Kentucky Hoppin' John

Hoppin' John is another in a long line of Southern classics that owe their existence to Africa, the original homeland of the black-eyed pea.

Arguments abound in the South about whether the black-eyed peas and the rice should be cooked together or separately in this age-old dish, a traditional New Year's Day good luck repast.

Bob Perry cooks them separately. And in an effort to claim local provenance, he chooses a Kentucky pork sausage for seasoning. Pork of some sort—whether ham hock, hog jowl, or fatback—is an essential ingredient in any hoppin' John, no matter the cooking method.

Makes 12 to 16 servings

1 pound smoked country pork sausage	3 short sprigs of thyme
1 medium onion, chopped (about ½ cup)	1 tablespoon kosher salt
	1 teaspoon ground black pepper
1 pound dried black-eyed peas, soaked overnight and drained	2 cups raw long-grain converted white rice

Cut the sausage into ½-inch slices and peel the cloth from around each piece. Fry the sausage slowly in a Dutch oven over medium-low heat until heated through. Dice the sausage, transfer it into a bowl, and set it aside.

Add the onion to the sausage drippings and cook, stirring often, until it softens, about 8 minutes. Add the black-eyed peas and cover with cool water. Stir in the sausage, thyme, salt, and pepper. Bring to a boil, reduce the heat to medium-low, cover, and simmer until the peas are nearly tender, about 40 minutes. Stir in the rice. Cover and cook until the rice is tender and has absorbed most of the liquid, about 20 minutes, never lifting the lid. Remove the pan from the heat and let the rice steam, still covered, for 10 minutes. Fluff with a fork and serve hot.

Bob Perry of Lancaster, Kentucky

Limpin' Susan

The name is the franchise. This Carolina cousin to hoppin' John, documented in the early 1950s, generally includes okra. Other variations include limpin' Kate or skippin' Jinny, which blend cowpeas with hominy instead of the rice used in John and Susan preparations. Taking his cues from the Lowcountry, Scott Barton uses dried, smoked shrimp in place of bacon and rice grits in place of traditional rice.

Makes 6 servings

3½ cups chicken, shellfish, or vegetable
    stock
2 tablespoons olive oil or peanut oil
4 ounces dried, smoked shrimp
1 small yellow onion, diced (about 1 cup)
1 celery stalk, diced (about ½ cup)
2 medium tomatoes, peeled, seeded, and
    diced (about 2 cups)
1 pound okra, trimmed and cut into
    thick rounds (about 4 cups)

Kernels from 1 ear fresh sweet corn
    (about ½ cup)
½ cup raw Carolina Gold Rice Grits,
    picked through and rinsed
½ teaspoon smoked paprika
Salt and ground black pepper
Ground cayenne pepper
1 bunch green onions, trimmed and
    thinly sliced (½ cup)
2 tablespoons chopped flat-leaf parsley

Bring the stock to a simmer in a medium saucepan and keep warm over low heat. Heat the oil in a large saucepan over medium heat. Stir in the shrimp and heat through. Stir in the onion and celery and cook, stirring often, until the vegetables soften, about 5 minutes. Stir in the tomatoes and cook, stirring, until they begin to release their juice. Stir in the okra and corn. Stir in the rice grits and smoked paprika. Stir in the hot stock. Season with salt, pepper, and cayenne. Bring to a boil, reduce the heat, cover the pan, and simmer until the rice is tender and has absorbed the liquid, about 18 minutes. Remove from the heat and adjust the seasoning. Stir in the green onions and parsley and serve hot.

Scott Barton of New York, New York

Red Jambalaya

Sally Davenport now lives in the mutton barbecue city of Owensboro, Kentucky, but she grew up amid her Cajun family in Kinder, Louisiana—rice country. Many Cajun dishes are prepared in one pot, and for this jambalaya, Davenport says she uses a large vessel in order to feed attendees at the International Barbecue Festival in Owensboro and upwards of 250 people at telephone company picnics. Her jambalaya, which can be made ahead of time, is baked in the oven and doesn't have to be constantly tended.

Makes 10 to 12 servings

1 pound smoked pork sausage, sliced into bite-sized pieces
1 pound boneless pork chops, cut into bite-sized pieces
1 pound boneless chicken thighs, cut into bite-sized pieces
2½ cups raw converted white rice
3 (8-ounce) cans tomato sauce, divided
1 (10-ounce) can diced tomatoes and green chiles (such as RO*TEL)
1 (10.5-ounce) can beef broth
1 (10.5-ounce) can condensed French onion soup

½ cup chopped green bell pepper
½ cup chopped fresh mushrooms
½ cup chopped celery
2 garlic cloves, minced
3 bay leaves
¼ pound (1 stick) butter
4 green onions, chopped
4 tablespoons chopped parsley
1 teaspoon Creole seasoning
1 tablespoon lemon pepper
½ cup water
Hot sauce

Preheat the oven to 350°F. Brown the sausage in a Dutch oven over medium-high heat, then transfer with a slotted spoon into a bowl. Brown the pork chops and add to the bowl. Brown the chicken. Return the sausage and pork chops to the pot. Stir in the rice, 2 cans of the tomato sauce, diced tomatoes and green chiles, beef broth, onion soup, bell pepper, mushrooms, celery, garlic, bay leaves, and butter. Bring to a simmer, stirring until the butter melts. Cover and bake for 45 minutes.

Meanwhile, stir together the green onions, parsley, Creole seasoning, lemon pepper, the remaining can of tomato sauce, and water in a bowl. Season with hot sauce. Stir in to the rice mixture after 45 minutes and then continue to bake until the rice is tender and has absorbed the liquid, about another 30 minutes. Fluff with a fork and serve hot.

Sally Davenport of Owensboro, Kentucky

Avery Island Jambalaya

"Eula Mae is a classic Cajun cook," says Paul McIlhenny. "She cooks only from memory, using recipes developed over a lifetime of experience in her kitchen."

McIlhenny once asked Eula Mae to prepare a special dish for his daughter's wedding reception. When he brought in a cooler filled with ducks and geese, she created this jambalaya. Chicken may be used in place of the wild game.

Makes 25 servings

10 quail	2 cups chopped green bell peppers
12 doves	½ cup chopped celery
12 teals	4 garlic cloves, peeled
4 geese	1 pound boiled ham, cubed
2 cups all-purpose flour	1 pound smoked pork sausage,
Salt and ground black pepper	chopped
½ cup oil, divided	5 cups raw long-grain white rice
1 teaspoon ground cayenne pepper	1 cup chopped green onions (white and
1 teaspoon hot sauce	tender green parts)
3 cups chopped yellow onions	1 cup finely chopped parsley leaves

Cut the birds into pieces that are a reasonable size to handle. Season the flour with salt and pepper. Lightly coat the meat in the flour and shake off any excess. Heat 2 tablespoons of the oil in a very large stockpot (or two smaller pots) over medium-high heat. Working in batches, brown the meat on all sides, adding more oil as needed. Transfer the browned pieces into a large bowl. When all of the meat is browned, pour off the fat from the pot. Return the browned meat to the pot and cover with cold water. Bring to a boil, reduce the heat, and simmer for 2 hours. Transfer the meat with a slotted spoon into a large bowl and set it aside until cool enough to handle. Pour the stock through a fine sieve into a large pot. Measure out 8 cups of stock and set it aside. (Save any remaining stock for another use.) Pull the meat from the bones and discard the skin and bones. There should be around 3 pounds of cooked meat. Season the meat with 1 teaspoon salt, 1 teaspoon pepper, cayenne, and hot sauce and mix well. Heat 3 tablespoons of the oil in a large Dutch oven or stock pot over medium-high heat. Brown the pulled meat well, stirring occasionally, then transfer it to a bowl and set aside. Add the onions, peppers, celery, and garlic and cook, stirring often, until light golden, about 10 minutes. Return the meat to the pot, add the ham and sausage, and cook, stirring often, for 10 minutes. Add the 8 cups of reserved stock and bring to a boil. Stir in the rice, reduce the heat to medium-low, cover, and cook until the rice is tender and the liquid has been absorbed, about 1 hour. Stir in the green onions and parsley. Adjust the seasonings, if necessary. Serve hot.

Eula Mae Doré of Avery Island, Louisiana

Savannah Red Rice

"Savannah Red Rice stands as a defining dish of the Georgia coast," says Glenn Roberts, who calls neighboring South Carolina home. Emphasizing vegetables, herbs, and spices, these composed rice dishes often reduce meat, fish, poultry, and game to condiment status. Roberts calls this "a rebuke to the legions of bad recipes in its name."

If you get lucky, or if you're already a talented rice cook, the bottom crust will be crisp and the rice on top will be plump and infused with flavor. Minced mushrooms and a dash of vinegar stand in for the historically correct mushroom ketchup. They also prove a distinct improvement over the sweet tomato ketchup present in many modern recipes.

Makes 4 to 6 servings

1 cup chicken stock
1 cup organic strained tomatoes or
    tomato juice
2 teaspoons red wine vinegar
1 Turkish bay leaf, crumbled
2 small whole chipotle chiles in
    adobo sauce
¼ cup (2 ounces) smoked, sliced bacon,
    finely chopped
1 small yellow onion, minced
    (about ½ cup)

¾ teaspoon dried thyme
1 teaspoon fine sea salt
½ teaspoon freshly ground
    black pepper
1 stalk celery, finely diced
    (about ⅓ cup)
4 ounces small button mushrooms,
    finely diced (about 1 cup)
1 garlic clove, minced
1 cup (7 ounces) raw Carolina Gold rice,
    well rinsed and drained

Stir together the stock, tomatoes, vinegar, and bay in a small saucepan. Drop the chipotles and any adobo sauce clinging to them into the pan and mash them against the sides with a wooden spoon. Cover and bring to a simmer over low heat for 10 minutes to infuse the flavors. Remove the pan from the heat.

Add the bacon to a cold, well-seasoned 9-inch cast-iron skillet. Fry the bacon over medium heat until crisp, stirring frequently, about 8 minutes. Add the onion and thyme and sauté until golden, stirring frequently, about 5 minutes. Stir in the salt and pepper. Stir in the celery and cook until barely tender; increase the heat, add the mushrooms, and cook until they have released their juices and the juices have evaporated, about 2 minutes.

While the mushrooms are cooking, bring the stock mixture back to a low simmer. Have a stainless conical strainer and a 9-inch lid wrapped with aluminum foil (to assist with the seal) at the ready.

Add the garlic to the bacon mixture and sauté until its aroma blooms, about 10 seconds. Stir the rice into the vegetables and sauté until the grains are opaque, 30 seconds or so. Pour the hot broth through the strainer into the skillet, pushing with the back of a wooden spoon to get every bit of liquid into the rice. Stir and reduce the heat to low. Cover tightly and cook 20 minutes without lifting the lid. Remove from the heat and rest 10 minutes without lifting the lid. Serve hot.

Glenn Roberts of Columbia, South Carolina

Spinach and Rice Casserole

When this casserole is served for lunch at Jimmy and Nicky Koikos's Bessemer, Alabama, restaurant, there's a standing list of customers who expect to be notified—by phone or fax. What's unusual is that the café serves up Southern fare and seafood as channeled by generations of Greek cooks. Although feta cheese may not be a staple in most Southern larders, we submit that, having tasted this recipe, it ought to be.

Makes 12 servings

1 large egg
1 (32-ounce) bag frozen chopped spinach, thawed and squeezed dry
½ cup chopped green onions
1 cup cooked white rice
¼ cup crumbled feta cheese

½ cup grated Parmesan cheese
2½ cups milk
1 chicken bouillon cube
¼ pound (1 stick) butter, melted
¼ cup all-purpose flour

Preheat the oven to 350°F. Generously butter a 9-by-13-inch baking dish.

Lightly beat the egg in a large bowl. Stir in the spinach, green onions, rice, feta, and Parmesan and mix well. Scrape into the prepared baking dish. Heat the milk in a saucepan to a bare simmer over medium heat. Add the bouillon cube and stir to dissolve. Remove from the heat. Whisk together the melted butter and flour in a small bowl until smooth. Whisk into the warm milk and then pour over the spinach mixture. Bake until the casserole is set and golden brown on top, 20 to 25 minutes. Serve hot.

Jimmy and Nicky Koikos of Bessemer, Alabama

Rice Pudding

Tennessean Martha Stamps made her reputation cooking seasonally inspired local foods. Fortunately for rice pudding lovers, rice has a year-round shelf-life.

Whiskey-loving cooks can count themselves lucky that Martha took more than one grain into account when formulating this recipe.

Makes 8 servings

¾ cup raw white rice
2 cups water
1 teaspoon salt
⅓ cup raisins
1 tablespoon whiskey

2 cups whole milk
4 large eggs
½ cup sugar
½ teaspoon ground cinnamon
¼ teaspoon ground mace

Preheat the oven to 325°F. Grease a ½-quart baking dish and set it aside.

Bring the rice, water, and salt to a boil in a saucepan over high heat. Stir and cover. Reduce the heat to low and simmer for 15 minutes. Remove from the heat, uncover, and set aside.

Place the raisins in a small bowl. Pour the whiskey over the raisins and set aside.

Heat the milk in a saucepan until scalding (180°F). Remove the pan from the heat and set aside.

Whisk together the eggs, sugar, cinnamon, and mace in a large bowl. Stir in the raisins and whiskey. Stir in the rice. Whisking constantly, add the milk in a slow, steady stream. Pour the pudding into the prepared baking dish. Bake until the tip of a thin knife inserted into the center comes out clean, about 1 hour. If the pudding is set but the top is not browned, set under the broiler for a few minutes. Serve warm.

Martha Stamps of Nashville, Tennessee

Calas

These rice fritters are history on a plate. The word *calas* itself and the cooking technique can be traced to Africa. In the eighteenth and nineteenth centuries, women of African descent sold calas on the streets of New Orleans on their days off from domestic chores, sometimes storing up the profits to buy their freedom. History books record their calls: "Belle calas, tout chauds" (Beautiful calas, nice and hot).

More recently, calas were in danger of becoming a lost tradition, a tradition that New Orleanian Poppy Tooker has made it her mission to revive. And she's enjoying great success.

Makes about 18

6 tablespoons all-purpose flour
3 heaping tablespoons sugar
2 teaspoons baking powder
¼ teaspoon salt
¼ teaspoon ground nutmeg
2 large eggs, lightly beaten

¼ teaspoon vanilla extract
2 cups cooked long-grain white rice,
   at room temperature
Vegetable oil, for frying
Confectioners' sugar,
   for dusting

Whisk together the flour, sugar, baking powder, salt, and nutmeg in a bowl. In another bowl, whisk together the eggs and vanilla. Whisk the egg mixture into the flour mixture, stirring only until combined. Fold in the rice; do not overmix. Let stand at room temperature for 20 minutes.

Pour oil into a large pot or deep fryer to a depth of at least 4 inches. Heat the oil to 360°F.

Working in batches, drop heaping tablespoons of the rice mixture into the hot fat and fry until golden brown, 3 to 4 minutes, turning as needed. Transfer with a slotted spoon to drain on paper towels. Let the oil return to 360°F between batches. Dust the calas with confectioners' sugar and serve hot.

Poppy Tooker of New Orleans, Louisiana

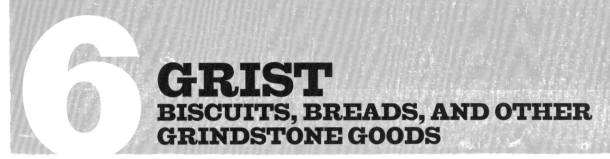

6 GRIST
BISCUITS, BREADS, AND OTHER GRINDSTONE GOODS

In the North man may not be able to live by bread alone.
But in the South, and particularly in Charleston, he comes
mighty near to it, provided the bread is hot.
—Blanche S. Rhett, *Two Hundred Years of Charleston Cooking*

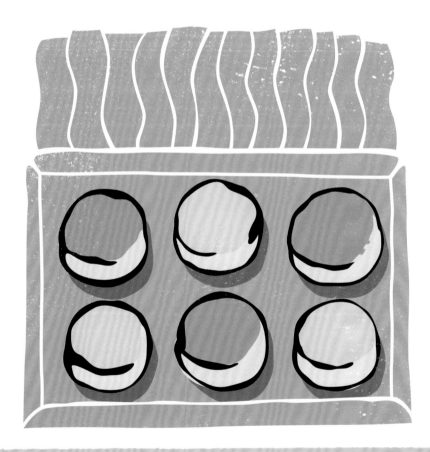

GRIST, not to be confused with that hot cereal grits, is anything that goes into or comes out of a mill. The simplest grist mill of two rocks remains, after thousands of years, the technique for producing the finest meals and flours.

Small, water-powered grist mills once dotted the region. They were central to the community, serving as a locus for visiting with friends and neighbors or gathering news while the miller ground the corn crop into meal.

Outside of the lowlands, corn was the antebellum grain of choice, and it remains the distinguishing component of the region's culinary tradition. Corn provides the basis of our breads, pones, grits, dumplings, and fritters. It also gives crunch to skillet-fried vegetables and thickens vegetable puddings. In its fresh form, corn is beloved. Distilled as corn whiskey, it is, as historian Joe Gray Taylor once put it, "one of the most notable contributions of the Scotch-Irish to American culture."

A staple for the earliest Americans, corn could be grown in a small home garden around the perimeter of the house. Large cultivated fields were not necessary for it to thrive. Most important, however, were corn's high yields and short growing cycle.

Although Southerners agree on their love of—and beholdenness to—corn, spirited disagreements erupt when the discussion turns to corn color. Edna Lewis said that white corn "has a clear, clean taste that's a little sweeter." European settlers focused their early breeding efforts on yellow corn to increase yields for animal feed. Without the effects of aggressive breeding insensitive to flavor, antebellum white corns have remained closer to their Native American predecessors.

Whether white or yellow, corn determined the style of bread that dominated the South. Corn was unresponsive to the leavening powers of yeast. Settlers learned to enjoy the simplest, unleavened cornmeal and water breads the way that they tasted best, steaming hot out of the ashes.

Later, the iron skillet became the preferred cooking vessel, and Southerners enjoyed hot breads as many as three times a day. When wheat did become widely available in the South, many home cooks proved uninterested in producing time-consuming and laborious yeasted and kneaded breads.

The marriage of soft wheat flour and modern chemical leavening, however, produced the beloved biscuit, which took only minutes to stir together. Neither biscuits nor cornbread were good keepers. Thus hot, home-baked breads became the pride of the South.

"It's an old tale that the South is known as the land of the hot biscuit and the cold check," Marjorie Kinnan Rawlings wrote in *Cross Creek Cookery*, her 1942 catalog of northern Florida foodways. "Yet a part of the placidity of the South comes from the sense of well-being that follows the heart-and-body-warming consumption of breads fresh from the oven. We serve cold baker's bread to our enemies, trusting that they will never impose on our hospitality again."

Angel Biscuits

Angel biscuits, also known as bride's biscuits, are virtually foolproof. They owe their airiness to two, or sometimes three, leavenings: yeast, baking soda, and, occasionally, baking powder. Somewhere between crusty European breads and traditional biscuits, but unlike either, this type of failsafe belt-and-suspender recipe began appearing in cookbooks in the 1950s and was all the rage through the 1970s.

Makes about 30 biscuits

1 (¼-ounce) packet active dry yeast
2 tablespoons lukewarm water (105° to 115°F)
5 cups Southern soft-wheat self-rising flour
¼ cup sugar

½ teaspoon baking soda
1 cup vegetable shortening
2 cups buttermilk
Nonstick cooking spray
4 tablespoons (½ stick) butter, melted

Dissolve the yeast in the lukewarm water in a small bowl. Set aside until the yeast looks foamy.

Stir together the flour, sugar, and baking soda in a large bowl. Use a pastry blender or your fingertips to cut in the shortening until the pieces are the size of peas.

Stir the buttermilk into the dissolved yeast. Stir into the flour mixture using a fork, just until moistened. Some or all of the dough can be refrigerated at this point. The dough is good for up to a week and actually develops more flavor over time.

When ready to bake, lightly coat a baking sheet with nonstick cooking spray and set it aside. Knead the dough lightly, about six turns. Roll out on a lightly floured surface to a ½-inch thickness. Stamp out biscuits with a 2-inch cutter. (Don't twist the cutter or the biscuits will rise taller on one side.) Gather, roll, and cut the scraps. Arrange the biscuits with sides touching on the prepared baking sheet. (This helps them rise higher and remain soft.) Cover with a damp lint-free towel or plastic wrap that has been lightly coated with nonstick cooking spray. Let the biscuits rise in a warm place until they have doubled in bulk, about 1 hour if at room temperature or 1½ hours if the dough has been refrigerated.

Preheat the oven to 425°F. Bake until the biscuits are lightly browned, about 15 to 20 minutes. Brush the tops with the melted butter and serve hot.

Belinda Ellis of Raleigh, North Carolina

Awendaw Spoonbread

This recipe is an antecedent to the modern spoonbread, likely taking its name from an ancient Native American settlement just north of Charleston, South Carolina. The Awendaw area is still faintly connected to its colonial foodways, and a few home cooks still prepare this dish on a hearth. Sadly, Awendaw's classic crisp crust, produced by dry hearth heat, cannot be achieved in a home oven. Kay Rentschler, however, hints at the glory of the original with this recipe, developed after much trial-and-error research.

Makes 6 to 8 servings

3 large eggs
½ cup (3 ounces) white or yellow stone-ground quick grits
2 cups water
2 tablespoons unsalted butter, at room temperature

1¼ teaspoons fine sea salt
½ teaspoon ground black pepper
2 cups whole milk
1 cup fine white or yellow cornmeal
1½ teaspoons baking powder
¼ cup heavy cream

Position the oven racks to the upper and middle positions and preheat the oven to 450°F. Butter a 9-inch cast-iron skillet, a 9-inch cake pan, or a 1½-quart casserole dish and set it aside.

Whisk the eggs in a medium bowl and set aside. Place the grits in a heavy 2½-quart saucepan (preferably one with fluted sides) and cover with the water. Stir once. Allow the grits to settle a full minute, tilt the pan, and skim off and discard the chaff and hulls with a fine tea strainer. Bring to a simmer over medium-high heat, stirring constantly with a wooden spoon, until the first starch takes hold, 5 to 8 minutes. Reduce the heat to low and cook, stirring frequently, until the grits are just tender and hold their shape on a spoon, about 25 minutes. Stir in the butter, salt, and pepper. Whisk in the milk in three additions. Cover the saucepan and bring the grits to a simmer over medium-high heat, whisking frequently. Remove the pan from the heat and whisk in the cornmeal. Whisk about 1 cup of the hot grits into the beaten eggs to temper them, then whisk this back into the grits. Whisk in the baking powder.

Scrape the batter into a prepared pan and smooth the top. Spoon the cream over the top. Place the pan in the oven and bake 10 minutes. Lower the oven to 375°F and bake until the spoonbread is nicely risen and golden brown, 15 to 20 minutes more. Serve without delay.

Kay Rentschler of Charleston, South Carolina

Beaten Biscuits

A symbol of aristocratic cooking, the beaten biscuit made its way to Appalachia at the turn of the twentieth century, when public health officials targeted cornbread as a source of diet-based diseases. Activists from the Progressive movement then set out to create a social revolution in Appalachia, switching mountain cooks from cornbread to beaten biscuits. Critics called it the Beaten Biscuit Crusade.

These biscuits required not only wheat flour, a prohibitive luxury to many, but also elaborate equipment, including a marble slab for beating the dough a laborious three hundred strokes (five hundred for company). Beaten biscuits, thus, served to separate the privileged from the poor and, following contemporaneous public heath logic, the healthy from the unhealthy. Elizabeth Engelhardt insists that "these biscuits must be beaten," by which she means "hammered, smacked, hit, bludgeoned."

Makes about 24

4 cups all-purpose flour, plus more for cutting
1 teaspoon salt

4 tablespoons chilled lard
1 cup cold water

Preheat the oven to 325°F. Lightly grease a baking sheet with butter or lard and set it aside.

Sift the flour and salt into a large bowl. Rub the lard into the flour until the mixture is granular. Stirring constantly, add the cold water in a slow, steady stream. Stir just until the dough comes together. Turn out onto a well-floured surface and knead briefly until smooth. Beat the dough approximately 20 times with a sturdy mallet, cleaver, or rolling pin to create a long rectangle. Fold into thirds, turn 90 degrees, and repeat. Opinions vary on how many times to repeat, but at least 200 strokes are necessary; consider more for special occasions. The dough will get smooth and elastic and may seem sticky, but don't add extra flour unless the mallet is getting stuck.

Roll the dough to a ½-inch thickness. Using a small biscuit cutter dipped in flour, cut out the biscuits and transfer them to the prepared baking sheet. Prick the top of the biscuits with a fork. Bake until firm, 20 to 30 minutes. The biscuits should remain white or very light golden. Although they can be served hot, these thin and crispy biscuits are usually served at room temperature.

Elizabeth Engelhardt of Austin, Texas

Benne Seed Biscuits

In the Carolina Lowcountry, sesame seeds are known by their African name, benne, and are regarded as a symbol of good luck. Sesame-seed-studded biscuits, sometimes thin and crackerlike, sometimes sweetened, sometimes referred to as cocktailers, are a mainstay of Lowcountry parties. Often filled with paper-thin slivers of country ham, they can also be smeared with butter, pimento cheese, or shrimp paste. Jean Anderson adapted this recipe from one given to her by a local cook.

Makes about 4½ dozen

2 cups sifted all-purpose flour, plus more
    for rolling
2 teaspoons baking powder
½ teaspoon baking soda
I teaspoon salt
½ teaspoon ground cayenne pepper

⅓ cup firmly packed lard or vegetable
    shortening
I tablespoon butter
½ cup lightly toasted benne (sesame)
    seeds (see note below)
½ cup buttermilk

Preheat the oven to 425°F. Combine the flour, baking powder, baking soda, salt, and cayenne in a large mixing bowl. Use a pastry blender or your fingertips to cut in the lard and butter until the mixture has the texture of coarse meal. Add the benne and toss thoroughly. Make a well in the middle of the dry ingredients, pour in the buttermilk, and stir briskly with a fork just until the mixture comes together to form soft dough. Turn onto a lightly floured surface and knead lightly, 8 to 10 turns. Use a lightly floured rolling pin to roll to a thickness of about ½ inch.

    Cut into 1-inch rounds using a small, floured biscuit cutter (or even a bottle cap) and space about ½ inch apart on ungreased baking sheets. Bake in the lower third of the oven until lightly browned, 15 to 20 minutes. Split, butter while hot, and serve warm. Or, if you prefer, cool to room temperature, split, and fill with the thinnest slivers of country ham. Pass with cocktails or set up on a party buffet.

Note: To toast sesame seeds, preheat the oven to 275°F. Spread the seeds in an ungreased pie pan and bake on the middle rack just until the color of pale amber, 8 to 10 minutes. Stir the benne frequently as they toast so that they brown evenly. Cool the seeds to room temperature before using.

Jean Anderson of Chapel Hill, North Carolina

Buttermilk Biscuits

There are many different beloved Southern biscuits: Fall-apart-soft, melt-in-your-mouth biscuits. Flat, crispy, old-timey biscuits. Fat, fluffy, cathead biscuits. Layered, crunchy-bottomed biscuits with tender middles. However, there exist a few necessities everyone can agree on: soft wheat flour, buttermilk, very cold ingredients, a gentle touch, and a hot oven.

Much ink has been spilled over the proper fat for biscuit making. The general consensus is: Butter tastes best but lacks structure. Lard tastes most authentic and yields the best layers. Shortening is the easiest medium for the novice and produces the most tender biscuit with decent layers but offers little taste value. A combination of fats, such as half lard and half butter, mixed for their respective qualities, is a favorite among many bakers.

Tough biscuits, the most common pitfall of bakers, are the result of inadequacies in the English language. (Also, recipe instructions are poor replacements for observation.) Many recipes call for biscuit dough to be "kneaded." In bread making, kneading refers to the method of folding and compressing to develop gluten and sturdy structure—exactly what you are trying to avoid when making biscuits. Note that while the motion of gathering biscuit dough by pulling and pushing is similar to kneading, it lacks all of the vigor.

Growing up in Florence, Alabama, Natalie Chanin ate biscuits every day. With grits. With bacon. These days she's more likely to serve star-shaped biscuits with freshly cooked fruits and whipped cream. Maybe with butter and honey.

Makes about 1 dozen

2 cups all-purpose flour, plus more
    for rolling
2 teaspoons baking powder
1 teaspoon salt

¼ pound (1 stick) unsalted butter, lard,
    and/or shortening cut into cubes and
    chilled
¾ cup buttermilk
2 tablespoons unsalted butter, melted

Preheat the oven to 425°F. Stir together the flour, baking powder, and salt in a bowl. Use a pastry blender or your fingertips to cut in the chilled butter until the pieces are the size of peas. Stir in the buttermilk with a fork or wooden spoon to form soft dough. Turn out the dough onto a lightly floured work surface. Gather and fold the dough over two or three times, just until it comes together. Use a lightly floured rolling pin to roll the dough to a ½-inch thickness. Use a lightly floured 2¼-inch round cutter to stamp out biscuits as close together as possible. Gently pat the dough scraps together and stamp out more biscuits. Transfer the biscuits to a large baking sheet. Bake until the biscuits are golden, about 20 minutes. Brush the hot biscuits with the melted butter and serve without delay.

Natalie Chanin of Florence, Alabama

Miracle Drop Biscuits

Sheri Castle calls these cream biscuits miracles, as in, "It's a miracle that anybody can make a decent drop biscuit with only two ingredients." Sheri recommends this recipe for harried weekdays, lazy weekends, and everyday sopping. She also admits, with a grin, that these are the biscuits she makes most often at home.

Makes 6 biscuits

2 cups Southern soft-wheat self-rising flour
1¼ cups well-chilled heavy cream

Preheat the oven to 475°F. Line a baking sheet with a silicone baking mat or parchment paper and set it aside. Place the flour in a medium bowl and make a well in the center. Pour the cream into the well and stir with a fork to make soft, slightly wet dough. If necessary, finish bringing the dough together with a rubber spatula, but handle the dough as little as possible. Drop the dough into 6 equal lumps on the prepared baking sheet. Bake until the tops are golden, about 12 minutes. Serve hot, although they're not bad at room temperature, even the next day.

Sheri Castle of Chapel Hill, North Carolina

YOU ALREADY KNOW THIS, BUT JUST IN CASE...

Makes 4 servings

BASIC GRITS

1 cup traditional stone-ground grits ½ teaspoon salt
5 cups water 2 tablespoons butter

Put the grits into a medium bowl, cover with cold water, stir vigorously, and let stand for 1 minute. Skim off and discard the chaff that rises to the surface. Drain the grits in a fine sieve. Bring the 5 cups of water to a boil in a large enameled cast-iron or other heavy saucepan. Add the salt and slowly stir in the grits. Reduce the heat to medium-low and simmer, stirring often to prevent a skin from forming on the surface and to keep the grits from sticking to the bottom of the pot, until they are thick, soft, and creamy, 1½ to 2 hours. Stir more often toward the end of cooking. Add a little water if the grits get dry before they are done. Stir in the butter and season with salt. Serve hot.

SLOW-COOKER GRITS

1 cup traditional stone-ground grits ½ teaspoon salt
5 cups water 2 tablespoons butter

Set the slow cooker to high. Put the grits into a medium bowl, cover with cold water, stir vigorously, and let stand for 1 minute. Skim off and discard the chaff that rises to the surface. Drain the grits in a fine sieve. Pour the grits into the slow cooker and stir in the 5 cups of water, the salt, and the butter. Cover, set the slow cooker to low, and cook until the grits are thick, soft, and creamy, about 8 hours. Do not remove the lid or stir during the first 2 hours. Season with salt and serve hot.

Cheese Grits Casserole

It's hard to beat a steaming bowl of grits, the ground product of dried hominy, cooked simply with spring water (or, if you're lucky, the mildly alkaline water from Georgia and Carolina Sea Island aquifers), flavored with a great deal of fresh butter and plenty of salt (black pepper, if you wish). That said, the soul who first grated Cheddar cheese into a pot of grits ensured that the dish would earn a wider audience. Beckett Howorth belongs to that latter camp. He folds in beaten eggs and half-and-half, creating a kind of countrified soufflé.

Makes 4 to 6 servings

5 tablespoons butter, divided
Basic grits or slow-cooker grits, hot
   (page 107)
1 small garlic clove, minced
Ground white pepper

4 ounces sharp Cheddar cheese, grated
   on the large holes of a box grater
   (1 cup)
3 tablespoons half-and-half
1 large egg, well beaten

Preheat the oven to 325°F. Grease a deep 2-quart baking dish with 1 tablespoon of the butter and set aside.

Stir together the hot cooked grits, garlic, and the remaining 4 tablespoons of butter in a bowl. Season with white pepper. Stir in the cheese, one third at a time. Stir in the half-and-half. Stir in the egg and mix well. Pour into the prepared casserole. Bake until light golden on top and bubbling, about 45 minutes. Set aside to cool briefly before serving.

Beckett Howorth of Oxford, Mississippi

Grits and Grillades

Grillades are, in essence, slow-cooked cutlets of beef, veal, or pork. Many versions exist, all made from the humblest cuts. Although widely known as a New Orleans brunch dish served over grits, grillades have as much in common with smothered pork chops from north of I-10 as they do with other Cajun or Creole analogues.

Follow the lead of Ashley Hansen, who says that the dish can be easily multiplied to feed a crowd: "I make a huge batch, invite everyone I know, then put some up for family, and then some for the freezer."

Makes 8 servings

3 pounds round steak or veal shoulder
Salt and ground black pepper
½ cup all-purpose flour, divided
3 tablespoons vegetable oil
2 medium yellow onions, chopped
   (about 3 cups)
2 celery stalks, chopped (about 1 cup)
1 red bell pepper, diced (about 1 cup)
1 green bell pepper, diced (about 1 cup)
3 cups beef stock

1 (15-ounce) can diced tomatoes
¼ cup bitters
3 large garlic cloves, minced
5 sprigs fresh thyme
1 teaspoon minced habanero chile
2 tablespoons brown sugar
1 bay leaf
Basic grits or slow-cooker grits, hot,
   for serving (page 107)

Cut the meat into ½-inch-thick slices. (This is easiest if the meat is very cold.) Season the meat with salt and pepper, then coat in ¼ cup of the flour, and shake off any excess. Heat the oil in a large Dutch oven over medium-high heat. Working in batches, brown the beef on both sides. Transfer with tongs to a shallow bowl and set aside.

Add the onions, celery, and bell peppers to the pot. Cook, stirring to scrape up the browned bits from the bottom of the pot, until the vegetables soften, about 8 minutes. Reduce the heat and add a splash of the stock if the vegetables start to scorch. Transfer the cooked vegetables to a large bowl and set aside.

Spoon off or add enough oil to have 3 tablespoons of fat in the pot. Make a roux by whisking in the remaining ¼ cup of the flour into the fat. Reduce the heat to low and cook, stirring constantly, until the roux browns, about 10 minutes. Stir in the stock, tomatoes, bitters, garlic, thyme, habanero, brown sugar, and bay leaf. Return the meat, vegetables, and accumulated juices to the pot and stir. Bring just to a boil, reduce the heat, cover the pot, and simmer until the meat is spoon tender, 2½ to 3 hours. Discard the bay leaf. Season with salt and pepper. Serve hot over grits.

Ashley Hansen of New Orleans, Louisiana

TANKIE'S CORNBREAD, as told by her great-grandson, Joe York

My grandmother cooks cornbread with almost every meal, except breakfast, which always features five-dot butter toast. The recipe for her cornbread came, as you might expect, from her mother, Francis Brown, a.k.a. Frankie, a.k.a. Tankie. As a side note, this cornbread was one of the only remnants of her former diet that Frankie could continue to eat during her long, losing battle with Alzheimer's (mostly she survived on baby food and ivs, an unforgivable reality of an unforgiving disease).

Fearing that the genetic lottery might have the same losing numbers in store for my grandmother Lurlene Brown Smith (so far so good, she's in her eighties and sharp as a shark tooth), I asked her to show me how to make the cornbread I have come to regard as the greasy tabernacle of everything I know to be sacred.

That said, I have a tendency to overstate, to embellish, to be what it is in my nature to be: absurd. Never was this more apparent than when my grandmother gave me her cornbread recipe. I had always assumed she ground the meal by hand, churned the buttermilk in the woods at night while we slept, and baked it in a cast-iron skillet she forged herself at the local blast furnace when the union was on strike. Instead, this is how she does it:

Makes 1 eight-inch cake

She heats her oven to 480°F (or so). She takes a huge spoon and scoops a glob of Crisco into a cast-iron skillet (I'm guessing it's an 8-inch since that's what mine is, and she gave it to me) and then puts it in the oven, where the shortening heats up and liquefies.

In a large bowl, she mixes 2½ cups buttermilk, 2½ cups Aunt Jemima White Cornmeal Mix, ½ cup White Lily Self-Rising Flour, and as much Clabber Girl baking powder as will sit in a lump on top of a dime without falling off.

By now the shortening is steaming hot. She pulls the skillet from the oven and sprinkles a little flour into the hot shortening and mixes it around. (This, she says, prevents sticking, and it does.) Next she pours about a third of the hot shortening into the batter and stirs it in. (If the grease doesn't sizzle when it hits the batter, it's not hot enough, so try pouring just a spoonful first to test, and then pour in a third of what's there.) Then she pours the batter into the skillet, where the remaining hot shortening awaits.

Now the tricky part. As the batter settles into the skillet, again sizzling, the hot shortening will travel up the sides of the skillet and form small pools around the top of the batter. With a spoon, lightly press down at the edges of the batter, filling the spoon with the shortening, and distribute the shortening evenly across the top of the batter, smoothing the surface with the spoon as you go. Make sure you get it good and greasy.

Now you just put the skillet back in the oven and let it cook for about 25 minutes, until the cornbread has a nice, more-brown-than-golden crust. Take it out of the oven and flip the skillet upside down over a cooling rack and the best cornbread you ever ate will pop right out. You can also dump it out onto a dinner plate and then slide a butter knife under it—that will raise it up enough to cool and release the steam so that the crispy crust won't be softened. If for some reason it doesn't pop right out, run a butter knife along the inside walls of the skillet and it should cooperate.

Apply copious amounts of butter and/or sorghum and/or honey and enjoy. It should be white and fluffy on the inside and brown and crunchy on the outside, just like Tankie used to make.

That's it. No, there are no eggs. Yes, there is flour. No, it's not healthy. Yes, it's delicious. And yes, I said, "Aunt Jemima White Cornmeal Mix."

Besides being my favorite thing ever, this recipe stands as a testament to a very real and very underappreciated side of Southern foodways, the side where hard-working women took mixes and boxes and cans of things they could find at the grocery and "doctored" them into the foods they had always eaten and in the process spent a little less time at the stove and a little more at the table.

I hope when you eat it you'll feel the way I do when I sit at my grandmother's table: full.

Corn Dumplings

Also known as Indian dumplings, these cornmeal or corn dumplings were one of the first foods English settlers in coastal Virginia and North Carolina learned to make from native ingredients. They have persevered for four hundred years. Although scarce nowadays, they are occasionally found floating on top of a pot of greens.

Nowhere are corn dumplings eaten with more variation than in eastern North Carolina, where they are added in the final fifteen minutes of cooking to most any stovetop dish: collard greens, green beans, speckled butterbeans, rutabagas, field peas, vegetable soup, beef stew, neck bones, even seafood stew. In his lifetime, Flavius B. Hall Jr. has witnessed the popularity of the corn dumpling wane. This is his family recipe.

Makes 8 to 10 dumplings

1 cup fine or medium cornmeal
1 tablespoon all-purpose flour
¼ teaspoon salt
¼ teaspoon ground black pepper
   (optional)

½ to 1 cup hot potlikker or water
1 large egg, lightly beaten (optional, but
   will lighten the dumplings)
¼ cup chopped green onions (optional)

Mix the cornmeal, flour, salt, and pepper in a bowl. Stir in the potlikker a little at a time, just enough to make smooth batter that is stiff enough to hold together. Vigorously stir in the egg, if using. Stir in the green onions, if using. Let the batter rest for a few minutes. Spoon up enough batter into your hand to pat out a 2-inch-round flat dumpling about ½-inch thick. It is easier to make the dumplings when your hands are wet. Use up all the batter. Lay the dumplings on the surface of the simmering liquid of cooked vegetables, soup, or stew. Cover the pot and simmer until the dumplings are firm and cooked through, about 12 minutes. If the dumplings seem too wet on top, gently turn them over or baste with some hot liquid. Take up the dumplings and place them on top of the vegetable or stew in a serving bowl.

Flavius B. Hall Jr. of New Bern, North Carolina

Fresh Corn Fritters

"Flat, almost pancakelike cakes made with fresh corn cut from the cob, these, fried in oil, are the type of fritter I grew up eating," says Crescent Dragonwagon, a native of New York who cut her teeth (and her corn) in Arkansas. Crescent argues that, at the height of corn season, when the sun is burning bright and the temperature is spiraling, these are just the bites to cook, when you want to taste sweet corn but don't want to heat up the house by turning on the oven.

Makes about 24 fritters

2 eggs
¼ cup milk
Kernels cut from 2 ears of fresh corn
    (about 1 cup), plus scrapings of liquid
    from running the back of a knife
    along the cob
2 tablespoons stone-ground white or
    yellow cornmeal

¼ cup unbleached white flour
1 teaspoon sugar
¼ teaspoon salt
2¼ teaspoons baking powder
Vegetable oil, for frying

Whisk together the eggs and milk in a large bowl. Stir in the corn and any corn liquid.

Sift together the cornmeal, flour, sugar, salt, and baking powder in a medium bowl. Stir the flour mixture into the egg mixture to make batter that is thick but still can be dropped from a spoon.

Pour oil into a heavy cast-iron skillet to a depth of ½ inch. Heat the oil to 350°F. Drop the batter by tablespoonfuls into the skillet. It will sizzle as it goes into the oil. If the first fritter doesn't sizzle, wait and let the oil get a little hotter before adding more fritters. Don't crowd the skillet—crowding will bring down the heat—no more than 4 to 6 fritters, not touching, at a time. Adjust the heat as needed to keep the oil at 350°F. Let the corn fritters cook until they are golden and crispy on the bottom, about 2 minutes. When it's time to flip them, the edges will be firmer and colored just slightly and the top of the fritter will no longer be moist. Turn them over and cook about 2 minutes more. As they cook, line a tray with paper towels or torn-open brown paper grocery sacks. Place the cooked fritters on the paper and blot them quickly with another piece of paper. Serve immediately, nice and hot.

Crescent Dragonwagon of Putney, Vermont

Hush Puppies

Hush puppies appear on barbecue plates throughout the Carolinas. In the rest of the South, hush puppies are served almost exclusively with fried fish, which is how Ed and Edna Scott—the first African Americans to own a catfish processing plant—became hush puppy experts. After retirement, Ed Scott began cooking for church and benefit dinners, dredging catfish in his wife's famous breading mix and frying them till they floated. When the catfish were almost ready, Scott would drop hush puppy batter by the spoonful into the hot oil. As the fish drained, he chased the puppies around the pot with a pair of tongs.

Makes about 4 dozen

Vegetable oil, for frying
3 cups self-rising cornmeal
⅔ cup self-rising flour
1 small yellow onion, minced or grated
    (about 1 cup)

1 small green bell pepper, minced
    (about ¾ cup)
2½ cups buttermilk
1 large egg, lightly beaten

Pour oil into a large, deep, cast-iron or heavy-bottomed skillet to a depth of 3 inches. Heat the oil to 350° to 360°F. While the oil is heating, stir together the cornmeal, flour, onion, and bell pepper in a large bowl. Stir in the buttermilk and egg and mix well.

Working in batches, use a small ice cream scoop or spoon to drop 1-inch balls of batter into the hot oil. Cook the hush puppies, turning them occasionally with metal tongs or a slotted spoon, until they are browned and crisp, about 5 minutes. Push loose any hush puppies that stick to the bottom or the side of the skillet as they fry. Transfer with a slotted spoon to drain on paper towels. Serve hot.

Ed Scott of Drew, Mississippi

Pimento Cheese Hush Puppies

Mary Beth Lasseter, a Georgian by birth and a Mississippian by residence, is a fiend for hush puppies. And for pimento cheese. At an early Southern Foodways Symposium, during a dinner at Taylor Grocery, her friend John Currence took a guest turn at the fry basket in the Taylor kitchen and set out to please her. What emerged was this dish, a Southern staple for the twenty-first century.

Makes about 2 dozen

PIMENTO CHEESE

6 ounces extra sharp Cheddar cheese, grated (1½ cups)

4 ounces cream cheese, at room temperature

⅓ cup chopped bread-and-butter pickles

3 tablespoons pickle juice

1 teaspoon ground cayenne pepper

1 teaspoon hot sauce

¼ cup drained and chopped pimentos

¼ cup homemade mayonnaise

Salt and fresh cracked pepper

SEASONED FLOUR

1 cup all-purpose flour

1 teaspoon onion powder

1 teaspoon garlic powder

½ teaspoon ground cayenne pepper

½ teaspoon paprika

¼ teaspoon ground cumin

1 teaspoon salt

½ teaspoon ground black pepper

EGG WASH

2 large eggs

¼ cup whole milk

1 teaspoon salt

1 teaspoon ground black pepper

½ teaspoon hot sauce

SEASONED CRUMBS

3 cups panko bread crumbs or seasoned cornmeal

1 teaspoon salt

½ teaspoon ground black pepper

Melted lard or peanut oil, for frying

To make the pimento cheese: Mix the Cheddar cheese, cream cheese, pickles, pickle juice, cayenne, hot sauce, pimentos, and mayonnaise, as well as salt and pepper to taste, in the bowl of a stand mixer fitted with the paddle attachment. Cover and refrigerate until firm and well chilled. Mold the chilled pimento cheese into scant ½-ounce balls that are about 1½ inches in diameter. Refrigerate until well chilled.

To make the seasoned flour: Sift together the flour, onion powder, garlic powder, cayenne, paprika, cumin, salt, and pepper into a bowl and set aside.

To make the egg wash: Whisk together the eggs, milk, salt, pepper, and hot sauce in a bowl and set aside.

To make the seasoned crumbs: Whisk together the panko, salt, and pepper in a bowl and set aside. If you use the seasoned cornmeal instead of the panko, the final product will be more like a traditional hush puppy.

To form and cook the hush puppies: Dredge the pimento cheese balls by coating them in the seasoned flour, then the egg wash, and then the seasoned crumbs. There must be no bare spots. Fry at once, or cover and refrigerate for up to several hours. The pimento cheese must stay cold and firm.

Pour melted lard or peanut oil into a deep, heavy skillet or Dutch oven to a depth of at least 3 inches. Heat the oil to 325°F. Carefully lower the hush puppies into the hot fat. They must be submerged. Don't move them or poke at them; otherwise, they will spring a leak and all the pimento cheese will ooze out, ruining both the hush puppies and the oil. Fry until nicely browned, 5 to 7 minutes. Transfer with a slotted spoon to drain on paper towels. Important: Let the hush puppies cool for several minutes before eating or you will end up at the hospital needing a skin graft in your mouth. And we all know where they get that skin for grafting.

John Currence of Oxford, Mississippi

Mississippi Delta Hot Tamales

The history of the Delta hot tamale is murky. As best as can be determined, it came to be a Mississippi favorite in the early years of the twentieth century when Mexican laborers began making their way up from Texas to work bumper cotton harvests. In the Delta cotton fields, Mexican laborers shared their bundles of pork and corn with African American laborers. And a hybridized food was born.

Though tamale recipes vary from place to place and person to person, in the Delta, you will generally find rough cornmeal in place of masa. And you will find that pork is the traditional filling. More recently, beef has come on strong and some tamale makers have begun wrapping their tamales in parchment paper as well as corn shucks.

Makes 7 to 8 dozen

MEAT FILLING

6 to 8 pounds boneless meat (pork
    shoulder, chuck roast, or chicken)
¾ cup vegetable oil
¼ cup chili powder
2 tablespoons paprika
2 tablespoons salt

2 teaspoons black pepper
1 teaspoon ground cayenne pepper
1 tablespoon onion powder
1 tablespoon garlic powder
1 teaspoon ground cumin

CORN HUSKS

1 to 2 packages dried corn husks

MASA DOUGH

8 cups maseca (masa mix) or yellow
    cornmeal
4 teaspoons baking powder
2 teaspoons salt

1⅔ cups lard or vegetable
    shortening
6 to 8 cups warm meat broth
    (from cooking the meat)

To make the meat filling: Cut the meat into large chunks and place in a large, heavy pot. Cover with cold water. Bring to a boil over high heat. Cover the pot, reduce the heat to medium-low, and simmer until the meat is very tender, 2 to 2½ hours. Remove the meat and reserve the cooking liquid. When the meat is cool enough to handle, remove and discard any skin or large chunks of fat. Shred or dice the meat into small pieces. There should be about 14 to 16 cups of meat. Heat the vegetable oil in a large, heavy pot over medium heat. Stir in the chili powder, paprika, salt, pepper, cayenne, onion powder, garlic powder, and cumin. Add the meat and stir to coat with the oil and spices. Cook, stirring often, until the meat is warmed through, 7 to 10 minutes. Set aside.

To prepare the corn husks: While the meat is cooking, soak the husks in a large bowl or sink of very warm water, until they are softened and pliable, about 2 hours. Gently separate the husks into single leaves, trying not to tear them. Wash off any dust and discard any corn silks. Keep any shucks that split to the side, since two small pieces can be overlapped and used as one.

To make the masa dough: Stir the maseca, baking powder, salt, and lard together in a large bowl until well blended. Gradually stir in enough warm broth (from cooking the meat) to make soft, spongy dough that is the consistency of thick mashed potatoes. The dough should be moist but not wet. Cover the bowl with a damp cloth.

To assemble the tamales: Remove a corn husk from the water and pat it dry. Lay the husk on a work surface. Spread about ¼ cup of the masa in an even layer across the wide end of the husk to within 1 inch of the edges. Spoon about 1 tablespoon of the meat mixture in a line down the center of the masa. Roll the husk so that the masa dough surrounds the filling and forms a cylinder or package. Fold the husk under to close the bottom and complete the package. Place the completed tamales in a single layer on a baking sheet. Repeat until all the masa and filling is used. Simmer or steam the tamales.

To simmer: Stand the tamales upright, closed side down, in a large pot. Place enough tamales in the pot so that they do not fall over or come unrolled, or tie the bundle together with kitchen twine. Carefully fill the pot with enough water to come just to the top of the tamales, trying not to pour water directly into the tamales. Bring the water to a boil over high heat. Cover the pot, reduce the heat to medium-low, and simmer until the masa is firm and pulls away from the husk easily and cleanly, about 1 hour.

To steam: Stand the tamales upright, closed side down, in a large steamer basket. Cover the tamales with a damp towel or additional husks. Steam the tamales over simmering water until the masa is firm and pulls away from the husk easily and cleanly, about 1 to 1¼ hours. Serve the tamales warm, in their husks.

Amy Evans Streeter (and friends) of Oxford, Mississippi

Everlasting Refrigerator Rolls

The dough for everlasting rolls keeps in the refrigerator for a week. This basic yeasted bread dough is made from a potato starter, one that was once beloved all over the region for its soft and fluffy texture, slightly sweet and sour flavor, and endless versatility. You can use this dough as a base for many other breads, including cinnamon rolls and the less widely known butter rolls, a specialty of the northern reaches of Mississippi, gilded with butter and sugar.

Makes about 3 dozen rolls

1 large white potato, peeled and cut into large chunks
⅔ cup shortening
1½ teaspoons salt
⅔ cup sugar
2 eggs, beaten

1 (¼-ounce) packet active dry yeast or 1 (½-ounce) yeast cake
1 cup milk
6 to 8 cups sifted all-purpose flour
Melted butter, for brushing

Cook the potato in boiling, salted water in a small saucepan until tender but not waterlogged, 10 to 15 minutes. Measure out ½ cup of the cooking water and set it aside. Drain the potato in a colander and transfer to a small bowl and mash until smooth. Transfer 1 cup of the mashed potato into a large bowl. (Discard or eat the rest.) While the potato is still warm, stir in the shortening, salt, and sugar. Add the eggs and beat vigorously until the mixture is smooth and creamy.

Gently reheat the reserved potato cooking water to lukewarm (105° to 115°F) and pour into a small bowl. Add the yeast and stir until it dissolves. Set aside to proof until the yeast looks foamy.

Meanwhile, heat the milk to scalding (180°F), let it cool to lukewarm, and then stir it into the potato mixture. Stir in the yeast mixture. Stir in enough flour to make a stiff dough. Dump it out onto a lightly floured surface and knead well until the dough is smooth. Return the dough to the bowl and brush the top with melted butter. Cover tightly with plastic wrap and refrigerate for up to six days.

You can bake all of the rolls at once, or in batches, as needed. About 90 minutes before baking, shape as much dough as you plan to bake into small rolls that are about 1½ inches in diameter. Place in a greased baking pan (such as a cake pan), leaving space between the rolls because they will double in size as they rise. Cover with a damp lint-free towel or plastic wrap that has been lightly coated with nonstick cooking spray. Let rise in a warm place until they double in bulk. Preheat the oven to 400°F. Brush the tops of the rolls with melted butter. Bake until nicely browned, 15 to 20 minutes. Brush again with melted butter and serve hot or at room temperature.

Carol Darden and Norma Jean Darden of New York, New York

White Loaf Bread

Store-bought white bread is considered nothing but a mere foil for the good stuff. It's the ballast in a sandwich of homegrown tomatoes and homemade mayonnaise. It's the handle by which we grab hold of chopped or pulled pork. But then there's the good stuff, homemade white loaf bread, about which novelist Lee Smith is quite passionate:

> I make this bread often myself because the smell of it baking in the oven brings my mother back to me so vividly. In my memory she's always in her kitchen, and she's always cooking, smoking a Salem cigarette, and drinking a cup of coffee from the percolator, which is always going in the corner; Johnny Cash sings "Ring of Fire" on the radio while the coal train roars along the mountainside behind our house. Somebody else is always in the kitchen with us—a neighbor from down the road, a friend from out of town, some of our innumerable cousins—eating and drinking, rocking and talking, always talking, giving us the real lowdown on somebody.

Makes 2 loaves

2½ cups whole milk
3 tablespoons sugar
1 teaspoon salt
4 tablespoons vegetable shortening

2 (¼-ounce) packets active dry yeast
2 large eggs, well beaten
7 to 8 cups all-purpose flour
4 tablespoons (½ stick) butter, melted

Grease two 9-by-5-inch loaf pans and set them aside. Heat the milk, sugar, salt, and shortening to scalding (180°F) in a saucepan over medium-high heat and then pour it into a large bowl and let it cool to lukewarm (105° to 115°F). Stir in the yeast and set it aside to proof until the yeast looks foamy. Stir in the eggs and mix well. Stir in enough flour to make fairly stiff dough. Cover the bowl with a damp lint-free towel or plastic wrap that has been lightly coated with nonstick cooking spray. Let the dough rise in a warm place until it doubles in bulk. Punch down the dough and knead it well on a lightly floured surface until the dough is smooth, elastic, and a little bouncy, about 7 to 10 minutes. Divide the dough in half and shape into loaves in the prepared pans. Cover with a clean cloth and let rise in a warm place until the dough doubles in bulk.

Preheat the oven to 350°F. Bake until the loaves are golden brown, 35 to 40 minutes. Turn them out onto a wire rack and brush all over with the melted butter. Cool to room temperature before slicing.

Lee Smith of Hillsborough, North Carolina

7

YARDBIRD
CHICKENS AND EGGS

Chicken run fast

Chicken run slow,

Chicken run by a Methodist preacher,

Chicken never run no mo.

—"Chicken Reel," an Ozark folk song

YARDBIRD sounds old-fashioned. And it is. Pretty much everyone in the South used to have a couple of chickens in the yard. Laying hens meant fresh eggs. If you kept a couple of hens, those hens would keep you in eggs every day. If you kept more than a couple of hens, you would be covered up in eggs. And maybe you'd have a chicken to fry on Sunday.

This sums up the South's history with poultry: *Columbus brought chickens to America in 1493. They took off.* But such a telling overlooks some key points. There was a time, not too long past, when chickens were an indulgence. By which we mean that chickens were expensive. Until the middle years of the twentieth century, fresh chicken was, in large part, a treat reserved for big spenders. Our forebears didn't kill a chicken every day. They saved chickens for special occasions, like when the preacher was coming for Sunday supper.

Speaking of preachers, Psyche Williams-Forson, a scholar of African American foodways, once observed that there are four things that can bring a preacher down. She calls them the four *C*s: cash, chicks, Cadillacs, and chicken. Fried chicken to be specific. Too much praise for one sister's cooking and the congregation starts to speculate that the preacher is availing himself of more than her gospel bird.

Southerners took to chickens because they are not difficult to keep or expensive to feed. They were the protein, along with pigs, that farm cooks relied on. As the chicken industry expanded across the region in the middle years of the twentieth century, chickens became the base for so many iconic dishes.

Some critics say that the expansion of chicken farming has yielded an inferior fowl, one that is oversized and lacks the tenderness and taste that young pullets had when they scratched in farmyards. Noting the trend toward larger, less flavorful fowl in 1949, Ralph McGill of the *Atlanta Constitution* declared a preference for "barnyard subdebs, rarely more than ten to twelve weeks old and weighing from a pound and a half to two pounds."

If young chickens take well to frying, older chickens take well to stewing. Lowcountry dishes that incorporate rice, such as pilau (that rice dish with seemingly infinite spellings perhaps most widely known as pilaf), country captain, and bog, are variations on the stew theme of chicken, vegetables, rice, and spices. They are one-dish meals that owe a substantial debt to African culinary traditions.

We include eggs here too, since they are the products of chickens. You'll find such dishes as Eggs Derby, worthy of white linen tablecloths at brunch, and Sriracha and Citrus Rémoulade, for oilcloth-covered kitchen tables at supper.

But let's get back to the main event: fried chicken. It's a dish that speaks to heart and home and skillet. Here in the South, fried chicken is a dish so iconic, so particular, so defined by place and memory that it would take an entire book to explore the subject—or at least a chapter. (Counterintuitively, it's a dish that has been co-opted by a rash of fast-food operators.) However, instead of compiling a second cookbook, we have provided not only one standard-bearer recipe but also an homage to one of the finest cooks ever to stand before a fryer—Austin Leslie of New Orleans.

Fried Chicken with New Orleans Confetti

Over many decades, before his untimely death in 2005, Austin Leslie made several New Orleans restaurants famous with his gloriously fried chicken. Evaporated milk was his secret weapon. A scattering of minced garlic and parsley, and pickle chips, provided a royal garnish. Austin's legacy lives on in our minds' palates—and in our kitchens.

Makes 6 to 8 servings

1 (3- to 4-pound) chicken, cut into 8 to
   10 pieces
2 tablespoons salt
2 tablespoons black pepper
2 tablespoons Louisiana-style seasoning
   blend
Peanut oil, for frying

1 large egg, beaten
1 (12-ounce) can evaporated milk
1 cup water
1 cup all-purpose flour
10 dill pickle slices
1 garlic clove, minced
1 bunch parsley, finely chopped

Wash the chicken in cool water and pat it dry with paper towels. Season the chicken with salt, pepper, and seasoning blend. Place the chicken in a single layer on a tray and refrigerate uncovered for at least 1 hour and up to 24 hours.

Pour oil into a deep skillet or Dutch oven to a depth of at least 3 inches. Heat the oil to 350°F.

Whisk together the egg, evaporated milk, and water in a bowl. Put the flour in a shallow bowl. Dredge the chicken by dipping it in the egg mixture and then into the flour. Starting with the heaviest pieces and working in batches to avoid crowding the skillet, slip the chicken into the hot oil. Adjust the heat to maintain the temperature of the oil as the chicken fries. Fry the chicken, turning with tongs, until the juices run clear when pierced to the bone with the tip of a sharp knife and the crust is deep golden brown and crispy, about 15 minutes per batch. Drain the chicken on a wire rack for 10 minutes, then serve hot, garnished with the pickles and a confetti of the garlic and parsley.

Austin Leslie of New Orleans, Louisiana

Cheerwine Barbecue Chicken

We are crazy for small-batch soft drinks—Blenheim, Dr. Enuf, Ale-8-One. Cheerwine, a fizzy cherry-flavored soda, calls Salisbury, North Carolina, home. Sara Gibbs, who calls Kentucky home, reaches across state lines and slathers her chicken in a tangy-sweet sauce built on a base of the Southern soft drink with the unlikeliest of names. She also likes to drink the stuff.

Makes 8 servings

16 meaty chicken thighs with bones
   and skin (7 to 8 pounds total)

Cheerwine barbecue sauce
   (recipe follows)

Combine the thighs and 1¼ cups of the sauce in a large bowl and mix well so that the thighs are coated. Cover and marinate in the refrigerator for 4 to 8 hours.

For oven barbecued thighs: Bake on a well-greased baking sheet at 350°F until the meat reaches an internal temperature of 170°F, about 1 hour, basting the thighs with the remaining 1¼ cups of sauce halfway through.

For grilled barbecued thighs: Light a charcoal fire in the bottom of a covered grill. Allow to burn down until the coals are red in the center and gray on the outside. Spray the grate with nonstick spray and place over the coals. Place the thighs on the grate and grill the chicken, covered with the grill lid, over medium-high heat (350° to 400°F) for 15 minutes, turning occasionally. Brush with more sauce and grill until the meat reaches an internal temperature of 170°F, about another 15 minutes, basting with more sauce as needed.

CHEERWINE BARBECUE SAUCE

Makes about 2½ cups

1 tablespoon butter
½ teaspoon minced garlic
1 cup ketchup
1 cup Cheerwine (not diet)
3 tablespoons Worcestershire sauce

¼ cup A-1 sauce
¼ teaspoon ground cayenne pepper
½ teaspoon ground black pepper
½ teaspoon dry mustard
2 tablespoons distilled white vinegar

Melt the butter in a heavy 2-quart saucepan over medium heat. Add the garlic and cook, stirring, for 30 seconds. Whisk in the ketchup, Cheerwine, Worcestershire sauce, A-1 sauce, cayenne, pepper, mustard, and vinegar. Bring the sauce to a boil; reduce the heat to medium-low and simmer until the sauce is slightly thickened, about 20 minutes. Cool to room temperature, cover, and refrigerate until chilled.

Sara Gibbs of Taylorsville, Kentucky

Chicken and Dumplings

Cappy Ricks, a retired pediatrician from Atlanta, and his late wife, Betty, an avid gardener, attended the first SFA symposium at their alma mater in 1998. And, thankfully, they kept coming back. When we set out to collect recipes for this book, we immediately asked Cappy what he would like to contribute. He sent us a hand-written recipe.

He wrote, "I really love to make chicken and dumplings and feel like I have a good method. But it's not a quick recipe—it takes time to make it right—and while Betty and I figured out the chicken portion of the recipe, the black pepper dumplings come from Bill Neal's book *Biscuits, Spoonbread, and Sweet Potato Pie.*"

Makes 6 to 8 servings

CHICKEN STOCK

1 (3½- to 4-pound) stewing hen	2 whole cloves
2 ribs celery with leaves, coarsely chopped	12 peppercorns
	2 bay leaves
2 large carrots, halved	1 teaspoon dried thyme leaves
1 large onion, quartered	1 tablespoon butter

BLACK PEPPER DUMPLINGS

2 cups all-purpose flour, plus more for rolling	1½ teaspoons sugar
	½ teaspoon coarsely ground black pepper
1 teaspoon salt	4 tablespoons lard
1 tablespoon baking powder	½ to ⅔ cup milk

1 medium onion, chopped (about 1½ cups)

2 large carrots, peeled and sliced (about 3 cups)

3 to 3½ cups cooked chicken meat, from making the stock

Salt and ground black pepper

1 bunch green onions, trimmed and thinly sliced (about ¼ cup), to garnish

To make the chicken stock: Remove and set aside the neck and giblets from the chicken. Put the chicken, celery, carrots, onion, cloves, peppercorns, bay leaves, thyme, and butter in a large stockpot and cover with cold water. Bring to a boil over medium-high heat. Reduce the heat to medium-low and simmer until the chicken is done, about 30 minutes. Remove from the heat and allow the chicken to cool in the stock. Remove the skin and pull the meat from the bones and set the meat aside. Return the skin and bones to the pot. Add the neck and giblets. Bring the stock back to a boil and cook until it reduces to 4 cups. Strain the stock through a mesh sieve and discard the solids. Return the stock to the pot.

To make the dumplings: Sift the flour, salt, baking powder, sugar, and pepper together into a bowl. Use your fingertips to work in the lard until the mixture is crumbly. Gradually stir in enough milk to make dough stiffer than for regular biscuits. Mix well. Turn out onto a well-floured surface and roll to a ⅛-inch thickness. Cut the dough into 1- by 1½-inch dumplings.

To make the chicken stew: Bring the stock back to a simmer over medium heat. Stir in the onion and carrots; simmer until the vegetables are tender, about 15 minutes. Shred the cooked chicken into bite-sized pieces and add them to the pot. Season with salt and pepper.

Return the stew to a low boil. Drop the dumplings into the stew. Cover the pot and simmer until the dumplings are puffed and firm, 5 to 8 minutes. Serve hot, garnished with green onions.

Cappy Ricks of Atlanta, Georgia

Chicken and Roasted Root Vegetable Pot Pie

Phoebe Lawless is a serious baker and an improvising cook. Her pot pie recipe encourages us to use what we find at the market—as many, or as few, varieties of root vegetables as we want. In the world according to Phoebe, the recipe changes, depending on the cook, the market, and what the farmers are pulling up.

Please note that the pastry crust includes two heaping tablespoons of crispy pork cracklings. Don't stint.

Makes 2 nine-inch deep-dish pies

PASTRY

2 cups unbleached all-purpose flour, plus more for rolling
½ teaspoon salt
1½ teaspoons sugar
2 heaping tablespoons crispy pork cracklings

¼ pound plus 2 tablespoons (1¼ sticks) unsalted butter, cubed and chilled
4 to 6 tablespoons ice water

FILLING

1 (3½- to 4-pound) chicken
Salt and ground black pepper
1 bay leaf
4 cups assorted diced root vegetables (such as parsnips, rutabaga, turnips, parsley root, sweet potatoes, or whatever is in season)
1 to 2 tablespoons extra-virgin olive oil
3 tablespoons bacon grease or butter
1 medium onion, diced small (about 1½ cups)

2 celery stalks, diced (about 1 cup)
Pinch of crushed red pepper flakes
A few sprigs of fresh herbs (such as sage, parsley tops, thyme, or rosemary)
3 tablespoons all-purpose flour
1 cup milk
2 cups chicken stock (from cooking the chicken)
Zest of 1 lemon

EGG WASH

1 large egg
2 tablespoons water

To make the pastry: Put the flour, salt, sugar, and cracklings in the bowl of a food processor fitted with a metal blade and pulse to combine. Scatter the butter over the flour mixture and pulse until the pieces of butter are the size of peppercorns. Pour into a large bowl. Slowly stir in enough ice water with a fork to form large, moist clumps of dough. Bring the dough together, then divide in half. Wrap each piece tightly in plastic wrap and chill for at least 20 minutes.

To make the filling: Place the chicken, a generous pinch of salt and pepper, and bay leaf in a large pot. Cover with cold water. Bring to a boil, reduce the heat to medium-low, and simmer for 1 hour. Remove the chicken from the liquid and set it aside to cool. When it is cool enough to handle, pick the meat from the carcass, being careful not to shred it; leave the meat in nice-sized pieces and set it aside. Strain the stock and set it aside.

Preheat the oven to 375°F. Place the root vegetables on a baking sheet. Drizzle with the olive oil and toss to coat. Season with salt and pepper. Roast until tender, about 20 minutes. Set aside. Leave the oven on.

Heat the bacon grease in a large saucepan over medium-high heat. Stir in the onion, celery, crushed red pepper flakes, and herb sprigs. (I don't bother picking off the thyme or rosemary leaves for this application as the leaves usually fall off the stem after a little stewing.) Season lightly with salt and pepper. Cook, stirring often, until the onions and celery soften, about 8 minutes. Sprinkle in the flour and cook, stirring constantly, until the flour starts to brown, about 4 minutes. Slowly stir in the milk and cook, stirring constantly, until the sauce thickens, about 3 minutes. Stir in 2 cups of the chicken stock. (Use any remaining stock in another recipe.) Season with salt and pepper. Bring to a boil. Remove the pot from the heat. Discard any herb stems and/or leaves. Stir in the chicken, roasted vegetables, and lemon zest. The filling should be the consistency of stew, so add more stock if needed. Season with salt and pepper. Set aside to cool to room temperature.

To make the pie: Divide the cooled filling between 2 nine-inch deep-dish pie plates. Roll out each piece of pastry into an 11-inch round on a lightly floured surface. Cover the filling with the pastry, turn under the edges, and crimp into place. Make an egg wash by whisking together the egg and the 2 tablespoons of water in a small bowl. Brush the pastry with the egg wash. Cut a few small slits in the pastry to let steam escape. Bake the pies at 375°F until the filling is bubbly and the pastry is golden, 25 to 30 minutes. Let cool for 10 minutes before serving hot.

Phoebe Lawless of Durham, North Carolina

Chicken Bog

Where rice grows, such as in coastal Georgia, South Carolina, and Louisiana, one-pot dishes incorporating rice, vegetables, spices, and meats are common. Pilaus and bogs may seem almost identical, but South Carolinians argue that the difference seems to be in how the rice is cooked.

Historian Karen Hess described chicken bogs as pilaus "made in large batches, which would always cause it to end up wet." The term *bog*, then, could refer to the dish's sogginess/bogginess. Or it could be merely elemental, as in chicken bogged down in rice. Louis Osteen doesn't contemplate such abstractions. He cooks.

Makes 6 servings

6 cups peeled, seeded, and diced ripe tomatoes
3 tablespoons extra-virgin olive oil
Salt and ground black pepper
4 cups chicken stock
2 tablespoons unsalted butter
2 tablespoons peanut oil
6 chicken thighs, bone in and skin on but trimmed of excess fat

1 cup finely chopped yellow onion
1 cup finely chopped celery
½ teaspoon minced garlic
2 cups raw converted long-grain white rice
1 large sprig fresh thyme
2 small bay leaves
2 teaspoons hot sauce

Preheat the oven to 350°F.

Toss the diced tomatoes and olive oil together in a bowl. Season with salt and pepper. Set aside.

Warm the stock in a small saucepan over low heat and keep warm until it is needed.

Heat the butter and peanut oil over medium heat in a medium ovenproof pot with a lid. Add the chicken thighs and brown both sides, about 2 minutes per side. Transfer the thighs to a plate, season with salt and pepper, and set aside. Pour off all but 2 tablespoons of the pan drippings. Warm the drippings over medium heat, stir in the onion and celery, and cook until softened, about 8 minutes. Add the garlic and rice and cook, stirring constantly, until the garlic is soft and the rice is translucent, about 3 minutes. Stir in the tomato mixture, the warm stock, thyme, bay leaves, and hot sauce. Season with salt and pepper. Return the chicken to the pot and nestle it down into the rice mixture. Cover and bake until the chicken and rice are done and the liquid is absorbed, 35 to 40 minutes. This is a moist dish, not one where the grains of rice are dry and fluffy. Discard the sprig of thyme and bay leaves. Check the seasoning and serve hot.

Louis Osteen of Lakemont, Georgia

Country Captain

Though its exact origins are unknown, this traditional curried chicken dish has long been associated with Georgia—"Savannah in particular, since it was a port for the spice trade," explains Scott Peacock. "Good spices are the key to a great country captain, and I have my own formula for curry powder."

"Country captain is a good dish for entertaining," writes Scott. Guests may "embellish their dinner with an assortment of condiments and garnishes, including currants, peanuts, crumbled bacon, chutneys, and crispy onion rings."

Makes 4 to 6 servings

Kosher salt
1 (3½-pound) chicken, cut into 8 pieces
    and brined for 8 to 24 hours
1 teaspoon dried thyme
Ground black pepper
¼ cup vegetable oil
6 slices bacon
2½ cups chopped onion
1 cup chopped celery, preferably with
    leaves
2 cups diced green bell pepper

1 tablespoon finely chopped garlic
2 cups canned whole tomatoes, drained
    (reserving ¾ cup of the juice) and
    chopped
2 tablespoons unsalted butter
2 tablespoons plus 2 teaspoons
    homemade curry powder
    (recipe follows)
⅓ cup currants
2 bay leaves

Make enough brine to cover the chicken by dissolving kosher salt into cold water in the proportion of ¼ cup salt to 4 cups water. Place the chicken in a nonreactive bowl and pour in enough brine to cover the chicken. Refrigerate for at least 8 and up to 24 hours.

Rinse the chicken pieces and pat dry with paper towels. Sprinkle with dried thyme and 5 grinds of black pepper. Heat the oil in a Dutch oven or large, wide pan over high heat until quite hot but not smoking. Place the chicken pieces skin-side-down in the hot oil and cook, turning once, until deep golden brown on both sides. Transfer the chicken pieces to a large bowl and set aside. Pour off the fat in the pan.

Add the bacon to the pan and cook over medium-low heat until it is deeply colored and quite crisp. Transfer the bacon with a slotted spoon to drain on paper towels, ready to use as a condiment on the finished dish. Add the onion to the pan and cook, stirring occasionally, for 2 to 3 minutes. Add the chopped celery and bell pepper and cook, stirring, for 5 minutes. Stir in the garlic and cook for 2 minutes. Stir in the tomatoes and reserved juice. Simmer, partially covered, for 10 minutes, stirring often.

Heat the butter in a small pan until hot and foaming. Stir in the curry powder and cook, stirring, for 2 minutes, then stir into the simmering vegetable mixture. Stir in the currants and bay leaves. Season well with salt and pepper. Simmer, tightly covered, for 30 minutes, stirring occasionally. Taste carefully for the seasoning.

Preheat the oven to 325°F. Spoon about 1 cup of the sauce into the bottom of an ovenproof casserole or baking dish that is just large enough to hold the browned chicken pieces in a single layer. Arrange the chicken over the sauce, then spoon the remaining sauce over the top. Place a piece of parchment paper directly on top of the chicken and a single layer of foil directly on top of the parchment. Cover the dish with a tight-fitting lid or a double thickness of foil. Bake until the chicken is quite tender, about 1½ hours. Taste the sauce again for any final seasoning adjustments. Serve the chicken hot with the sauce spooned over it, along with rice and at least 4 curry condiments.

CURRY CONDIMENTS

Crumbled bacon
Thinly sliced green onions
Crispy thin onion rings
Currants or raisins
Toasted coconut

Finely chopped white and sieved
  yolk of hard-boiled egg,
  served separately
Chutneys, one or more varieties
Chopped peanuts

HOMEMADE CURRY POWDER

Makes about ¼ cup

1 tablespoon ground ginger
1 teaspoon chili powder
½ teaspoon ground cumin
1 teaspoon ground cardamom
½ teaspoon ground turmeric
1 teaspoon paprika

1 teaspoon ground coriander
1 teaspoon ground cinnamon
½ teaspoon ground cloves
¼ teaspoon ground cayenne pepper,
  or to taste

Whisk together all of the ingredients in a small bowl. For fresher, more vibrant flavor, mix the curry in small batches as needed and use quickly, although it can be stored in a small, tightly sealed jar at room temperature.

Scott Peacock of Decatur, Georgia

Country-Fried Chicken Livers

Versailles, France, had its Sun King, and Versailles, Kentucky, has Jared Richardson, Fry King. Cooked in the manner of country-fried steak, his livers come cornmeal-breaded. Served hot from a cast-iron skillet with an elegant sauce, they belong on your best dinner china. Eaten cold the next morning, they prove the perfect topping for scrambled eggs.

Makes 4 to 6 servings

1 pint fresh chicken livers, rinsed, trimmed, and deveined
1 to 1½ cups buttermilk
2 tablespoons hot sauce
Peanut oil or vegetable oil, for deep frying

2 cups all-purpose flour
½ cup white cornmeal
1 teaspoon kosher salt
½ teaspoon ground cayenne pepper
Snipped, fresh chives, for garnish (optional)

Place the livers in a bowl. Pour in enough buttermilk to cover and stir in the hot sauce. Cover and refrigerate for at least 30 minutes and up to 2 hours.

Pour oil into a deep skillet or large pot to a depth of 3 inches. Heat the oil to 340°F.

Stir together the flour, cornmeal, salt, and cayenne in a bowl. Drain the livers and let the excess buttermilk drip off. Coat the livers in the flour mixture. Working in batches to avoid crowding the pot, fry the livers in the hot oil until they are golden brown, 3 to 4 minutes. Transfer with a slotted spoon to drain on paper towels or a brown paper bag. Serve hot, garnished with chives, if using.

Jared Richardson of Versailles, Kentucky

Deviled Eggs

Rick Ellis transforms hard-cooked egg yolks into velvet by pushing them through a sieve and then whipping them with—surprise—butter. The secret ingredient adds a rich heft to the mixture and a stability to the eggs' beautiful golden filling. The rest of Rick's recipe is classic, down to a sprinkling of paprika.

Makes 2 dozen

1 dozen medium eggs
¼ cup mayonnaise
¼ cup Dijon mustard
4 tablespoons (½ stick) butter, at room
temperature

1 teaspoon fresh lemon juice
¼ teaspoon ground cayenne pepper
Salt and ground white pepper
Paprika, to garnish

Place the eggs in a large saucepan and cover with cold water. Bring to a boil over high heat. Remove from the heat, cover the pan, and let sit 15 minutes. Drain and rinse under very cold running water until completely cool. Peel the eggs.

Cut the eggs in half lengthwise. Remove the yolks and set the whites aside. Rub the yolks through a fine sieve into a bowl. Add the mayonnaise, mustard, and butter and mix until smooth. Stir in the lemon juice and cayenne. Season with salt and white pepper. Be a little bold here as the flavors dull slightly when the eggs are chilled. Place the filling mixture in a pastry bag, although a zip-top bag with a corner snipped off works too. Pipe the filling into the egg whites, sprinkle with paprika, and chill until ready to serve.

Rick Ellis of New York, New York

Eggs Derby

This may be the most decadent recipe in the entire collection—all good things baked into one dish so creative and rich that making it causes the cook to chuckle periodically at the luxury and process. Don't wait for Derby Day.

Makes 6 servings

6 hard-cooked eggs, peeled
4 tablespoons finely chopped country
ham
1¼ teaspoons salt, divided
¼ teaspoon ground black pepper
¼ teaspoon dry mustard
¼ teaspoon celery seed
1 cup plus 1 to 3 tablespoons heavy cream
2 large sweetbreads

4 tablespoons (½ stick) butter
8 ounces fresh morels
4 tablespoons all-purpose flour, divided
1 cup sweetbread stock (from cooking the
sweetbreads)
4 to 6 tablespoons bourbon
½ cup Parmesan cheese, grated
½ cup sharp Cheddar cheese, grated
½ cup slivered almonds

Preheat the oven to 350°F. Cut the eggs in half lengthwise. Remove the yolks and set the whites aside. Stir together the yolks, ham, ¼ teaspoon of the salt, pepper, mustard, and celery seed. Stir in 1 to 3 tablespoons of the cream, just enough to make the filling smooth yet remain fairly stiff. Spoon the filling into the whites. Arrange the filled eggs in a single layer in a small gratin dish or shallow baking dish.

Have ready a small bowl of ice water. Place the sweetbreads in a small saucepan and cover them with cold water. Stir in the remaining 1 teaspoon of salt. Bring to a boil, reduce the heat, and simmer until the sweetbreads are plump and feel slightly firmer to the touch, about 3 minutes. Transfer the sweetbreads with a slotted spoon to the bowl of ice water and set aside until cool enough to handle. Discard all but 1 cup of the cooking liquid to use as stock. Drain the sweetbreads. Cut away any fat and pull away as much of the membranes and connective tissue as possible without breaking them up. Cut the sweetbreads into thumb-sized pieces. Place in a bowl, add 1 cup of cream, and set aside.

Melt the butter in a skillet over medium-high heat. Stir in the morels and cook, stirring often, until tender and lightly browned, about 10 minutes. Whisk the flour into the reserved sweetbread stock until smooth, then slowly stir into the morels. Cook until the sauce slightly thickens, about 5 minutes. Remove from the heat. Stir in the sweetbreads, cream, and 4 tablespoons of the bourbon. Taste, then add the rest of the bourbon if you like the kick. Season with salt and pepper.

Pour the sweetbread mixture over the eggs. Sprinkle with the Parmesan, Cheddar, and almonds. Bake until the cheese is browned and bubbly, about 10 to 15 minutes. If the cheese isn't browned after 15 minutes, run the dish under a broiler for a few seconds. Serve piping hot.

Kathy Cary of Louisville, Kentucky

Baked Eggs

Shirley Corriher believes in indulgences, as a gander at this recipe proves. "Baked eggs are special—a white ramekin with a pale gold cheese crust that gives way to a creamy mixture of crumbs and egg white moistened with yolk and spiked with nutmeg and a little nip from hot sauce," she says. "I make them on leisurely Sundays as a luxurious little treat."

Makes 1 to 2 servings

2 tablespoons butter, at room
   temperature
¼ cup fine dry bread crumbs
2 large eggs
Freshly grated nutmeg

Hot pepper sauce
Salt and ground black pepper
¼ cup heavy or whipping
   cream
2 tablespoons Gruyère, grated

Preheat the oven to 350°F. Butter two small ramekins or custard cups. Distribute the bread crumbs evenly around the sides and bottom of the cups. Crack 1 egg into the center of each cup, taking care to not break the yolks. Sprinkle each egg with a pinch of nutmeg, a dash of pepper sauce, and a light sprinkle of salt and pepper. Spoon 2 tablespoons of the cream over each egg to distribute the seasonings and sprinkle each with 1 tablespoon of the Gruyère. Bake until the whites are set and the yolks are as firm as you like, 8 to 10 minutes—the time depends on your oven and how you like your eggs.

Shirley Corriher of Atlanta, Georgia

Sriracha and Citrus Rémoulade

Good rémoulade upstages anything it smothers. And while this sauce landed in the yardbird section because of its inclusion of eggs, we like to think we put it here because a rooster graces the red Sriracha bottle—a bottle that Texas native Bryan Caswell reaches for often. We recommend trying the rémoulade with roasted potatoes, on fried-egg sandwiches, and even as a tartar sauce substitute with fried fish dinners.

Makes about 2½ cups

2 tablespoons dashi
2 tablespoons freshly squeezed
    orange juice
2 tablespoons freshly squeezed
    lemon juice
2 tablespoons freshly squeezed
    grapefruit juice

2 tablespoons Sriracha
    hot sauce
2 large egg yolks
1⅔ cups canola oil
Salt

Combine the dashi, orange juice, lemon juice, grapefruit juice, Sriracha, and yolks in the bowl of a food processor fitted with the metal blade. Pulse to blend. With the machine running, slowly add the oil, processing just until emulsified. Season to taste with salt. Store covered and refrigerated.

Note: Dashi is a Japanese stock generally made from kombu (kelp) and dried bonito flakes. You may make your own or buy packets of instant dashi at Asian and specialty grocery stores.

Bryan Caswell of Houston, Texas

8 PIG
FROM SNOOT TO TAIL

There is no stronger test of an observant Jew's true commitment to his or her faith than the aroma that wafts over east Memphis from Corky's Restaurant when the barbecue pits are slow-roasting pork ribs.
—Marcie Ferris, *Matzo Ball Gumbo*

PIG, and the flesh derived from pig, has long captured the attention—and appetites—of Southerners, no matter their religion.

The Spanish introduced pigs to Florida in 1539. Soon thereafter, the animals were being raised in Georgia, where they came to be appreciated for their efficient conversion of feed to flesh. "If the 'king' of the antebellum southern economy was cotton," wrote Sam Bowers Hilliard, in *Hog Meat and Hoecake*, "then the title of 'queen' must go to the pig." Indeed, pork came to be so pervasive a part of the antebellum diet that one observer claimed, "Hog's lard is the very oil that moves the machinery of life."

In the pages that follow, we catalog the South's serial love affair with the pig. And we remember the people behind the pig, the men and women whose histories and hard work yield the objects of our adulation. In several cases these men and women are restaurant chefs who bring to their professional kitchens lessons learned on the farm and in the home. Red beans and rice is not emblematic of the Commander's Palace kitchen, for example, but any New Orleans chef is at some point bidden to prove his merit by producing a mama-worthy pot of beans. He may use a ham bone and smoked sausage; she may throw in pigs' tails and tasso. The late Jamie Shannon favored pickled pork. Donald Link technically serves his boudin blanc in a restaurant, but he in no way fancifies the traditions and techniques of his family's many home boudin makers. When it comes to the pig, restaurant cookery in the South draws heavily from home cookery.

Paul Prudhomme grew up eating fresh pork only when it was available in the immediate aftermath of a hog killing. His parents struggled as sharecroppers to raise thirteen children, all of whom labored with them to feed the family. They made each animal last by smoking sausages, salt-curing pieces of fat streaked with lean, and putting up grillades in jars of hog lard. Only after he became a professional chef did Prudhomme trade lard for butter.

The late pit boss J. C. Hardaway smoked pork in Memphis, Tennessee, pork that inspired Lolis Elie to write, "In J. C. Hardaway, the shoulder sandwich has discovered its Stradivarius." But lest we overglamorize the labor behind that sandwich, Elie adds that, while Hardaway eventually enjoyed some amount of fame, "Years of standing up twelve hours a day, cooking, serving, and cleaning took its toll. His advanced age and failing health made it difficult for him to fully enjoy the accolades that were his in later life."

In the South, pork is often the basis for breakfast, lunch, and dinner. It's equal parts inspiration and vice. Poet Kevin Young, who has called boudin "God's chewing gum," writes in his "Ode to Pork" about the dark side of the omnipresent pig:

> I know you're the blues
> because loving you
> may kill me.

In the recipes that follow, rest assured, no deaths occur. But we do pay homage to the ceremonial import of the hog killing.

Carnitas

Miguel Torres moved from Celaya, Mexico, to North Carolina in 1999, at the age of sixteen. He often prepares these carnitas for the staff's family meal at Lantern Restaurant. Miguel explains that, in Mexico, carnitas are generally cooked at home, as part of a special celebration, and often by a hired cook. Typically, carnitas are the product of a whole hog that has been chopped into big chunks—skin, bones, and all. For his carnitas, he uses the ribs, hocks, and picnic meat left over from whole roasted pigs.

Makes 18 to 24 servings

1 teaspoon ground cumin
7 bay leaves
1 teaspoon whole black peppercorns
1 teaspoon whole coriander seeds
2 tablespoons salt
5 pounds pork shoulder, cut into 1½-inch chunks
2 pounds pork ribs, cut through the bone into 2-inch pieces

3 cups lard
1 cup whole milk
3 cups pork stock or water
Zest and juice of 1 orange
1 cup Coca-Cola
Warm corn tortillas, pickled jalapeño peppers, chopped raw onion, and chopped cilantro, for serving

Stir together the cumin, bay leaves, peppercorns, coriander, and salt in a large bowl. Add the meat and toss to coat. Melt the lard in a large, heavy Dutch oven over medium-high heat. Cook the meat until golden brown, about 20 minutes, stirring occasionally to prevent it from sticking to the bottom of the pot. Add the milk and stock. Reduce the heat, cover the pot, and simmer, stirring occasionally, until the meat is spoon tender and falls off the bones, about 1 hour. Discard the bones and bay leaves. Stir the zest, juice, and cola into the meat. Increase the heat and cook at a low boil until the cooking liquid evaporates and the meat is crispy and dark brown on the outside, 30 minutes. Spoon off the fat and serve hot with warm corn tortillas, pickled jalapeños, raw onion, and cilantro.

Miguel Torres of Durham, North Carolina

Chitlins

Audrey Petty grew up in Chicago with parents who had moved north from Arkansas and Alabama. "We all had roots and people down South. And we ate like it, too," she recalls.

In the Petty household, eating like it meant that Audrey and her mother enjoyed chitlins around the holidays, while her father and two sisters bellyached about the stench, a smell that she describes as "vinegary and slightly farmy." In this recipe, modeled after her mother's, the potato absorbs some of the odor but is never eaten (other cooks use white bread for the same purpose).

"For all their potent smell, the flavor was calm and subtle," Audrey remembers. "Precious, strange, and furtive food; I longed for them even as I consumed them."

Makes 8 servings

9 to 10 pounds fresh or thawed chitlins
Salt
1 large onion, peeled and chopped
1 russet potato, peeled
1 green bell pepper, chopped
4 garlic cloves, peeled

½ cup apple cider vinegar
¾ teaspoon crushed red pepper
    flakes
2 bay leaves
Freshly ground black pepper
Hot sauce

Put the chitlins into a large colander and rinse under tepid running water in the sink. Transfer to a very large bowl or pot. Cover the chitlins by at least two inches with tepid water. Stir in 1 tablespoon of salt for every gallon of water. Wash the chitlins one section at a time. Drain in a colander set in the sink, rinse them again under tepid running water, then drain again.

Put the chitlins in a large pot and cover with cold water. Add the onion, potato, bell pepper, garlic, vinegar, red pepper flakes, and bay leaves. Season with salt and pepper. Partially cover the pot and bring to a boil over high heat. Reduce the heat to medium-low and cook, partially covered, until the chitlins are very tender, about 6 hours.

Pour off most of the cooking water from the pot, leaving just enough to keep the chitlins moist. Discard the potato and bay leaves. Cut the chitlins into 1-inch pieces, return them to the pot, and bring them to a simmer. Using a slotted spoon, serve the chitlins (drained fairly well and apart from the vegetables) in bowls, and douse with hot sauce to taste.

Audrey Petty of Urbana, Illinois, inspired by Naomi Petty of Chicago, Illinois

Pork Backbone Stew

Back when hog killings were more frequent events, the backbone was often cooked immediately, a rare and fresh delicacy. Butchers in Acadiana still stock their meat cases with the cut.

"That's one of the most popular things we serve," says Floyd Poche of Poche's Market. "You know, you can't hardly find backbone stew anywhere you go. We serve it two days a week, and it usually sells out. We start cooking at maybe five in the morning and let it cook slow and long for about four hours, so it makes a real good gravy—rice and gravy. That's Cajun country."

You can substitute another bone-in cut, such as country-style pork ribs, for backbone.

Makes 6 servings

8 cups pork stock
½ cup dark roux, homemade or store bought
1 tablespoon liquid browning and seasoning sauce, such as Kitchen Bouquet
2 cups finely chopped onions
2 cups finely chopped green bell pepper

1½ cups finely chopped celery
3 teaspoons salt
2 teaspoons garlic powder
½ teaspoon ground cayenne pepper
5 pounds pork backbones, cut into 2-inch pieces
1 tablespoon cornstarch dissolved in ¼ cup cold water, if needed

Bring the stock to a boil in a large pot over high heat. Add the roux a tablespoonful at a time, stirring until smooth after each addition. Stir in the browning sauce, onions, bell pepper, and celery. Stir together the salt, garlic powder, and cayenne in a small bowl and sprinkle it generously over the backbones, then add them to the pot. Reduce the heat and cook at a low boil, stirring occasionally, for 1 hour. Reduce the heat and simmer until the meat is falling-off-the-bone tender, about 1 hour more. If the stew gets too thick, add more stock or water. If the stew is too thin when the meat is done, stir in the cornstarch-and-water slurry. Season with salt and cayenne. Serve hot over cooked rice.

Note: If making the roux at home, use equal parts fat and all-purpose flour—vegetable oil works well. Heat the oil in a large skillet or Dutch oven over medium heat. Whisk in the flour, stirring until smooth. Cook, stirring slowly and constantly, until the roux is dark brown. Remove from the heat and let cool.

Floyd Poche of Breaux Bridge, Louisiana

Boudin Blanc

Another remnant of the home hog killing (called a boucherie in Louisiana), boudin is a soft Cajun pork-and-rice sausage that used to provide a home to parts of the pig that didn't belong anyplace else. These days, while liver remains an ingredient in many versions, most commercial Cajun boudins contain meat from the shoulder or Boston butt.

Donald Link, a Cajun of German ancestry whose surname appears to have been prophetic, says this about the places where boudin tends to be found: "These stores are open at six o'clock in the morning for boudin, and that's something I don't think that a lot of people really understand about boudin—that it's an all-day food."

Curing salt acts as a preservative and helps keep the boudin's liver flavor in check. Without it, the liver takes a bitter turn within a day of preparation.

Makes 4 pounds

2 pounds pork shoulder, cut into 1-inch cubes
8 ounces pork liver, cut into 1-inch cubes
1 small onion, chopped
2 celery stalks, chopped
1 medium poblano, chopped
3 medium jalapeño chiles, chopped
6 garlic cloves, coarsely chopped
4 tablespoons salt
2 tablespoons ground black pepper
1 tablespoon ground white pepper

½ teaspoon curing salt (also known as pink salt)
2 teaspoons ground cayenne pepper
1 teaspoon chili powder
7 cups cooked white rice (about 2½ cups uncooked rice)
1 cup chopped parsley
1 cup chopped green onions (white and tender green parts)
2 to 3 yards natural hog casing for forming links (optional)

Stir together the pork shoulder, liver, onion, celery, poblano, jalapeños, garlic, salt, black pepper, white pepper, curing salt, cayenne, and chili powder in a large bowl. Refrigerate for at least 1 hour and up to overnight.

Place the pork mixture in a large stockpot and add enough water to come 2 inches above the meat. Bring to a boil, reduce the heat, and simmer until the meat is tender, about 1 hour and 45 minutes. Remove the pot from the heat and strain, reserving the liquid. Let the meat cool slightly and then run it through a meat grinder set on coarse grind. (You can also chop the meat mixture with a knife if you don't have a meat grinder, which is what I usually do anyway.) Transfer the ground meat into a large bowl and add the rice, parsley, green onions, and the reserved cooking liquid. Use your hands or a rubber spatula to mix vigorously for 5 to 10 minutes. Feel free to use a mixer if you have one. I have one yet I still mix it by hand for some reason I can't explain. When the boudin-rice mixture is first mixed together, it looks very wet, and it's pretty spicy—don't worry. After poaching, the rice becomes much firmer and absorbs the excess moisture and much of the spice. The moist texture and extra spice early on will ensure that your final boudin is moist and full of flavor.

At this point you can feed the sausage into rinsed natural casings. (They come packed in salt.) To do this, slide about two to three yards of casing onto the nozzle. Tie a knot in one end of the casing once the boudin starts to come out. Guide the sausage onto a sheet pan that has a little water on it to keep the casings from drying out and cracking. Twist the sausage into 6- to 8-inch links, depending on how big you like your sausage. Poach the links gently in hot (not bubbling) water for about 10 minutes. Serve hot.

Variation: To make boudin balls, let the mixture cool completely and roll into balls the size of golf balls. Lightly roll them in flour, then in buttermilk, and then in bread crumbs. Fry in small batches at 350°F until they turn golden brown, 3 to 5 minutes. Serve hot.

Donald Link of New Orleans, Louisiana

Chaudin

Marcelle Bienvenu grew up attending her grandfather's annual boucherie in St. Martinville. She recounts the day's porcine bounty: "The head and the feet were kept to make fromage de tête cochon, hogs-head cheese. The fat outer skin was diced to fry as gratons or cracklings. . . . The butchers, with their large, sharp knives, went about cutting out the roasts and pork chops, passing cuts of meat on to the women, who then made the boudin rouge and the boudin blanc. . . . Even the stomach of the pig was used to make chaudin."

Minus a pig's stomach, you can form the stuffing mixture into a sort of meatloaf in a roasting pan, then bake as instructed.

Serves 6

1 pig stomach
2½ pounds lean ground pork
1 large onion, minced (about 2 cups)
1 large green bell pepper, finely chopped (about 1¼ cups)
2 garlic cloves, peeled and minced
1 bunch green onions, finely chopped (about 1 cup)
3 slices of bread, broken into pieces and soaked in a little milk

1 sweet potato, peeled and diced (about 2 cups)
1 stalk celery, chopped (about ½ cup)
1 large egg, lightly beaten
½ teaspoon ground cayenne pepper
1 teaspoon salt
½ teaspoon black pepper
3 tablespoons cooking oil
1 tablespoon cornstarch dissolved in ¼ cup cold water

Clean the pig's stomach well, picking off any bits of fat and membrane clinging to the lining or surface. Soak in enough cold water to cover for 2 hours, rinse, and pat dry.

Combine the ground pork, onion, bell pepper, garlic, green onions, soaked bread, sweet potato, celery, egg, cayenne, salt, and pepper in a large mixing bowl. Use your hands to mix the ingredients together. You might want to fry a little of the mixture in a small skillet with some oil to check the seasoning.

Stuff the stomach with the mixture and sew it closed with a large needle and heavy thread. Heat the oil in a heavy cast-iron pot with a lid. Lightly brown the stomach on all sides, then add enough water to cover the stomach. Cover the pot and simmer over low heat for 2 hours. Uncover and cook until the cooking liquid reduces to about 1½ cups. Transfer the chaudin to a serving platter. Pour the cornstarch slurry into the cooking liquid and cook, stirring, until it thickens to make gravy. Slice the chaudin along with the skin and serve hot, topped with a little gravy. Have some hot crusty French bread around to eat along with it.

Marcelle Bienvenu of St. Martinville, Louisiana

Country Breakfast Sausage

When we put out a call for recipes to members and friends, we received three from the 2008 hog killing that went down at Morris Farm in Henry County, Georgia. One for a country ham cure. One for a killing-day pig stew. One for bulk breakfast sausage. We chose to run the latter for its simplicity and also for the traditional inclusion of rubbed sage. Just reading through the instructions makes you want to scramble some eggs and grab the biscuit cutter.

   If you're not starting with a whole hog, you'll likely need to shave the ingredient amounts, but we wanted to honor the Morris family's tradition, printing the recipe in the quantities required of a true hog killing.

Makes 50 pounds

50 pounds fresh pork
11 ounces salt
1½ ounces ground black pepper
1½ ounces rubbed sage

½ ounce ground cayenne pepper
1 ounce crushed red pepper flakes
1 cup packed light brown sugar

Cut the meat into 1-inch cubes. Don't try to make lean sausage. It should be about 40 percent fat to make good sausage. Stir together the salt, pepper, sage, cayenne, pepper flakes, and brown sugar in a large bowl. Add the meat and mix thoroughly. Grind the meat by running it through a sausage mill. Use a very small grinding plate, about ¹⁄₁₆-inch. Keep the meat very cold—as near to 34°F as possible—while grinding. Store refrigerated for up to 3 days or frozen for several months. You may press this sausage into links or fry it up loose. Eggs are the obvious accompaniment, but it would also be good in casseroles or on pizza.

Gene and Ouida Morris of McDonough, Georgia

HOW TO FRY OUT FAT FOR CRACKLINGS, by Kathy Starr

Makes 30 to 40 servings

1 dishpan full of hog fat (skin and fat)
   and trimmings

2 quarts water
1 teaspoon baking soda

Put the hog trimmings and water in a backyard cast-iron pot. Cook slowly on low heat for a couple of hours, stirring constantly so they won't glue together and stick to the bottom of the pan. This mixture will cook out to good pork fat. Cook the meat until all the cracklings cook and move from the bottom of the pan and float on top of the grease. This is a sign that the cracklings are ready. Remove the cracklings with a large slotted spoon or spider strainer. When cooled, the grease becomes lard. Store the cracklings in an airtight container for up to 3 days. The lard will keep in the refrigerator for 3 months or in the freezer for a year.

Pork Roast (a.k.a. Liquid Pork)

Pork roast was in regular rotation at the family dinner table during Lolis Elie's youth. His mother, who stuffed the meat with lots of garlic, would buy a roast with the skin still on so that, once cooked, the surface would crisp up like cracklings.

Lolis began to tweak his mother's recipe as an adult, adding habanero peppers for heat and extending the cooking time. He pulls the pork rather than slicing it like a traditional roast. So tender is his rendition that smitten friends christened it "liquid pork." Lolis's family is not so flexible. "I have made this recipe for my extended family for Christmas dinner. They have insisted on slicing it," he says.

Makes 8 to 10 servings

1 (7- to 7½-pound) bone-in pork
   shoulder or fresh ham with skin
1 garlic head, cloves peeled and quartered
   lengthwise
1 tablespoon salt
2 teaspoons ground black pepper
1 teaspoon ground cayenne pepper or
   minced Scotch bonnet peppers, or to
   taste

6 medium onions, chopped
   (about 8 cups)
2 bell peppers, chopped (about 2 cups)
2 stalks celery, chopped (about 1 cup)
2 carrots, chopped (about 2 cups)
¾ cup peanut oil or vegetable oil
1 cup all-purpose flour

Preheat the oven to 350°F.

Cut narrow 1-inch-deep slits all over the pork shoulder with the tip of a sharp paring knife, twisting the knife slightly to widen the openings. Press a piece of garlic into each slit. Generously season the outside of the meat with salt, pepper, and cayenne. Heat a very large Dutch oven over high heat. Add the meat and brown it on all sides. Add a little oil if the meat sticks, but it should turn easily when sufficiently seared. Transfer the meat to a large bowl. Add the onions, peppers, celery, and carrots to the pot, stirring to coat in the drippings. Return the meat to the pot and nestle it into the vegetables. Set aside.

Heat the oil in a heavy cast-iron skillet over medium heat for about 2 minutes. Sprinkle the flour over the oil and stir until smooth. Stir slowly and constantly, cooking the roux until it is the color of peanut butter, about 12 minutes. Pour the roux over the meat and vegetables.

Cover the Dutch oven with the lid or tightly with foil. Roast for 2½ hours. Uncover and add ½ cup water. Continue to roast, uncovered, until the skin is browned and the meat is falling apart, 3½ to 4 hours more. Check about every 30 minutes and add more water as needed; you want the meat to remain moist and for a gravy to form in the pan. When the meat is done, taste the gravy and adjust the seasoning. Let stand at room temperature for 30 minutes before lifting off the skin. If the skin is not crisp, place it on a baking sheet in a 475°F oven until crisp, about 10 minutes. Pull the meat from the roast with a fork. Serve with gravy and pork skin.

Lolis Elie of New Orleans, Louisiana

NORTH CAROLINA BRUNSWICK STEW

David Cecelski of Durham, North Carolina, explains the origins of this recipe:

> The best stew I've ever had was fixed by Ben Averitt of Oxford, North
> Carolina, who, as a boy, worked many summers on his uncle Ruben Jones's
> tobacco farm in Granville County. In those days, cooking stew and curing
> tobacco went hand in hand. Every fall since 1967, Ben, as an adult, has held
> a stew for his friends and neighbors replete with old-time music-making and
> some fine autumnal tonic. Until his wife, Amy, got sick with cancer, Ben grew
> all the ingredients for his stew himself. Ben and Amy canned the tomatoes
> and beans and froze fresh corn, and Ben shot the squirrels in his backyard.

Makes 25 gallons, enough for a good crowd

By first light, have water boiling in a very, very large pot. Add 2 cleaned squirrels, 8
pounds of pork, 8 pounds of beef, 7 fresh frying chickens (never frozen), 2 pounds of
onions peeled and chopped, and 2 pods of red cayenne pepper. Cook at a roiling boil
until midmorning. Add 1 gallon of baby butterbeans. Add water as necessary. Keep at
a boil. Pick bones out as the meat settles. Add 3 tablespoons of salt and pepper every
time you add ingredients. Around 1 o'clock, add 10 pounds of potatoes, peeled and
quartered. Around 3 o'clock, scoop out the cayenne peppers and add 8 quarts of tomatoes, skinned and seeded. An hour later (30 minutes before serving time), add frozen
kernels cut from 120 ears of corn. Just before serving, add 1 pound (4 sticks) of butter, ½ cup of vinegar, 1 cup of sugar, and a small bottle of Heinz ketchup. Cook for 15
minutes and serve.

Red Beans and Rice

The lore in New Orleans runs that red beans and rice first became a Monday staple back when Monday was laundry day. The low-maintenance, long-simmering bean dish allowed cooks to monitor closely their more pressing and time-consuming household chores. These days, on Mondays, red beans and rice still burbles in kitchens all over town.

Of red beans and rice, Jamie Shannon wrote, "You can use just about any type of meat you want: smoked turkey necks, drumsticks, tasso, seasoned meat, pigs' tails, salt pork, or your favorite sausage—you name it. (Pickled pork is my favorite.) I like my beans meaty, so that I can serve this as a complete meal."

Makes 8 servings

1 pound dried red kidney beans
1 tablespoon butter
1 pound smoked pork sausage, cut into ¼-inch-thick slices
2 medium onions, medium diced (about 3 cups)
5 ribs celery, medium diced (about 1½ cups)
2 bell peppers, medium diced (about 2 cups)
¼ teaspoon ground cayenne pepper, or to taste

1½ tablespoons Creole meat seasoning (recipe follows)
8 cups cold water
1 pound smoked ham hocks
3 bay leaves
Kosher salt and freshly ground black pepper
Hot, boiled rice, for serving
Hot sauce, chopped green onions, and French bread, for serving (optional)

Rinse and pick through the beans thoroughly. Place in a bowl and cover with cold water. Soak at room temperature for at least 6 hours and up to overnight. Drain and rinse. Soaking speeds the cooking process and helps the beans break down.

Melt the butter in a large, heavy pot. Add the sausage and cook until brown, about 5 minutes. (The small amount of butter will keep the sausage from sticking before the fat renders out.) Add the onions, celery, and bell peppers and sauté until tender. Add the cayenne and Creole seasoning and stir. Add the water, ham hocks, and bay leaves. Bring to a boil, stirring occasionally. Reduce to a simmer and cook until the beans are tender, about 1½ hours. Be careful not to scorch the beans—add more water while cooking if necessary. Discard the bay leaves. Season with salt, black pepper, and cayenne. Serve with boiled rice and, if desired, with hot sauce, chopped green onions, and French bread.

CREOLE MEAT SEASONING

Makes 1 cup

4 tablespoons salt
3 tablespoons onion powder
3 tablespoons garlic powder

3 tablespoons paprika
3 tablespoons freshly ground black
   pepper
¾ teaspoon ground cayenne pepper

Combine all of the ingredients in a bowl and mix thoroughly. Store in an airtight
container. It will keep indefinitely.

Jamie Shannon of New Orleans, Louisiana

Souse Meat

The noun *souse* denotes any pickled meat . . . or person. In the southern United
States, where it sometimes goes by the name head cheese, *souse* refers more specifically
to a jellied product made with pigs' heads, ears, and feet—a delicacy whose origins
can be traced to the custom of seasonal hog killings.

   In many cookbooks, pigs' feet are soused whole, and several authors instruct that,
while heads and feet are to be cleaned and scraped, the hair must never be singed, for
it causes discoloring. While mace, nutmeg, sage, and thyme are common souse seasonings, Mildred Council (a.k.a. Mama Dip) uses just salt and peppers and then tarts
her sauce near the end of preparation, adding sweet pickle.

Makes 8 servings

4 large pig feet, cleaned
2 to 3 pig ears, cleaned
2 tablespoons salt
½ teaspoon black pepper
1 teaspoon crushed red pepper flakes

1 tablespoon pickling spice
2 cups apple cider vinegar
¾ cup sweet pickle cubes
¼ cup sugar

Put the feet and ears in a pot and add water to cover by 2 inches. Add the salt, pepper,
red pepper, and pickling spice and bring to a boil. Boil for 10 minutes. Reduce the
heat and let simmer until the meat is tender and about to fall off the bones, usually
about 3½ hours. Transfer the meat with a slotted spoon into a bowl to cool enough to

handle. Pull the meat from the bones and cartilage. Finely chop the meat and discard the bones and cartilage.

Strain 2 cups of the cooking liquid into a saucepan and discard the rest. Stir in the vinegar, pickles, and sugar. Bring to a simmer on medium-high heat, stirring to dissolve the sugar. Remove from the heat and stir in the chopped meat. Pour into an 8-inch-square dish. Refrigerate until set, about 8 hours. Slice and serve.

Mildred Council of Chapel Hill, North Carolina

Stuffed Pork Chops

> I walked and I walked and I walked and I walked
> I stopped for to rest my feet
> I sat down under an old oak tree
> and there went fast asleep
> I dreamt about sitting in a swell café
> as hungry as a bear
> My stomach sent a telegram to my throat:
> There's a wreck on the road somewhere
> I heard the voice of a pork chop say,
> "Come on to me and rest"
> Well you talk about your stewing beef
> I know what's the best
> Well you talk about your chicken, ham, and eggs;
> turkey stuffed and dressed
> But I heard the voice of a pork chop say,
> "Come on to me and rest."

These lyrics, transcribed from "I Heard the Voice of a Pork Chop," a song recorded in Memphis in 1928 for Victor Records, are peculiar. But are they any more peculiar than the following recipe from Paul Prudhomme?

The lyrics ring true. Who among us has not heeded the comforting call of a pork chop? And so does this amalgam of seemingly contradictory ingredients. Prudhomme manages to produce a satisfying and balanced dish—one that reflects the custom of stuffing meats that is prolific in markets throughout his native Acadiana.

Makes 6 servings

2 unpeeled medium apples, coarsely
   chopped
7 tablespoons unsalted butter, at room
   temperature, divided
3 tablespoons light brown sugar
1 teaspoon vanilla extract
½ teaspoon ground nutmeg
1 tablespoon salt
1 teaspoon onion powder
1 teaspoon ground cayenne pepper
1 teaspoon garlic powder
½ teaspoon white pepper
½ teaspoon dry mustard

½ teaspoon rubbed sage
½ teaspoon ground cumin
½ teaspoon black pepper
½ teaspoon dried thyme leaves
12 ounces ground pork
1 cup chopped onions
1 cup chopped green bell peppers
2 teaspoons minced garlic
1 (4-ounce) can diced green chiles
1 cup pork or chicken stock
½ cup very fine dry bread crumbs
½ cup finely chopped green onions
6 (1¾-inch-thick) pork chops

Preheat the oven to 400°F.

Puree the apples, 4 tablespoons (½ stick) of the butter, brown sugar, vanilla, and nutmeg in the bowl of a food processor fitted with a metal blade or in a blender, about 4 minutes. Make a seasoning blend by stirring together the salt, onion powder, cayenne, garlic powder, white pepper, dry mustard, sage, cumin, pepper, and thyme in a small bowl. (Alternately, Paul markets his own seasoning mix, available at grocers, Chef Paul Prudhomme's Meat Magic.) Melt the remaining 3 tablespoons of butter in a large skillet over high heat. Brown the ground pork, about 3 minutes. Stir in the onions, bell peppers, garlic, and 2 tablespoons of the seasoning blend and cook 5 minutes, stirring and scraping the bottom of the pan. Stir in the green chiles and cook until the mixture is well browned, 6 to 8 minutes, stirring occasionally and scraping the bottom of the pan as needed. Add the stock and cook 5 minutes, stirring frequently. Stir in the bread crumbs and cook 3 minutes. Add the apple mixture and the green onions and cook for 2 minutes, stirring constantly. Remove the skillet from the heat.

Prepare the pork chops by cutting a large pocket (to the bone) in the larger side of each chop to hold the stuffing. Sprinkle the remaining seasoning blend evenly on both sides of the chops and inside the pockets, pressing it onto the meat. Prop the chops with their pockets up in a 9-by-13-inch baking pan. Spoon about ¼ cup of stuffing into each pocket. Place any remaining stuffing in a small baking pan. Bake the chops until the meat is done, about 1 hour and 10 minutes. Add the pan of leftover stuffing to the oven during the last 20 minutes of cooking. Serve hot.

Paul Prudhomme of New Orleans, Louisiana

Pork and Sauerkraut

Robb Walsh says that his Ruthenian grandmother, Catherine Timura, made her own sauerkraut in the basement, boiled it down on the stove with pork, and thickened the dish with a roux as preferred by his grandfather. This recipe calls for the pork and sauerkraut to be roasted, an improvement adapted by Robb's mother. Robb buys artisan sauerkraut for this dish but says that jarred or bagged sauerkraut from the refrigerator case of the supermarket will do. Pork spare ribs or pork steaks may be substituted for the country-style ribs.

Makes 6 to 8 servings

3 pounds country-style pork ribs
1 tablespoon garlic powder
1 teaspoon coarse black pepper
½ teaspoon salt
5 tablespoons vegetable oil, divided

2 quarts fresh-pack sauerkraut
1½ cups chicken stock
4 tablespoons all-purpose flour
1 cup chopped onions

Preheat the oven to 350°F.

Rinse the pork and pat dry with paper towels. Make the seasoning blend by stirring together the garlic powder, pepper, and salt in a small bowl. Sprinkle some of the seasoning blend lightly and evenly all over the ribs.

Heat 1 tablespoon of the oil in a Dutch oven over medium-high heat. Brown the pork on all sides, transfer it to a plate, and set aside. Reduce the heat to low and add the sauerkraut, stirring to remove the browned bits from the bottom of the pot. Stir in the chicken stock. Return the pork to the pot. Cover and roast until the pork is tender, about 1 hour. Uncover and continue roasting until the pork is falling-apart tender and browned on top and the liquid is slightly reduced, about 15 minutes more. Transfer the pork to a plate with a slotted spoon, being careful not to break it up too much. Set the pot of sauerkraut aside.

Heat the remaining 4 tablespoons of oil in a sauté pan over medium heat. Whisk in the flour until smooth. Stir in the onions and any remaining seasoning blend. Cook, stirring constantly with a wooden spoon, until the roux is the color of dark gravy, 10 to 15 minutes. Set aside to cool a little.

Reheat the sauerkraut over medium heat, stirring to loosen the browned bits from the bottom of the pot. The mixture should be soupy, so if it's too dry, add a little water. Add the roux a tablespoon at a time to the sauerkraut, stirring well each time. Continue to add roux until the sauerkraut thickens to the consistency of gravy. Season with salt and pepper.

To serve, place the hot sauerkraut in a bowl and arrange the pork on top. Serve hot with mashed potatoes.

Robb Walsh of Houston, Texas

Filé Marinade

Lionel Key learned the art of making filé—which involves curing and pulverizing the leaves of the sassafras tree—from his great-uncle Joseph William Ricard. "Uncle Bill," who was born blind, passed on the tradition, which is said to have been established by the Choctaw Indians. He also passed down the same large mortar and pestle for grinding filé that his own uncle made by hand in 1904.

"Gumbo filé is a thickening and a seasoning that we use for our gumbos here in Louisiana," Lionel says. But that's not the sole use. He offers this recipe for an herbaceous marinade to be used on pork.

Makes about 1½ cups

¾ cup extra-virgin olive oil
¼ cup distilled white vinegar
¼ cup distilled water
1 tablespoon meat tenderizer
   (such as Accent)

1 tablespoon garlic powder
5 teaspoons ground filé

Place all of the ingredients in a glass jar and shake well to mix. Store in the refrigerator and use as soon as possible.

Lionel Key of Baton Rouge, Louisiana

PORK SHOULDER AND SAUCE, by J. C. Hardaway, by way of Lolis Elie

Too few consider the architecture of a barbecue sandwich. Here, Lolis Elie recounts what it was like to dine at Hawkins Grill in Memphis, Tennessee, where J. C. Hardaway was once the pit master:

> Sitting on a hot grill, there was a pork shoulder wrapped in aluminum foil. As Al Green or Albert King or Frankie Beverly played on the jukebox, J. C. cut a few slices and set them to warm on the grill. On the same grill, he toasted the hamburger buns. While the meat cooked, he splashed it with barbecue sauce from an old Palmolive dish detergent bottle. The meat was then placed on a worn chopping board, chopped with a dull cleaver, placed on the toasted bun, topped with a mayonnaise-based coleslaw, cut in half, stuck with a toothpick, and served.

Makes 12 to 18 servings

One (7- to 8-pound) pork shoulder (Boston butt), untrimmed

Salt
Barbecue sauce (recipe follows)

Put the shoulder on the pit fat-side down, directly over the coals (recommended woods: hickory, red oak, or white oak). Let it brown for about 1 hour. Salt the lean side of the shoulder, turn it over, and salt the fat side. Cook the meat for 6 to 7 more hours, turning it every 15 to 20 minutes. If the coals flame, use plain water to dampen them.

BARBECUE SAUCE

Makes about 3½ quarts

1 (18-ounce) bottle hickory-smoke-flavored barbecue sauce (Hardaway used Kraft)
1 (3.5-ounce) bottle liquid smoke

3 cups sugar
8 cups red or white vinegar
1 (16-ounce) bottle ketchup

No cooking needed. Stir all of the ingredients together in a large bowl until the sugar dissolves. Store covered and refrigerated.

Root Beer Glazed Ham

Visitors who waltz into Jim and Diane Gossen's Grand Isle, Louisiana, fishing camp on the weekend of the annual Tarpon Rodeo fishing competition marvel at Jim's prize ham, baked to a glossy black sheen, resting on the kitchen's butcher block.

Jim believes that simmering the meat achieves a textural complexity that baking alone doesn't yield. He also likes the strong herbal flavor that root beer extract—versus the soda itself—imparts.

Makes 20 to 24 servings

1 (15- to 16-pound) bone-in ham
A good glug of canola oil
1 cup yellow mustard
1 cup packed light brown sugar

2 teaspoons root beer extract
⅓ cup light corn syrup
½ teaspoon ground cloves

Place the ham in a large stock pot and add enough water to make the ham float. Bring to a boil, reduce the heat, and simmer slowly until the ham reaches an internal temperature of 160°F, about 2 hours. Remove the pot from the heat and let the ham rest for 30 minutes.

Preheat the oven to 475°F. Brush the inside of a large roasting pan with the oil and set it aside.

Remove the ham from the water and pat it dry. Use a sharp knife to score the ham by making ½-inch-deep cuts in the meat in a diamond pattern across the top of the ham and as far down on the sides of the ham as you can get without turning it over. Place the ham in the prepared roasting pan.

To make the glaze, stir together the mustard, brown sugar, root beer extract, corn syrup, and cloves in a saucepan. Cook over medium heat, stirring until the sugar melts and the sauce is smooth. Set aside ¼ cup of the glaze and brush the rest over the ham.

Bake the ham until the top begins to crackle and the score marks open up, about 25 minutes. You are not cooking the ham now but simply honing the glaze. Pour the remainder of the glaze over the ham and continue to bake until the glaze turns black in spots and starts to crisp up, about 20 minutes more.

Place the pan on a wire cooling rack. Let the ham rest for at least 20 minutes before carving. Serve warm or at room temperature.

Jim Gossen of Houston, Texas

Deep-Fried Bacon

The original dispute between the Hatfields and the McCoys revolved around the owner-ship of a hog. We're fairly certain that both parties had bacon in mind. We would have held a grudge too.

When we asked Mary Beth Lasseter for a recipe contribution, she submitted the fol-lowing options: "a seafood gumbo recipe from my Grandma Eanes (from New Orleans); a tea cake recipe from my Grandpa Lasseter (from South Georgia); a red velvet cake recipe from my mama (also from South Georgia); and a battered and deep-fried bacon recipe from my daddy (served with black-eyed peas on New Year's Day)."

In other words, we had no choice.

Makes 6 to 8 servings

Oil or lard, for deep frying
1 cup all-purpose flour, divided
½ cup milk

½ to ⅔ cup thick buttermilk
½ to 1 teaspoon ground black pepper
1 pound sliced bacon

Preheat the oven to 350°F. Set a wire rack inside a rimmed baking sheet and set it aside. Pour oil into a deep heavy pot to a depth of at least 2 inches. Heat the oil to 350°F.

Place ½ cup of the flour on a plate. Pour the milk into a shallow bowl. Put the remaining ½ cup of flour in another shallow bowl and stir in enough buttermilk to make thick batter. Season the batter with pepper. (I like a heavy hand.)

Working in batches, dust each slice of bacon with flour, dip it in milk, and then coat it in batter, letting any excess drip off. Lower the battered bacon into the hot oil and fry, turning as needed, until crisp and golden brown, about 3 minutes. Transfer to the rack to drain. Let the oil return to 350°F between batches. Skim out the floating bits of lost batter as needed so they won't burn up and ruin the oil.

When all of the bacon is fried, place the pan of bacon (still on the rack) in the oven and cook until it is all hot and crispy, 5 to 7 minutes. Serve hot.

David Lasseter of Valdosta, Georgia, and Mary Beth Lasseter of Vicksburg, Mississippi

HOW TO BUILD A BACON FOREST, by Melissa Booth Hall of Oxford, Mississippi

Notes from an SFA staff meeting in advance of the 2007 Southern Foodways Symposium:

JOHN T. EDGE, SFA DIRECTOR: "Wouldn't it be cool to have a bacon forest? So that when you entered the final dinner of the symposium, you come in through a canopy of cooked strips of bacon?

SFA STAFF: "No, not cool at all."

JOHN T. EDGE: "But could we build one?"

Among SFA staff members, the pejorative phrase "jumping the shark" was used nearly every time the forest was discussed.

Turns out, though, that the answer is a resounding yes. It is possible to build a porcine arboretum. In fact it's not really that hard at all.

Makes 3 trees

6 three-foot planters (we suggest the plastic kind, for weight considerations)
6 two-foot lengths of clay drainage pipe (the rectangular kind found at gardening centers)
Lots of rocks, broken bricks, gravel, or sand (Concrete is an obvious temptation for the bacon-forest builder. Resist it. The resulting pot is too heavy and has a permanence best reserved for outdoor decorative features that will not attract foxes, bears, or mountain lions.)
6 tree branches at least 6 feet in length (we gathered most of ours after a particularly windy thunderstorm)
18 pounds of bacon
200 Christmas tree hooks

Take one planter. Place one vertical length of clay drainage pipe in the bottom center of the planter. Fill around the outside of the drainage pipe with two or three inches of rocks. Place 1 tree branch inside the clay drainage pipe. Fill the inside of the pipe with rocks, gravel, bricks, or sand until the tree branch can stand upright without support. Move the planter to its final resting spot and then fill the pot to the top with rocks, gravel, bricks, or sand. Repeat for the five remaining planters.

Once the branches are standing in their pots, start cooking the bacon. For this volume of bacon, oven preparation is best. Preheat the oven to 400°F. Place wire racks inside baking sheets. Put as much bacon as will fit (without overlapping) on each sheet. Bake the bacon for 15 minutes (or until browned). Remove the bacon from the racks and place on paper towels to drain. Repeat until all the bacon is fully cooked.

To decorate: Place each piece of bacon on a Christmas tree hook and hang. Make sure to put the hook through the meat of the bacon. Bacon slices hooked through the fat will fall quickly and become a walking hazard (think banana peel on the sidewalk). Your own aesthetic will guide the hanging. And, really, there are few things wrought with natural beauty like the bacon tree.

To display: Best viewed in natural light. Particularly gorgeous in the late afternoon when the rays from the setting sun cause the fat dripping from the bacon to glisten. For evening displays, build in enough time to add up-lighting.

To eat: Reach up, choose your slice, and go for it, making sure to avoid the metal hook. Monitor small children and pets while in the forest.

THE MISSING COW

WHILE attempting to portray our South through recipes and the stories behind them, we spent time in the chicken coop, lingered in the forest, and went hog wild (sorry) in the pig pen. But we didn't write a chapter chock-full of beef recipes.

Yes, Southerners do eat beef. Brisket is as central to the Southern Jewish identity as pork ribs are to that of Gentile Memphians, and the following musings from Eli Evans begin to explain why. We also present chicken-fried steak, courtesy of Robb Walsh, a dish that's common to Southerners of all stripes, from the cow-worshipping state of Texas. And Joyce King contributes her Arkansas family's beef stew, a downright American dish.

Historically, though, we were more likely to hunt or fish to feed a family. A few birds in the yard kept us in eggs and fortified Sunday's fried or roast chicken dinners. Extended families ate whole hogs, in whose lard they preserved every single part, long before the invention of refrigeration.

So, here we give the cow its due. But proportionately.

THE SECRET OF ATLANTA BRISKET, by Eli Evans

My mother, Sara, never really had the patience to cook. Besides, she had a business to run and, like all [eight] Nachamson girls, she was a great manager. Brisket was a weekly occasion, a marvelous, succulent, gravy-laden triumph that took hours to marinate and simmer and baste. Lifting the lid of the Dutch oven to savor the aroma and taste a sliver was as heady as a first kiss. When I was a kid, Ethel Benjamin and Zola Hargrave and Roady Adams, our family cooks, . . . used to let me help. And as the official family taster, I got to crunch the crispy ends that had burned a little as the rest of it finished cooking. I once heard someone mysteriously refer to it as "Atlanta Brisket," but I never really knew why or what its secret was until I moved to New York and discovered its magical powers. Each time I would leave home in Durham to go back to the City, Mom would hand me a large, ice-cold package—an already sliced brisket, each portion wrapped in tinfoil with gravy frozen in. Back in my bachelor apartment, I could take it out of the freezer one serving at a time and "eat great" in what she viewed as the barren canyons of Manhattan. Like magic, I could produce Southern Jewish "home cookin'" in the Big Apple. . . .

One day, after consulting Zola and Roady, I decided to try cooking it myself from scratch. I bought fresh onions, plus onion-soup mix, bay leaves, and paprika. But before I browned the meat in oil (to retain the juices), they told me the "secret" ingredient. It was so Southern, really. Fundamentally and soul-deep Atlanta bubbled up from its epicenter. . . . The secret was not fine wine, not Heineken's, not a special marinade handed down for generations from the old country. The secret was—dare I reveal it?—the exotic elixir was . . . Coca-Cola! Or, rather, marinating the meat overnight in the dark epicurean liquid, which has so much fizzy potency, breaks down the fibers and transforms this brisket into the tenderest, softest delicacy you ever put in your mouth. . . .

So try it. Just soak three pounds of meat in Coca-Cola overnight. Remove it and let it drain. Brown it in oil, then put it in a Dutch oven with sliced onions and onion-soup mix and bay leaves in an inch or so of water. Cook about two hours on low, basting and checking it every so often, and adding boiling water when needed (cold water splatters). Slice and serve with the onion mixture as gravy. It's great cold or reheated. And you can eat it for a week in sandwiches.

Savoring this maverick culinary invention will make you feel at one with the lifeblood of Atlanta, the very essence of its body politic, the pulse-beat of its universities and downtown spires and church steeples and cloverleafed interstates and white mansions dotting the rolling hills. As you savor Atlanta Brisket, you will also be absorbing the spiritual force of the dark, vivacious liquid in the female-shaped bottle that, way back when, built a city on the red clay of the Georgia Piedmont.

Chicken-Fried Steak with Cream Gravy

There are three types of chicken-fried steak in Texas, says Robb Walsh: The pan-fried steak of the West Texas cowboys is simply a steak dipped in seasoned flour and fried. The schnitzel-like chicken-fried steak of the Hill Country Germans is dipped in seasoned flour, then egg batter, then flour mixed with bread crumbs.

The original Southern-style chicken-fried steak is dipped in seasoned flour, then batter, then flour again. When it's done, it looks like fried chicken. That's how the dish got its name.

Here's a recipe for the Southern version. Serve it with mashed potatoes and vegetables or the way it comes at Texas truck-stop diners: with French fries and an iceberg wedge covered in ranch dressing.

Serves 4

4 tenderized round steaks, about 2 pounds total	Pinch of cayenne
1½ cups all-purpose flour	2 large eggs
1 tablespoon salt	1 cup buttermilk
1 tablespoon pepper	2 cups oil, for frying
	Cream gravy, for serving (recipe follows)

Preheat the oven to 250°F. Place a wire rack inside a rimmed baking sheet and put it in the oven.

Whisk together the flour, salt, pepper, and cayenne on a plate or in a shallow bowl. Whisk together the eggs and buttermilk in a shallow bowl. Heat the oil to 350°F in a large skillet. While the oil is heating, prepare the meat by dredging first in the seasoned flour, then in the egg mixture, and then again in the flour mixture, evenly coating the meat. Push the flour into the meat with the palm of your hand and be sure it sticks. Working with 1 or 2 steaks at a time, slide the meat into the hot oil and fry until crispy and golden brown, turning once, about 5 minutes per side. Drain the cooked steak on paper towels. Place the cooked steaks on the rack in the warm oven until all four are done. Serve with cream gravy over the top or on the side.

CREAM GRAVY

Makes 3 cups

5 tablespoons butter	1 tablespoon salt
5 tablespoons all-purpose flour	1 tablespoon coarsely ground black pepper
2½ cups milk	

Melt the butter in a skillet over medium-high heat. Whisk in the flour and cook, whisking slowly and evenly, until the roux is smooth and light brown, about 5 minutes. Whisking constantly, slowly add the milk and whisk until smooth. Simmer the gravy, whisking slowly, until it thickens, about 10 minutes. Season with the salt and pepper and serve hot.

Robb Walsh of Houston, Texas

Parsons Vegetable Beef Stew

Joyce King adapted her trusty beef stew recipe from one she found in the Memphis newspaper forty or so years ago. This is her go-to cold-weather dish, and she adds whatever fresh or frozen vegetables are on hand—corn, cabbage, turnips. "Anything in the winter venue," she says. Served with cheese biscuits, jalapeño cornbread, or saltines, this stew is a complete meal, "almost medicinal." She's never thrown a drop away.

Makes about 4 quarts

2 pounds lean beef stew meat or
 well-trimmed chuck roast cut into
 2-inch pieces
2 teaspoons salt
1 teaspoon ground black pepper
3 tablespoons unsalted butter, divided
1 cup chopped celery leaves
1 large onion, finely chopped (about 2
 cups)
1 (10.5-ounce) can beef consommé
2 tablespoons ketchup
1 tablespoon Worcestershire sauce
1 tablespoon sugar

4 dashes hot pepper sauce
1 pound white potatoes, peeled and cut
 into bite-sized pieces (about 3 cups)
1 pound carrots, cut into bite-sized pieces
 (about 3 cups)
1 pound small onions, cut into bite-sized
 pieces (about 3 cups)
2 celery stalks, cut into bite-sized pieces
 (about 1 cup)
2 cups shredded turnips, garden peas,
 snapped green beans, sliced okra,
 and/or other vegetables
 (optional)

Season the meat generously with the salt and pepper. Melt 1½ tablespoons of the butter in a large soup pot or Dutch oven over medium-high heat. Working in batches to avoid crowding the pot, sear the meat until well browned on all sides. As the pieces of meat become browned and cooked, transfer them to a bowl, adding more butter to the pot as needed. Add the celery leaves and chopped onion to the pot and stir to coat with the drippings. Stir in the consommé and stir to scrape up the browned bits from the bottom of the pot. Fill the can with water and add it to the pot. Stir in the ketchup, Worcestershire, sugar, and hot sauce. Return the meat and any accumulated juices to the pot and stir well. If the liquid does not come up level with the meat, add a little more water. Bring to a boil, reduce the heat, and simmer, partially covered, for 1 hour.

Stir in the potatoes, carrots, small onions, and sliced celery. Stir in the optional vegetables, if using. Simmer until the meat is spoon tender, 1½ to 2 hours. Season with salt and pepper and serve hot.

Joyce King of Blytheville, Arkansas

THE HOOK
PULLED FROM OUR WATERS

God made fish to be fried.

—Joe Gray Taylor, *Eating, Drinking, and Visiting in the South*

A BOY in south Mississippi strings trotlines across muddy rivers and waits all night for catfish to bite. The next morning he pulls yellow cats and blues off three-pronged hooks and rejoices. A grandmother in coastal Georgia anchors chicken backs and necks to the bottom of her basket and lowers it until it lies flat on the bottom of a brackish creek. Every few minutes she hoists the roped metal basket, hoping for blue crabs.

All day long, men with linebacker shoulders work oyster tongs, scissoring them into water in a motion that calls to mind the effort required to work a posthole digger. The metal teeth of the tongs interlace on the bottom of a Texas bay, scraping up oysters. Tennessee fisherwomen attired in hip waders whip hand-tied flies across the surface of a mountain stream, hoping for a bite from a rainbow trout. Arkansas grabblers risk snakes as they probe with their fingers underneath rocks to catch fish with bare hands. Worm-grunters along the Gulf Coast of Florida "roop" slabs of iron across wooden stobs until the earth itself vibrates and earthworms crawl from the depths to the surface, where they are scooped up for fish bait.

Fisherfolk rely on ingenuity. Safety pins double as fishhooks. Bean poles become fishing rods. From mountain streams and farm ponds, from oceans and bays, in brackish water and fresh, in rivers wide and narrow, Southerners have hooked, tugged, gigged, tonged, speared, and netted their meals.

And in the kitchen, they have applied that same inventiveness and resourcefulness to cooking the catch. Here, cooks across the region pass along their favorite ways to serve up the gifts of the waters. Their tools are cast-iron wash pots, deep fryers full of peanut oil, roadside smokers, slow cookers, slick black iron skillets, and Dutch ovens. Their recipes are newspaper-as-tablecloth plain and country-club-wedding-reception fancy.

Their recipes honor and memorialize what we, as a region, have inherited from the breakfast rituals of civil rights heroes, from the empty cabinets of Civil War widows, from small-town volunteer fire departments. These are recipes passed down by National Guardsmen, home economists, and bait-shop proprietors. In times of drought and dwindling water tables, they remind us further to protect and conserve the waters from which we derive such goodness.

Broiled Flounder

When Beth Shortt was growing up in Washington, North Carolina, on the Pamlico River, the only fish her family ate was flounder. "As far as I knew, flounder was fish the way cows are beef," she recalls. "There were three preparations. Fried usually required a group of Shriners, Masons, Elks, Moose, Lions, Rotarians, or Kiwanians and a home-made fryer made out of a fifty-five-gallon drum. Stuffed meant crabmeat, and that was a standard country-club item. And then there was broiled." She has since learned that there are more fish in the sea, but she still loves flounder.

Makes 4 servings

Nonstick cooking spray
4 flounder fillets
4 to 6 tablespoons mayonnaise
Salt and ground black pepper
Paprika

Ground cayenne pepper
Minced parsley and lemon wedges,
   for garnish

Position a rack in the top of the oven and preheat the broiler to high. Cover the broiler pan or other sturdy, shallow baking pan with aluminum foil. Lightly coat the foil with nonstick cooking spray.

Arrange the fillets skin-side down in a single layer on the prepared pan. Use a dinner knife or pastry brush to coat the top of the fillets with a thin, even layer of mayonnaise. Season with salt and pepper. Sprinkle with paprika for color and a little cayenne for heat.

Place the fish under the broiler and watch it carefully. Broil the fillets until they are opaque and break into large, moist flakes when lightly pressed, 5 to 8 minutes. The mayonnaise will seem to disappear, leaving a light golden glaze on the fish. Serve at once, garnished with parsley and lemon.

Beth Shortt of Oklahoma City, Oklahoma

Boiled-Peanut Beurre Blanc

"Finish with gremolata and boiled peanuts." How often have you heard that phrase? Or, for that matter, the words "boiled-peanut beurre blanc"? Such is the beauty of melding Southern and French techniques. And who better to teach us a thing or two about fresh takes on Southern food than a Canadian, happily assimilated in Georgia? Hugh Acheson says that any medium-bodied fish will work with the sauce. We believe it to be delicious with flounder.

Makes about 2 cups

2 shallots, minced (about ¼ cup)
1 cup champagne vinegar
1 cup white wine
Small bouquet of fresh thyme and
    tarragon sprigs tied together with
    kitchen twine
3 black peppercorns

¼ pound (1 stick) unsalted butter, cut
    into very small cubes and chilled
1 tablespoon gremolata (equal parts
    minced garlic, parsley, and
    lemon zest)
½ cup shelled boiled peanuts
Salt and ground black pepper

Stir together the shallots, vinegar, and wine in a medium saucepan. Toss in the herb bouquet and peppercorns. Bring to a boil over medium-high heat and cook until the mixture reduces by half. Reduce the heat to low. Discard the bouquet and peppercorns.

   Slowly add the butter, one cube at a time, madly whisking all the time, until all of the butter has been incorporated. Whisk in the gremolata and boiled peanuts. Season with salt and pepper. Serve at once or keep the sauce warm in a bain-marie (fancy French for hot-water bath).

Hugh Acheson of Athens, Georgia

Carolina Fish Muddle

"A muddle is a mess of fresh fish and friends gathered around a bubbling pot of seafood stew," explains Dan Huntley. In eastern North Carolina, along the Outer Banks and Pamlico Sound, fish muddles have been cooked (and staged) since the mid-1700s. Dan experienced his first muddle while on a fishing trip with his father to Oregon Inlet and Cape Hatteras. The feed was a simple fund-raiser staged by a Dare County volunteer fire department. A large cast-iron wash pot was placed over a mound of embers by the roadside. "I remember thinking that most everything in it was either caught or grown nearby," recalls Dan. "This was the *terroir* of the Outer Banks—salty and rich, like a dose of sea spray in your face."

Makes 4 to 6 servings

4 ounces bacon, diced
1½ pounds white potatoes, peeled and
    thinly sliced
2 garlic cloves, minced
1 pound yellow onions, thinly sliced
1 (8-ounce) can tomato sauce
½ teaspoon crushed red pepper flakes
1 bay leaf
1 teaspoon dried thyme
Salt and ground black pepper
1½ pounds fresh, white-fleshed, skinless
    fish fillets, cut into 1-inch chunks
3 large eggs

Fry the bacon in a large pot or Dutch oven over medium heat until it renders its fat, about 5 minutes. Discard all but 3 tablespoons of the drippings. Add the potatoes, garlic, and onions and cook, stirring often, until the onions soften, about 8 minutes. Stir in the tomato sauce, pepper flakes, bay leaf, and thyme. Add water to cover. Season generously with salt and pepper. Bring to a boil, reduce the heat, cover, and simmer until the potatoes are tender, about 20 to 30 minutes. Stir in the fish and a little more water to cover, if needed. Cover and simmer until the fish is done and the potatoes are breaking apart to thicken the muddle, about 20 minutes.

   Beat the eggs in a small bowl, then slowly stir into the muddle and mix well; simmer for 20 minutes. Season with salt and pepper. Discard the bay leaf. Serve hot.

Dan Huntley of Rock Hill, South Carolina

Pine-Bark Stew

This variation on a muddle, from the coast of North Carolina, was called such because it was cooked in big iron pots over fires kindled with pine bark. Or because of its dark brown color reminiscent of pine bark. Or, even more implausible, because cooks, lacking access to other ingredients, seasoned the stew with tender bits of pine. The latter myth begs the question: Are there tender bits of pine?

Makes 6 servings

½ cup chopped bacon
1 cup chopped onion
2 cups seeded and chopped tomatoes
1 cup ketchup
2 tablespoons Worcestershire sauce

2 cups peeled and 1-inch cubed potatoes
2 pounds red snapper or other firm white
 fish, cut into 1-inch cubes
2 teaspoons sea salt
½ teaspoon ground black pepper

Fry the bacon until crisp in a large Dutch oven or soup pot over medium heat. Transfer with a slotted spoon to drain on paper towels. Add the onion to the drippings and cook, stirring often, until tender, about 8 minutes. Stir in the tomatoes, ketchup, Worcestershire sauce, and potatoes. Add enough water to cover the vegetables. Bring to a boil, reduce the heat, cover, and simmer for 30 minutes. Stir in the fish, salt, and pepper and simmer until the potatoes are tender, 15 to 20 minutes more. Stir in the bacon, adjust the seasoning, and serve hot.

Rick McDaniel of Asheville, North Carolina

Slow Cooker Crab Dip

Think queso, that goo that's omnipresent in Americanized Mexican restaurants. Think fondue. What would tailgate parties be without peppers and processed cheese kept warm in a slow cooker? For that matter, where would this cookbook be without them?

Makes 16 servings

1 tablespoon butter
6 green onions, thinly sliced
1 red bell pepper, diced
1 pound block processed cheese (such as Velveeta), cut into 1-inch cubes
8 ounces Monterey Jack cheese, grated (2 cups)

1 (10-ounce) can diced tomatoes and green chiles, such as RO*TEL
1 pound crabmeat, picked and bits of shell removed
Hot sauce
Tortilla chips, crackers, toast points, or crudités, for dipping

Melt the butter in a small skillet over medium heat. Stir in the green onions and bell pepper and cook, stirring often, until softened, about 8 minutes. Transfer into a small slow cooker. Stir in the processed cheese, Monterey Jack, and tomatoes. Cover and cook on high until the cheeses melt, about 1 hour. Stir in the crabmeat. Cover and cook on low until the crab is warmed through and the flavors meld, about 1 hour. Season with hot sauce. Serve warm with crunchy things for dipping.

Ann Garner Riddle of Winston-Salem, North Carolina

Crab Stew

Peter Patout comes from a sprawling Louisiana food family. This recipe, which he gleaned from his aunt, Carolyn Roane, exemplifies the Louisiana cooking tradition of making something spectacular to feed many out of an ingredient list that doesn't look like much. The roux sets the visual and taste tone of this dish. Don't rush it.

Makes 12 to 16 servings

3 pounds fresh crabs
2 cups all-purpose flour
1 cup vegetable oil
3 cups chopped onions
8 cups hot tap water
1 (8-ounce) can tomato sauce

1 cup chopped bell pepper
1½ teaspoons salt
1 teaspoon ground cayenne pepper
¾ cup chopped green onion tops
½ cup chopped parsley
Hot, steamed white rice, for serving

Clean and pick the crabs, saving the fat. There should be 5 to 6 cups of crabmeat. Set the crab and fat aside separately.

Stir together the flour and oil until smooth in a large pot. Cook over medium heat, stirring constantly and slowly, until the roux is toasty brown, about 20 minutes. Add the onions and cook until softened, about 10 minutes. Slowly stir in the water and tomato sauce and mix well. Stir in the bell pepper and crab fat. Season with the salt and red pepper. Reduce the heat, cover, and simmer for 1 hour. Stir in the green onion tops and cook for 5 minutes. Gently stir in the crabmeat and parsley and heat through. Adjust the seasoning and serve hot over steamed rice.

Peter Patout of New Orleans, Louisiana

Crawfish Étouffée

Cynthia LeJeune Nobles grew up in Iota, Louisiana, on a rice and crawfish farm. "Our cooking rice came directly from the mill in bulk, and it wasn't uncommon for us to eat it twice a day," she recalls. The family didn't cotton to swanky rice cookers. Her parents taught all seven children how to eyeball the amount of water to pour into a pot full of raw rice.

When Cynthia was growing up, crawfish was a strictly springtime food. Rice fields flooded in the winter, and the water and nutritious rice stubble coaxed the crawfish out in early spring. "Sometimes we were so anxious for the first taste of crawfish," she remembers, "that we had to break through ice-covered ponds to lower our nets. For bait we used sliced pieces of melt, which is beef pancreas."

Makes 4 servings

¼ pound (1 stick) butter
2 large bell peppers, chopped (about 2 cups)
3 stalks celery, chopped (about 1½ cups)
1 large onion, chopped (about 2 cups)
2 garlic cloves, chopped
3 tablespoons all-purpose flour
1 (8-ounce) can tomato sauce
1½ cups water

1 pound peeled crawfish tails (if you peel your own, save the fat)
Salt and ground black pepper
Ground cayenne pepper
¼ cup chopped green onions, white and tender green parts
¼ cup chopped parsley
Hot, cooked white rice, for serving

Melt the butter in a large skillet over medium-high heat. Add the bell peppers, celery, onion, and garlic; cook, stirring often, until softened, about 8 minutes. Stir in the flour and cook, stirring constantly, until the flour is light brown, about 5 minutes. Add the tomato sauce and water and stir until smooth. Stir in the crawfish tails and fat. Reduce the heat, cover, and simmer for 45 minutes. Season with salt, pepper, and cayenne and simmer another 15 minutes. Stir in the green onions and parsley. Serve hot over rice.

Cynthia LeJeune Nobles of Baton Rouge, Louisiana

Oyster Dressing

"To the best of my knowledge, this recipe—a rich dressing of pork, beef, and six dozen oysters—comes from my mother's family," says Dale Abadie, a native of Edgard, Louisiana.

"But it likely was not unique to them. Others along Louisiana's River Road—especially that fifteen-mile stretch where the German and Acadian coasts overlap—appear to have used it, or close variations."

Dale remembers that this dressing was served almost exclusively for the Christmas and New Year's season, probably because it was used to stuff the holiday turkey, and that bird was available only rarely to the people of the area. Also, the colder weather at that time of the year ensured the safe handling and storage of the oysters. This dressing recipe is handed down from Camille Roussel LeBoeuf, Abadie's maternal great-grandmother.

Makes enough to stuff 1 turkey or 2 hens

3 pounds lean ground pork
2 pounds lean ground beef
3 to 4 teaspoons salt
2 teaspoons ground black pepper
2 cups chopped onion
4 garlic cloves, chopped
6 dozen shucked oysters, with their
    liquor

1 large loaf French bread,
    crust removed, torn into
    bite-sized pieces
2 cups finely chopped green
    onion tops
1 cup finely chopped parsley
2 teaspoons freshly ground
    allspice

Mix the pork, beef, salt, and pepper in a large bowl. Cook the meat mixture, onion, and garlic in a large skillet over medium-high heat, stirring often, until the meat is no longer pink. Pour off the fat. Lift the oysters out of their liquor and set aside on a cutting board. Add the bread to the liquor and set aside to soak. Chop the oysters and add them to the skillet. Stir in the green onions and parsley. Add the bread and oyster liquor to the skillet. Cook over low heat, stirring often to prevent scorching, until the mixture is very brown, 2 to 3 hours. Stir in the allspice. Cool completely before stuffing the bird.

Variations: Bake the stuffing in pie shells. Or, keep out a cup or so to serve with crackers or toast as hors d'oeuvres.

Dale Abadie of Oxford, Mississippi

Oyster Patties

"My aunt, Vernon Scott Watson, and her lifelong friend, Zelda Kroll Waltman, formed a catering business shortly after finishing their studies at Louisiana State Normal School," says Pam Eversmeyer.

Maybe they preferred cooking to teaching. Or, like many of their generation, maybe they saw the kitchen as one of the few spaces where they could flourish as entrepreneurs. "This recipe was one of their specialties," says Pam. "It was a fixture at every family occasion from Christmas Eve to wedding receptions."

Makes 4 to 6 entrée servings, or 50 hors d'oeuvres

3 dozen small shucked oysters with
   their liquor
¼ pound (1 stick) butter
2 bunches green onions, white and
   tender green parts finely chopped
   (about ½ cup)
½ cup finely chopped parsley
4 celery stalks, finely chopped
   (about 1½ cups)

3 tablespoons all-purpose flour
1 (10.5-ounce) can cream of mushroom
   soup
Salt and ground black pepper
1 to 2 tablespoons whole milk,
   as needed
Large patty shells, toast points,
   or crackers, for serving

Drain the liquor from the oysters into a bowl and set aside. Melt the butter in a large saucepan over medium heat. Add the green onions, parsley, and celery and cook until tender, about 5 minutes. Add the flour and stir until smooth; cook, stirring constantly, for 2 minutes. Stir in the soup and oyster liquor and cook until the sauce is smooth and thick, about 5 minutes. Add the oysters and cook just until the edges curl, about 5 minutes. Season with salt and pepper. If the mixture is too thick, thin with a little milk.

For a main course, spoon the hot filling into large, baked patty shells. For hors d'oeuvres, serve hot atop toast points or crackers.

Pam Eversmeyer of Metairie, Louisiana

Oyster Stew

"When I was growing up, my father always cooked his famous oyster stew around the holidays," says Sarah O'Kelley. The family lived inland, but a friend of O'Kelley's father owned a seafood restaurant and oyster bar in Columbus, Georgia, for which he brought in oysters from Apalachicola, Florida.

"When my father died unexpectedly, I felt lucky to have just asked him general instructions for this simple but tasty stew," says Sarah. "Since then I have made it every year on his birthday."

Makes 4 to 6 servings

1 quart freshly shucked oysters and
   their liquor
3 tablespoons butter
1 large yellow or white onion, chopped
   (about 2 cups)

3 cups whole milk
1 cup heavy cream
Salt and ground black pepper
Oyster crackers, for garnish

Drain the liquor from the oysters into a bowl and set aside. Melt the butter in a medium saucepan over medium-high heat. When the foam subsides, add the onion and cook until soft, about 8 minutes. Add the oyster liquor and cook until it reduces by half, about 10 minutes. Stir in the milk and cream and bring to a simmer. Stir in the oysters and cook until their outer edges begin to curl, about 5 minutes. Season with salt and pepper. Serve hot with oyster crackers.

Sarah O'Kelley of Folly Beach, South Carolina

SALMON CROQUETTES

These croquettes were a favorite of the late Arlam Carr Sr. of Montgomery, Alabama. His wife, Johnnie, cooked them for him for breakfast until his death at age ninety-five in 1995.

Johnnie Carr, who died in February 2008 at age ninety-seven, was a giant in the civil rights movement in Montgomery. After her childhood friend Rosa Parks was arrested in December 1955 for refusing to give up her seat on the bus to a white man, Johnnie helped organize the bus boycott and created a carpooling program to transport people to work. In 1967, she succeeded Martin Luther King Jr. as president of the Montgomery Improvement Association and held the position for over forty years.

Randall Williams submitted this recipe. To make them the way Johnnie Carr did, Williams says you need:

1 (14.75-ounce) can or 2 (6-ounce) cans
   of salmon (picking bones and skin out
   is optional)
6 Ritz crackers

½ cup hush puppy mix
1 egg
Salt and ground black pepper
Oil, for frying

According to Carr, "You put your salmon (save the juice from the can) in a container and crumble up the crackers and add some hush puppy mix, about a half a cup, and one egg. I don't use any onions but some people do. So you mix all that up and season it with your salt and pepper. Get your grease ready. You need enough to cover the bottom of the pan so they fry up nice and brown. Medium heat, not too high. Add some of the juice from the can if you need to so your salmon mix is a good consistency to make into patties. Mix it all up real good. Then take some and make patties and place in the hot fryer. Pat them down in the fryer with your spatula. Then brown on both sides and serve them hot. That's it."

She observed that some people like ketchup or hot sauce on their salmon croquettes, but her husband did not. "He didn't put nothing on his but his teeth," she remembered.

Seafood Gumbo

Carol Copeland received this gumbo recipe some forty years ago from a friend's grandmother in Shreveport, Louisiana. "I make the gumbo every time my family goes to Dauphin Island," a barrier island south of Mobile, Alabama. "We used to buy the shrimp from Petrona's market there until Hurricane Katrina took it away."

Makes 12 servings

6 tablespoons bacon drippings, divided
2 medium onions, finely chopped (about 3 cups)
½ cup all-purpose flour
6 cups chicken stock or shrimp stock
2 bay leaves
2 teaspoons ground cayenne pepper
1 tablespoon seasoned salt
1 teaspoon ground black pepper

1 tablespoon finely chopped parsley
1½ pounds okra, trimmed and cut into thin rounds
1 (28-ounce) can diced tomatoes
2 pounds shrimp, shelled and deveined
1 to 2 pints shucked oysters
1 pint crabmeat, picked over
1 tablespoon filé (optional)
Hot, cooked white rice, for serving

Heat 2 tablespoons of the bacon drippings in a large soup pot over medium-high heat. Add the onions and cook, stirring often, until they soften, about 8 minutes. Transfer the onions with a slotted spoon into a bowl and set aside. Add the remaining 4 tablespoons of bacon drippings to the pot. Add the flour and stir until smooth. Reduce the heat to low and cook, stirring slowly and constantly, until the roux is rich rusty brown, about 30 minutes. Stir in the stock, reserved onions, bay leaves, cayenne, seasoned salt, pepper, parsley, okra, and tomatoes. Cover and simmer, stirring occasionally, for 2 hours. Stir in the shrimp, oysters, and crab. Cook, uncovered, another 20 minutes. Stir in the filé, if using. Serve hot, over rice.

Carol Copeland of Athens, Alabama

Shad Roe with Hominy

According to John Egerton in *Southern Food*, shad was once so plentiful along the Atlantic Coast "as to be considered too common to eat—but in other times, the spring spawning season was greeted with joy by shad lovers from the St. Johns River in north Florida to the Virginia coast and beyond." He goes on to explain that "the Indians were said to use shad for fertilizer, but they also ate it, and ate shad roe (eggs) as well." This recipe comes from the files of the late Bill Neal, to whom Southern cooks and eaters owe a debt—for his marked influence on contemporary Southern cooking in general and for chronicling old recipes like this one in particular.

Makes 4 servings

3 tablespoons butter, melted
2 sets (pairs) fresh shad roe (about 1 pound)
Juice of 1 lemon
¼ cup water
Salt and ground black pepper
8 slices bacon
½ cup finely chopped onion

2 garlic cloves, minced
¼ teaspoon dried thyme
1½ cups peeled, seeded, and chopped tomatoes
2 tablespoons dry sherry
1 (16-ounce) can hominy, drained
2 tablespoons chopped parsley
Lemon wedges, to garnish

Preheat the oven to 350°F.

Pour the melted butter into a medium baking dish and carefully arrange the roe in it. Sprinkle with the lemon juice and pour the water around, but not over, the roe. Season with salt and pepper. Cover loosely with waxed paper and bake on the middle rack of the oven until the shad roe is just firm, about 20 minutes, depending on the size of the roe. Let cool. Gently separate the sets.

Fry the bacon in a large skillet, starting with a cold pan. Remove and crumble the bacon when cool, reserving it as a final garnish. Pour half of the rendered bacon fat into another skillet for sautéing the roe. Stir the onion into the remaining bacon fat and sauté, stirring often, until it is lightly browned. Stir in the garlic and thyme and cook, stirring, for 1 minute. Stir in the tomatoes and simmer for 20 minutes, adding water if necessary to maintain the consistency of a sauce. Stir in the sherry and boil rapidly for 2 minutes. Add the hominy and heat thoroughly. Keep warm.

Heat the skillet with the bacon fat over medium-high heat. Handling the roe carefully, sauté until golden brown on both sides. Working quickly, divide the tomato sauce and hominy evenly among 4 serving plates. Place the sautéed roe on top of the sauce and sprinkle with the fresh parsley and crumbled bacon. Garnish with lemon wedges and serve very hot.

Bill Neal of Chapel Hill, North Carolina

Shrimp Paste

April McGreger learned this recipe by reading the work of the late Eugene Walter, a native of Mobile, Alabama. In the 1953 novel *The Untidy Pilgrim*, Walter introduced the world to a skewed vision of his native city: "Down in Mobile they're all crazy, because the Gulf Coast is the kingdom of monkeys, the land of clowns, ghosts and musicians, and Mobile is sweet lunacy's county seat." Throughout his life Walter espoused the virtues of good food and drink. Of Mobile natives he observed, "It's a toss-up whether they rank the pleasures of the table or the pleasures of the bed first, but it's a concrete certainty that talk follows close after."

April likes serving leftover shrimp paste on crackers or toast or stirring it into hot grits.

Makes 2 cups

6 tablespoons plus ⅛ teaspoon salt,
   divided
3 bay leaves
Zest of 1 lemon
1 pound raw shrimp in their shells

¼ pound (1 stick) butter,
   at room temperature
Pinch of mace
Pinch of cayenne
Splash of dry sherry

Preheat the oven to 300°F. Bring 3 quarts of water, 6 tablespoons of the salt, bay leaves, and lemon zest to a boil. Drop in the shrimp and simmer just until opaque, 3 to 5 minutes. Drain well, discard the bay leaves, and spread the shrimp on a towel to cool. When the shrimp are cool enough to handle, peel and set the shells aside. Coarsely chop the meat and set aside. Spread the shells on a baking sheet and roast until dry and brittle, 15 to 20 minutes. Grind the shells to powder in a spice grinder or food processor.

Melt the butter in the top of a double boiler set over (not in) simmering water. Stir in the ground shrimp shells and 2 tablespoons of water. Simmer for 10 minutes, stirring now and then. Don't let it boil. Pour into a small bowl and refrigerate until the mixture hardens. Meanwhile, make an ice bath by placing a medium bowl inside a larger bowl that is filled with ice water and set it aside. Spoon the hardened butter mixture into a small saucepan and discard any liquid in the bottom of the bowl. Melt the hardened butter over medium heat. Stir in ⅛ teaspoon of the salt, mace, cayenne, and chopped shrimp. Transfer into the ice bath and refrigerate until chilled. Transfer into the bowl of a food processor fitted with the metal blade. Add the sherry and pulse until smooth. Scrape the shrimp paste into a 2-cup mold, bowl, or terrine. Smooth the surface with the back of a spoon or with a small offset spatula. Refrigerate until well chilled. Serve with crackers, toast points, or hot grits.

Variation: Seal the container of shrimp paste with butter. Melt ¼ pound (1 stick) of butter and cool slightly. Gently pour the butter over the paste. Cover tightly with foil and refrigerate until the butter hardens. The hardened butter seals the surface for up to one week.

April McGreger of Carrboro, North Carolina

Barbecue Shrimp and Sweet-Potato Tarts

This "pie" uses the buttered version of barbecue shrimp found at many New Orleans restaurants. It also relies on mashed sweet potatoes, which Greg Sonnier came to love while visiting relatives in Cajun country. "The taste of the dish is layered with the lemony, beer-buttered sauce and the orange juice and cinnamon-spiced sugariness of the sweet potatoes," says Greg. The tart shell is a typical pie crust, sold in convenience stores and first-class bakeries alike.

Makes 4 servings

SWEET POTATO FILLING

2 cups roasted, peeled, and mashed sweet
   potatoes (from about 1 pound of
   potatoes)
Zest and juice from 1 orange
¼ cup packed light brown sugar

Pinch of ground cloves
½ teaspoon pure vanilla extract
½ teaspoon ground cinnamon
Pinch of salt

BARBECUE SHRIMP AND SAUCE

¼ pound (1 stick) butter, cut into cubes
   and chilled, divided
2 teaspoons Cajun or Creole seasoning
   blend
1 teaspoon finely chopped rosemary
1 tablespoon finely chopped garlic
1 teaspoon cracked black pepper

16 jumbo Louisiana shrimp with heads
   (about 2 pounds), raw, peeled and
   deveined
¼ cup beer
1 tablespoon Worcestershire sauce
Juice of 2 lemons
½ cup seafood stock or shrimp stock

4 four- to five-inch tart shells, baked and
   cooled

4 sprigs fresh rosemary,
   for garnish

To make the filling: Place the mashed sweet potatoes, orange zest, orange juice, brown sugar, cloves, vanilla, cinnamon, and salt in a food processor fitted with a metal blade. Process until the mixture is smooth and well blended. Taste for salt and sugar and adjust as needed. Transfer the puree to a small saucepan and keep warm over low heat until ready to serve.

To make the shrimp and sauce: Melt 4 tablespoons of the butter in a large skillet over medium-high heat. Cook, gently swirling the pan, until the butter is lightly browned and smells toasty. Quickly stir in the seasoning blend, rosemary, garlic, and pepper. Add the shrimp and sauté until they are pink and just cooked through. Transfer with a slotted spoon to a plate and cover with foil to keep warm. Add the beer, Worcestershire sauce, lemon juice, and stock to the skillet. Bring to a boil and reduce the liquid by half. Finish the sauce by whisking in the remaining 4 tablespoons of butter, 1 cube at a time.

To assemble: Place the tart shells on serving plates. Fill the shells with the warm sweet-potato filling. Arrange 4 shrimp on each tart. Pour the sauce over and around the tarts. Garnish each with a sprig of fresh rosemary and serve at once.

Greg Sonnier of New Orleans, Louisiana

Smoked Mullet Dip

Mullet are a jumping fish. They are also oily-fleshed, which means that they stand up well to smoke.

"Marilyn Rose of the Florida Department of Natural Resources developed the ancestor of this recipe about thirty years ago," writes Francine Wolfe Schwartz. Since then, Francine has tweaked and twirled it: "This has graced many a party table in my home. It's my favorite hostess gift with a basket of crackers."

Makes about 4 cups

8 ounces cream cheese, at room temperature
2 teaspoons Worcestershire sauce
1 tablespoon fresh lemon juice
1 tablespoon minced shallot
1 tablespoon minced fresh dill

4 drops hot sauce
Ground black pepper
12 to 16 ounces skinless, boneless smoked mullet or other hot-smoked fish, crumbled
Chopped parsley and chives, for garnish

Combine the cream cheese, Worcestershire sauce, lemon juice, shallot, and dill in a food processor fitted with a metal blade and process until smooth. Season with the hot sauce and pepper and pulse to combine. Transfer the dip into a serving bowl. Fold in the mullet with a rubber spatula. Sprinkle with chopped parsley and chives. Serve with crackers or toasted baguette slices.

Francine Wolfe Schwartz of Fort Myers, Florida

Pan-Fried Soft-Shell Crabs

Soft-shells are crabs that have just molted, shedding their old shells in order to grow larger ones. In this form, the entire crustacean is edible. Folklore holds that soft-shell season begins around the time of the first full moon in May. With that in mind, Bret Jennings says, "Soft-shell crabs are a seasonal treat, and we always try to take advantage of them in their peak season."

Makes 6 appetizers or 3 entrée servings

1 cup buttermilk
3 cups cornmeal
½ cup all-purpose flour
1 tablespoon salt
1 teaspoon ground cayenne pepper
Corn oil for pan frying

6 soft-shell crabs, cleaned and rinsed
¼ cup sliced green onions, for garnish
¼ cup homemade or store-bought
   mayonnaise seasoned liberally with
   hot sauce, for garnish

Pour the buttermilk into a shallow bowl. In another shallow bowl, stir together the cornmeal, flour, salt, and cayenne. Pour oil into a deep cast-iron skillet to a depth of ½ inch. Heat the oil to 375°F.

Dip each crab into the buttermilk, then coat in the cornmeal mixture, shaking off the excess. Place the crabs upside down into the hot oil. Fry, turning once, until the crabs are crisp and very hot in the center, about 7 minutes. Reduce the heat if the oil gets smoky. Serve at once, garnished with the green onions and seasoned mayonnaise.

Bret Jennings of Chapel Hill, North Carolina

West Indies Salad

Some restaurants guard their trademark recipes. Not Bayley's, down near the Alabama Gulf Coast, where West Indies salad was likely born. In the 1960s, Bill Bayley appeared on a Mobile morning television show, telling everyone how to do it. He gave the recipe away to charity cookbook publishers too.

Many ditched the ice-water step (a very effective means of keeping the crabmeat chilled), thinking that would dilute the brackish tang of the crab. That's where they probably went wrong.

Serves 4 to 6

1 medium onion, finely chopped (about
   1½ cups), divided
1 pound fresh claw crabmeat, picked
   through for shells and cartilage

Salt and ground black pepper
½ cup vegetable oil
¼ cup apple cider vinegar
½ cup ice-cold water

Spread half of the onion in the bottom of a large, shallow bowl or serving dish. Scatter the crab over the onion, then top with the remaining onion. Season with salt and pepper.

Drizzle the oil and vinegar over the salad, then pour the cold water over it all. Cover and refrigerate for at least 2 hours and up to 12 hours. Toss slightly and adjust the seasoning with salt and pepper, if needed. Serve cold.

Bill Bayley of Theodore, Alabama

Fried Catfish

Martha Foose is a strong proponent of using cottonseed oil for fish frying. She likes its high smoke point and light flavor. She is also aware of the synergies of combining cotton (old Mississippi economy) and catfish (new Mississippi economy). She likes to serve hush puppies alongside, fried, of course, in the same oil.

Makes 4 to 6 servings

8 six-ounce catfish fillets
Salt and ground black pepper
2 cups corn flour (sometimes called fish
   fry) or very finely ground cornmeal

Refined cottonseed oil or peanut oil, for
   deep frying

Set a wire rack inside a rimmed baking sheet lined with newspaper or paper towels.

Rinse the fillets and pat them dry. Season both sides with salt and pepper. Place the corn flour in a shallow bowl and season it liberally with salt and pepper. Coat the fillets in the seasoned corn flour and set them on the wire rack to dry slightly while the oil heats.

Pour oil into a deep pot or fryer to a depth of at least 4 inches. Heat the oil to 375°F. Lower the fillets into the hot oil, being careful not to crowd the pot. The grease will rise and sputter violently. Fry the fish until light golden brown, slightly curled, and floating, about 4 minutes. Replace the wire rack with a clean one. Transfer the fish with a skimmer or slotted spoon to the clean rack to drain. Serve piping hot.

Martha Foose of Pluto Plantation, Mississippi

Rice-Fried Catfish

Lee Richardson moved from his home state of Louisiana to Arkansas in 2005, following "Hurricane Katrina's uninvited reorganization" of his life. He came upon the idea of coating catfish fillets in rice meal—rather than cornmeal—while driving between the two states, both of which are rich in both rice production and catfish farming. Lee uses a small flour mill to grind the rice into meal, but a food processor or clean electric coffee grinder works just as well.

Makes 4 to 6 servings

6 six-ounce catfish fillets
1 tablespoon kosher salt
1 cup buttermilk

1 teaspoon cayenne pepper
Vegetable oil, for deep frying
2 cups pulverized raw long-grain rice

Season the fillets liberally with the kosher salt and set them aside in a single layer for 10 to 15 minutes.

Whisk together the buttermilk and cayenne in a shallow container large enough to hold the fillets. Add the fillets, making sure that they are submerged and coated in buttermilk. Cover and refrigerate overnight.

Pour oil into a deep pot or fryer to a depth of at least 4 inches. Heat the oil to 350°F.

Spread the rice meal on a plate. Lift the fillets out of the buttermilk and let the excess drip off. Generously coat the fillets with rice meal. Lower the fillets into the hot oil, being careful not to crowd the pot. Fry the fish until golden brown and floating, 4 to 5 minutes. Serve immediately.

Lee Richardson of Little Rock, Arkansas

10

THE HUNT
DEER CAMP AND
QUAIL LODGE COOKERY

If we had our crops laid by . . . the only
extracurricular activities we engaged in were
to go coon hunting or to a revival meeting.
—Jerry Clower, "A Coon Huntin' Story"

EARLY TRAVEL ACCOUNTS and diary entries speak of the profusion of game in the forests and fields of the South. In the 1620s, Captain John Smith wrote of the area near Jamestown: "And now the winter approaching, the rivers became so covered with swans, geese, ducks, and cranes that we daily feasted with good bread, Virginia peas, pumpkins, and putchamins [persimmons], fish, fowl, and divers sort of wild beasts as fast as we could eat them."

The explorers who wrote such accounts learned hunting and cooking techniques from the American Indians, whose stewed meats were the precursors to such dishes as Brunswick stew and burgoo and whose elders cautioned hunters to take only what was needed from the forest. This ethos persists among hunters—and in Southern kitchens—still. As a result, not only in this chapter but throughout this cookbook, you will find recipes that use every part of the animal.

Although the consumption of wild game has declined, venison, wild turkey, duck, and squirrel—game enjoyed by American Indians prior to the Jamestown settlement—are still cooked and served and savored. White-tailed deer have inhabited the South for thousands of years. We still roast, stew, and barbecue deer meat, and we preserve it in the form of jerky. Venison remains one of the region's most prized game dishes, with often contentious arguments erupting over who gets the tenderloin.

On the Southern frontier, wild turkeys were, in the words of one historian, "almost as common as blackbirds." Seeking warmer climates and food, ducks still follow their annual pattern down the Mississippi River flyways, landing in the marshes of Arkansas to feed in the rice fields.

The most plentiful animal in our forests is still the squirrel. We stew its meat in iron cauldrons, smother it in gravies made with milk and water, and cook it in pots bobbing with floury dumplings.

Hunting has long been a means of survival, as well as an act of reverence. It connects us to the past, to an era when expertise with a rifle and trap was key to family nutrition. Whether spearing frogs in a pond at night with a cane pole–mounted gig or shooting squirrels from tree limbs for a community supper, hunters take pride in their connection to the land. "While people in other regions of the country may have equated the consumption of wildlife with unsuccessful farmers and shiftless backwoods folks," writes historian Wiley Prewitt, "Southerners have generally exalted the hunting, cooking, and eating of game."

Baked Wild Duck

Ann Cashion is a native of Mississippi now cooking in Washington, D.C. Both of her parents hunted when she was a child. Their favorite place to shoot wild mallards was Stuttgart, Arkansas, where the ducks fed on rice and were, therefore, less gamey than those in Mississippi.

This recipe, obtained by Ann's mother from the kitchen at the Stuttgart Inn, reflects the way she always prepared wild duck. "I remember how the lovely, classic aromas of beef consommé, duck fat, and sherry would fill the kitchen," says Ann, "and sharpen my appetite for the rich, dark duck flesh to be enjoyed that evening."

Makes 4 to 6 servings

2 wild ducks
Salt and ground black pepper
2 medium onions, coarsely chopped
 (about 3 cups)
2 stalks celery, coarsely chopped (about
 1 cup)
2 large carrots, coarsely chopped (about
 3 cups)
1 (10.5-ounce) can beef consommé
¾ cup dry sherry

Preheat the oven to 350°F. Season the ducks inside and out with salt and pepper. Put the onions, celery, and carrots inside the ducks. Pour the consommé and sherry into a roasting pan. Place the ducks breast-side-down into the liquid. Cover and bake for 2½ hours. Uncover, turn the ducks over, and brown the breasts, about another 15 to 20 minutes. Serve hot.

Margaret P. Cashion of Jackson, Mississippi, by way of Ann Cashion of Washington, D.C.

Braised Coon or Possum with Sweet Potatoes

"My father, Bill Smith Sr., lives in New Bern, North Carolina, where he was born and raised," says Bill Smith Jr. "From the time he got home from World War II until his retirement, he worked for the post office. For many years his routes took him through rural Pamlico County." His clients there were either fishermen or farmers. The Smith family was showered, especially at holidays, with game, fish, oysters, pickles, baked goods, homemade wine, and liquor. The elder Smith made a hobby of gathering recipes from those friends. This recipe for coon and possum was in his collection.

Serves 6 to 8

1 three- to five-pound raccoon, cut into serving pieces	2 tablespoons rubbed sage
Salt and ground black pepper	5 medium sweet potatoes, peeled, halved, and cooked

Bring a large pot of salted water to a boil over high heat. Add the coon and cook until tender, about 1 hour. Drain well, reserving 1 cup of the cooking liquid.

Preheat the oven to 350°F. Place the coon in a shallow baking pan. Season generously with salt and pepper and sprinkle with the sage. Tuck the sweet-potato halves around the sides. Pour the reserved cooking liquid over it all. Bake until heated through, about 20 minutes. Serve hot.

Variation: Substitute a possum for the coon.

Note: While fixing coon or possum, make yourself a "crow cocktail." Mix a shot of bourbon, ½ teaspoon fresh lemon juice, and a dash of grenadine. Shake well with cracked ice and strain into a 3-ounce cocktail glass. If you think you need more, double it.

Bill Smith Sr. of New Bern, North Carolina, by way of Bill Smith Jr. of Chapel Hill, North Carolina

Duck and Andouille Étouffée

Specialties of southwestern Louisiana, étouffées incorporate various meats, poultries, and seafoods, which are smothered in highly seasoned gravies. Here, Ken Smith marries duck, native to North America, with sausage, first introduced into Louisiana by French and German immigrants. Ken garnishes his étouffée with pepper jelly; the sweet-hot flavors play well off this rich dish.

Makes 8 to 10 servings

½ cup vegetable oil
½ cup all-purpose flour
4 cups sliced andouille sausage
1 cup finely chopped celery
1 cup finely chopped onion
2 garlic cloves, minced
½ cup finely chopped red bell pepper
½ cup finely chopped green bell pepper
8 cups rich duck stock or chicken stock
2 tablespoons tomato paste
12 teaspoons dried thyme

3 bay leaves
2 teaspoons salt
Ground black pepper
Ground cayenne pepper
¼ cup finely chopped parsley
5 cups chopped roasted duck meat
Hot, cooked rice or cornbread,
    for serving
Pepper jelly, homemade preferably,
    but store-bought is okay

Heat the oil in a large cast-iron Dutch oven over medium heat. Whisk in the flour, stirring until smooth. Cook, stirring slowly and constantly, until the roux is very dark brown. Don't burn it. Reduce the heat to low. Stir in the sausage, celery, onion, garlic, red bell pepper, and green bell pepper. Add the stock, 1 cup at a time, stirring well after each addition. Stir in the tomato paste, thyme, bay leaves, salt, and black pepper and cayenne to taste. Increase the heat to medium-high and simmer, uncovered, for 20 minutes, stirring occasionally. Stir in the parsley and duck. Simmer until heated through, about 20 to 30 minutes. Serve hot with rice or cornbread. Garnish, if you like, with a drizzle of pepper jelly.

Ken Smith of New Orleans, Louisiana

Duck Gumbo

The men in Georgeanna Milam Chapman's family have always been big duck hunters. Duck gumbo was a wintertime staple in her Tupelo, Mississippi, home. "We still serve it today on Christmas Eve," she says. "One year, when our freezer was well-stocked with ducks, I searched all my cookbooks for duck gumbo. But I couldn't find a recipe I liked. So I turned to this one from my grandmother, Pauline P. Bridgforth."

Makes 12 to 15 servings

3 whole ducks
4 teaspoons salt, divided
1 whole chicken
¼ cup vegetable oil, divided
1 green bell pepper, chopped
2 large yellow onions, chopped
1 celery stalk, chopped
1 (16-ounce) bag frozen sliced okra
2 tablespoons bacon drippings
2 tablespoons all-purpose flour

1 cup water
1 (6-ounce) can tomato paste
1 (3-ounce) bag crab and shrimp boil
   seasoning
Seasoned salt
Creole seasoning
Hot, cooked white rice, for serving
Chopped parsley and green onions, for
   garnish

Place the ducks in a large stock pot or Dutch oven. Cover with cold water, add 2 teaspoons of the salt, bring to a boil, reduce the heat, and simmer for 1 hour. Pour off the water. Add the chicken to the pot. Cover with cold water, add the remaining 2 teaspoons of salt, bring to a boil, reduce the heat, and simmer until the meat starts to fall off the bones, 45 to 60 minutes. Strain the stock into a large bowl. Pour 14 cups of stock back into the pot; discard any excess. When the birds are cool enough to handle, pull the meat off the bones and return it to the pot. Discard the bones and skin. Keep the stock warm over low heat.

Heat 2 tablespoons of the oil in a large skillet. Add the bell pepper, onions, and celery; cook, stirring often, until softened, about 8 minutes, then add to the pot of stock and meat. Heat the remaining 2 tablespoons of oil in the skillet. Add the okra and cook until it thaws and the liquid cooks away, then add to the pot.

Heat the bacon drippings in the skillet over medium heat. Add the flour and stir until smooth. Cook the roux, stirring slowly and constantly, until it is toasty brown. Add the water and tomato paste; stir until smooth, then add to the stock pot. Toss in the seasoning bag. Reduce the heat to low, cover, and simmer, stirring occasionally, until the gumbo is thick, 1 to 1½ hours. Discard the seasoning bag. Season with seasoned salt and Creole seasoning. Serve hot over rice, garnished with parsley and green onions.

Pauline P. Bridgforth of Tupelo, Mississippi, by way of Georgeanna Milam Chapman of Lexington, Kentucky

Fried Rabbit

"This recipe comes from my wife's side of the family," says Dean McCord, "namely her grandmother, Katherine Forbes Taylor." She lived most of her life in the coastal area of North Carolina, in the small village of Maple. "The population was fifty, including livestock, as my father-in-law often says. Miss Katherine's husband, Emest Taylor, owned the town's general store and often received wild game in exchange for the goods he sold. I don't think Miss Katherine or Mr. Emest shot the rabbits themselves, although Miss Katherine knew how to handle a shotgun."

Makes 4 servings

½ cup all-purpose flour
2 teaspoons salt
1 teaspoon ground black pepper

1 three- to four-pound rabbit,
    cut into serving pieces
1 cup lard

Stir together the flour, salt, and pepper in a shallow bowl. Coat the rabbit in the seasoned flour, shaking off the excess. Melt the lard in a large cast-iron skillet over medium heat. Add the rabbit and fry to light golden brown on both sides, 5 to 8 minutes total. Reduce the heat to low and cook until the juices run clear when the meat is pierced with a fork, 30 to 40 minutes, turning frequently. Serve hot.

Katherine Forbes Taylor of Maple, North Carolina, by way of Dean McCord
of Raleigh, North Carolina

Fried Squirrel with Gravy

Sarah Thomas ate a lot of squirrel when she was growing up in French Creek, West Virginia. "They grow way bigger there," she recalls. "This is how my mom, Nancy Loudin, taught me to cook squirrel. My dad and brothers always shot the squirrels through the head with .22 rifles to avoid anyone breaking a tooth on buckshot. We usually helped Dad skin out the squirrels. And there was often a battle over who got the tail."

Makes 4 servings

2 large squirrels
Salt and ground black pepper
1 cup all-purpose flour

Vegetable oil or lard, for frying
Milk, mixed with equal parts water
  (about 1 cup each)

Gut and skin the squirrels. If they were shot with buckshot, check thoroughly for any pieces of shot and remove. Soak the squirrels in a pan of water in the refrigerator for 1 to 2 hours, covering the squirrels. Cut into pieces but don't throw out the backs; there's good flavor there. Discard the heads. Put the pieces in a large pot and cover with water. Bring to a boil, reduce the heat, and simmer until the meat is tender but not falling off the bone, then drain. Season the squirrel pieces with salt and pepper and roll in the flour. Heat oil to shimmering in a cast-iron skillet and add squirrel pieces. Fry until golden brown on both sides. You are not cooking the meat here but rather adding flavor and texture. Remove the meat to drain on paper towels or a brown paper bag.

    Leave about 2 tablespoons of oil in the skillet and add 2 tablespoons of the flour left over from dredging the squirrel. Make a roux (turn the heat down or it'll get away from you). Once the flour is golden, add half milk and half water a good splash at a time, stirring furiously, until your gravy is the consistency you like. Season to taste with salt and pepper.

    Serve the squirrel and gravy with mashed potatoes and green beans cooked with bacon fat. Biscuits wouldn't be a bad idea either.

Sarah Thomas of Black Mountain, North Carolina

Molasses-Brined Wild Turkey Breast with Bourbon Pan Sauce

John Malik never forgot his first wild turkey. "Since that first taste," he says, "I would consider it perhaps the finest protein I have ever had." True wild game is very lean. Turkey is no exception. So brining really works wonders. The bourbon doesn't hurt either.

Serves 6 to 8

1 gallon water
2 bay leaves
1 tablespoon cracked peppercorns
1 cup kosher salt
¼ cup sugar
½ cup molasses
1 large bunch fresh thyme
1 bunch fresh parsley

1 lemon, sliced
1 orange, sliced
1 teaspoon ground cayenne pepper
1 wild turkey breast
1 cup bourbon
2 cups rich turkey stock or chicken stock
4 tablespoons (½ stick) butter
4 whole leaves of fresh sage

To make the brine, stir together the water, bay leaves, peppercorns, salt, sugar, molasses, thyme, parsley, lemon, orange, and cayenne in a large pot. Bring to a boil over high heat, stirring until the sugar dissolves. Remove from the heat and refrigerate until it cools to 45°F. If the pot will not fit into the refrigerator, fill a clean zip-top bag with ice cubes, close the bag tightly, and place it in the brine. The ice will cool the brine without diluting it. Submerge the turkey breast into the cold brine. (If the pot cannot hold both the brine and the turkey, pour the brine into a scrupulously clean ice chest, then add the turkey.) The meat must be submerged in the brine. The brine must stay cold. Brine the turkey for at least 8 hours or overnight.

When ready to cook, preheat the oven to 375°F. Remove the turkey from the brine and pat it dry. Discard the brine. Heat a large cast-iron skillet over high heat. Sear the breast on both sides, 5 to 6 minutes per side. Transfer to the oven and roast until the meat reaches 155°F on an instant-read thermometer inserted into the thickest part of the breast, 20 to 30 minutes. Transfer the breast to a cutting board and cover loosely with foil to keep warm.

Carefully pour the bourbon into the skillet. Cook over medium heat until the bourbon reduces to ¼ cup. Do not stand over the hot pan of bourbon. Stir in the stock and cook until the sauce reduces to the consistency of thin syrup. Add the butter and sage and swirl until the butter melts. Slice the turkey and serve with a ladle of the bourbon pan sauce.

John Malik of Greenville, South Carolina

Osso Buco of Frog Legs

John Folse says that osso buco, "literally translated from the Italian, means 'bone with a hole' and generally refers to the shank portion of an animal, especially veal, lamb, or pork." The meat surrounding the marrow-filled bone is perfect for long, slow braising in rich sauces, such as tomato or veal stock. When the very large frog legs of south Louisiana are too tough and stringy for deep-frying, he says, the braising method, often applied to Italian osso buco style, is ideal.

Makes 6 servings

½ cup olive oil
½ cup all-purpose flour
Salt and ground black pepper
6 pairs of frog legs, cleaned
½ cup diced carrots
½ cup diced potatoes
½ cup diced zucchini
½ cup diced summer squash
10 pearl onions
½ cup diced onions
½ cup diced celery

½ cup diced red bell pepper
¼ cup diced garlic
4 cups beef stock
½ cup red wine
Dash of Worcestershire sauce
Dash of hot sauce
1 tablespoon finely chopped fresh thyme
1 tablespoon finely chopped fresh basil
½ cup sliced green onions
¼ cup chopped parsley

Heat the oil in a 10-inch cast-iron skillet over medium-high heat. Place the flour in a shallow bowl and season with salt and pepper. Coat the frog legs in the seasoned flour, shaking off the excess. Sear the legs in the hot oil until lightly browned on both sides. Do not overcook. Add the carrots, potatoes, zucchini, squash, pearl onions, diced onions, celery, bell pepper, and garlic. Sauté, stirring often, until the vegetables wilt, about 5 minutes. Add the beef stock, one ladle at a time, until well blended. Stir in the red wine. Season with salt, pepper, Worcestershire, and hot sauce. Reduce the heat to medium-low, cover, and cook until the meat is tender, about 30 minutes. Stir in the thyme, basil, green onions, and parsley. Serve hot over pasta or rice.

John Folse of Donaldsonville, Louisiana

Smothered Quail and Stone-Ground Grits

"I love to serve this dish for breakfast or dinner," says Tim Patridge. He recalls how his mother often cooked it after his father went hunting. Later, when Tim was cooking at Callaway Gardens in Pine Mountain, Georgia, guests would bring their quail in from the hunt to be cleaned and prepared by the staff. With those guests in mind, Tim developed this recipe, from a family hand-me-down that lacked measurements.

Makes 8 servings

8 quail (4 braces)
2 teaspoons salt
1 teaspoon ground black pepper
½ teaspoon ground cayenne pepper
½ cup all-purpose flour
4 tablespoons lard or bacon drippings
2 cups diced onions

1 cup diced bell pepper
2 teaspoons chopped garlic
2 cups chicken stock or water
½ cup freshly brewed coffee
2 teaspoons Worcestershire sauce
Hot stone-ground grits, for serving

Season the quail with the salt, pepper, and cayenne. Lightly coat them in flour, shaking off the excess. Heat the lard in a large cast-iron skillet over high heat. Add the quail and brown them on all sides. Transfer to a plate and set aside. Reduce the heat to medium and add the onions, bell pepper, and garlic to the pan. Cook, stirring often, until softened, about 8 minutes. Stir in the stock, coffee, and Worcestershire sauce. Return the quail and any accumulated juices to the skillet. Reduce the heat to low, cover, and simmer until the quail are tender and the sauce thickens, 20 to 30 minutes. Serve hot, atop the grits.

Tim Patridge of Atlanta, Georgia

Venison and Noodles

They hunt. They fish. Gayle Brooks will tell you that to know her people you need to acquaint yourself with their forests and their waters, which they hunt with a passion. "Newcomers to west-central Florida may hear adults talk about 'getting the camp ready' or 'leaving for camp'" and assume these people are on their way to a resort, she says. But when they see the locals pulling four-wheel-drive vehicles with dog boxes or camping gear, they catch on that the destination is a hunt camp.

Gayle says that her people favor fried venison back strap but that the following preparation is a more suitable way to present your kill to company.

Makes 4 servings

2 pounds venison roast	1 stalk celery, chopped (about ½ cup)
¼ cup all-purpose flour	3 medium onions, sliced (about 6 cups)
1 teaspoon salt	1 tablespoon Worcestershire sauce
½ teaspoon ground black pepper	2 cups chopped tomatoes
3 tablespoons bacon drippings	Hot, cooked noodles, for serving

Cut the venison into 2-inch pieces. Stir together the flour, salt, and pepper in a bowl. Lightly coat the venison in the seasoned flour, shaking off the excess. Set aside in a single layer.

Heat the drippings in a large skillet over medium-high heat. Add the venison and brown it on all sides. Stir in the celery, onions, Worcestershire, and tomatoes. Reduce the heat to medium-low, cover, and simmer until the meat is very tender, 1½ to 2 hours. Serve hot over the noodles.

Gayle Brooks of Brooksville, Florida

11 PUT UP
PICKLED, BRINED, JARRED, AND CANNED

Given the choice between a cucumber and
a pickle, I'll take the pickle. Every time.
—Ann Cashion

PRESERVING FOOD was once a necessity. Decades past, a well-set winter table depended on the fruits (and vegetables) of summer. Women and their daughters, sisters, and friends crowded together on back porches to peel peaches and apples, snap beans, and shuck corn. They hovered around steaming kettles in the suffocating heat of late summer. It was exhausting, strenuous work necessary for their family's subsistence. In households everywhere groups of women processed food in volumes rarely seen today outside of commercial kitchens.

Hard work though it was, this time spent in kitchens was one of great optimism and abundance, when it seemed as if the harvest would never cease, when community was reinforced, as many hands turned the summer harvest into a staggering array of edible jewel-toned accomplishment to bow and beautify the shelves of the pantry.

The South's myriad relishes and pickles complemented an otherwise monotonous winter diet of dried peas and beans, cornbread, salt pork, and occasional roots and tubers.

Some preserving traditions have changed very little from their beginnings. In Appalachia, sauerkraut has long been a sustaining dish in wintertime, just as it was during the long, cold winters in northern and central Europe. Mountain folk preserve leather britches—a term that describes the pods hung to dry with their beans still inside them—in much the same manner employed by American Indians before the first European settlers arrived.

Then there are the one-offs, the peculiar dishes that reference particular traditions, such as spiced muscadines, the Deep South take on cranberry sauce, with antecedents in the spiced barberries of England, and mango'd muskmelon, the British colonists' attempt to recreate the East Indian mango chutney with New World muskmelons, cucumbers, and peaches. These queer and lovely and simple dishes stand as evidence of the dynamic cultural exchange that produced the cherished foods of our collective larder.

A note on canning: The U.S. Department of Agriculture continues to support research and education on canning and preserving through its Extension Service partnership at the University of Georgia. We consider these tax dollars well spent! Please use this excellent resource to familiarize yourself with home canning: National Center for Food Preservation (http://www.uga.edu/nchfpl). Alternately, invest in the *Ball Blue Book Guide to Preserving*.

Appalachian Pickle Beans and Corn

"I have never seen pickled beans this way (in the sauerkraut fashion) anywhere other than a few mountain counties in western North Carolina," says Sheri Castle. "My family always included corn with our beans, but others didn't. Around my hometown of Boone, North Carolina, folks ate as many pickled beans as they ate regular canned beans, although they're an acquired taste for outsiders. We once gave a quart to a new neighbor (who was 'from off') and found out later that she flushed them down the toilet because she thought that they had spoiled."

According to Sheri, soupy potatoes (creamed new potatoes) and cornbread are commonly paired with pickle beans in her neck of Appalachia, to cut the salt.

Makes 4 quarts

3½ quarts half-runner green beans, strung and broken into bite-sized pieces

4 to 6 ears fresh corn
¼ cup pickling salt
1 gallon filtered water or spring water

Important Note: You should start the pickling when the signs are above the belt (preferably in the head) and the moon is new. Farming and preserving food "by the signs" goes back to Celtic times. Mountain people held on to this practice longer than growers in most places because they held on to their folklore longer. To plant or preserve by the signs means consulting *The Farmers Almanac* for optimal timing before doing either, thereby ensuring better growth and preservation results. The idea is that the phases of the moon and the movement of the planets are messages from nature. These days, most people consider this methodology nonsense. Superstition. But quite a few rural families and all biodynamic farmers still consult the signs—believing that there's some common sense and a respect for nature behind it all—although they might not admit it. I still consult the signs when I pickle things. The terms used for the signs are the same words used for astrological signs and for parts of the body. For good fermentation with these beans, for example, the proper signs are *high on the body, away from the bowels and feet.*

The bean pods need to be very full of beans; if not, add a cup or two of shellies (fresh shell beans). Put the beans in a large pot and cover with water. Bring to a boil, reduce the heat to low, cover the pot, and simmer until tender, about 30 minutes. Add the corn in the last 5 minutes to parboil it. Drain the corn and beans and let cool. Cut the kernels off the cobs. Get as much of the kernels as possible with the first cut and do not scrape the cobs. Mix the beans and corn kernels and pour into a sterilized cloth sack (such as a flour sack or cotton pillowcase) and tie it up. Put the sack in a pickling crock. Make the brine by dissolving the pickling salt into the cold filtered water. (Old-timers made their brine salty enough to float an egg. They used 8 to 10 tablespoons of pickling salt per gallon of water, which is very salty.) Pour enough brine into the crock to cover the sack by at least 2 inches. Put a scrubbed and sterilized river rock or inverted dinner plate on top of the sack to hold it under the brine. Cover the crock with a clean cloth (such as a flour sack towel or cheesecloth) and secure it with twine. Store the crock in the cool corner of the basement, ideally around 65°F. Skim off the scum every 3 or 4 days. Do not worry if there is a little mold in the scum. Taste the beans after two weeks to see how they are doing. Use sterilized utensils, not your hands, lest you contaminate the brine. Most people prefer beans that have fermented between 2 and 3 weeks, although some people leave them in the brine as long as 6 weeks, but they will be extremely sour and salty.

Remove the beans from the sack and transfer to a sterilized glass container—or containers—with their brine. For storage up to 1 month, simply cover and refrigerate. For longer storage, pack the vegetables into hot sterilized quart jars, cover with brine, and close with hot sterilized lids and rings. Process in a hot-water bath for 20 minutes to seal.

When ready to serve, heat a big spoonful of bacon grease in a skillet. Pour in the pickle beans and juice. They'll pop a little at first. Serve hot.

Madge Castle of Boone, North Carolina, by way of Sheri Castle, of Chapel Hill, North Carolina

Fried Dill Pickles with Comeback Sauce

The origin point of fried dill pickles is unknown. Atkins, Arkansas, and Hollywood, Mississippi, are two claimants. Born after the introduction of commercial hamburger dills and spears, they are an ethereal combination of hot, crispy, salty, and sour. Comeback sauce is the shotgun marriage of Thousand Island dressing and rémoulade, popularized in Jackson, Mississippi, diners. It emerged as the house dressing of the Rotisserie, one of the city's early Greek-owned restaurants.

Makes about 2 cups of pickles, or 4 to 6 servings

2½ cups all-purpose flour
2 tablespoons garlic powder
2 tablespoons onion powder
1½ teaspoons ground cayenne pepper
3 teaspoons kosher salt
4½ teaspoons black pepper

1 tablespoon paprika
Peanut oil, for frying
1 (16-ounce) jar sliced dill pickles
Comeback sauce, for dipping (recipe follows)

Stir together the flour, garlic powder, onion powder, cayenne, salt, pepper, and paprika in a bowl. Pour into a small brown paper bag.

Pour oil into a deep, heavy skillet or Dutch oven to a depth of 3 inches. Heat the oil to 350°F.

Drain the pickles. Toss them into the bag of seasoned flour and shake to coat. Working in batches, put the coated pickles in a sieve and shake off as much excess coating as possible. Fry the pickles in the hot oil until golden brown, about 4 minutes. Transfer with a slotted spoon to drain on paper towels. Serve hot, with comeback sauce for dipping.

COMEBACK SAUCE

Makes about 2 cups

⅔ cup mayonnaise
½ cup chili sauce
¼ cup canola oil
1 tablespoon Worcestershire sauce
2 tablespoons fresh lemon juice
¾ teaspoon onion powder

2¼ teaspoons garlic powder
1½ teaspoons paprika
½ teaspoon ground black pepper
¾ teaspoon dry mustard
¾ teaspoon kosher salt

Stir together all of the ingredients in a large bowl until smooth. Cover and refrigerate until chilled.

Amy Crockett of Oxford, Mississippi

Gingery Crisp Watermelon-Rind Pickles

The ultimate waste-not-want-not pickle, watermelon-rind pickles work best with heritage varieties of watermelons, which usually have a thicker rind. If you have trouble getting ¾-inch-thick strips, you can cut your rind into cubes or even use tiny cookie cutters to cut it into decorative shapes, as the Victorians did.

Although considered inedible by some, watermelon rind has long been enjoyed as a vegetable in China, where it is stir-fried and pickled. Eastern Europeans have a taste for sour watermelon pickles. They include the fruit's flesh and store the pickles in large barrels. These pickles are full of warm spice and some ginger heat.

Makes 6 pints

2 teaspoons slaked pickling lime or
   mason's lime
Rind of one large watermelon
½ to 1 cup pickling salt
2 cups distilled vinegar or white wine
   vinegar

1 ounce fresh ginger, peeled and
   thinly sliced
1 large lemon, thinly sliced
2 three-inch cinnamon sticks
8 whole allspice berries
4 cups sugar

Dissolve the lime into 8 cups of water in a large jar or bowl. The mixture will be cloudy. Allow to rest undisturbed overnight. The insoluble calcium salts in the lime will settle to the bottom. The next day, carefully ladle off and reserve the clear top portion of liquid. This is the lime-water solution that is used to crisp the rind.

Peel off and discard the green outer skin from the watermelon rind. Cut enough of the white rind into 1½-by-¾-inch strips to make 3 quarts. Place the rind strips in a nonreactive pot and set aside.

Measure the lime water. For every 1 cup of lime water, stir in 2 tablespoons of pickling salt. When the salt is completely dissolved, pour this brine over the rind strips and refrigerate overnight. Pour off the brine and rinse the strips 3 times in fresh, cold water. Drain and return them to the pot. Cover with fresh cold water and bring to a full boil over high heat. Boil until tender, about 4 minutes. Drain the strips, pat them dry, and set them aside.

To make the syrup, stir together 2 cups of water and the vinegar, ginger, lemon, cinnamon, allspice, and sugar. Bring to a boil, stirring until the sugar dissolves. Add the rind, remove the pot from the heat, and let cool to room temperature. Refrigerate at least 12 hours and up to 24 hours. Bring the syrup and rinds back to a full boil over high heat. Reduce the heat and simmer until the rinds are translucent, 5 to 10 minutes. Pack the hot rinds and syrup into sterilized pint jars, leaving ¼ inch of headspace. Close the jars with hot 2-piece lids and refrigerate to store up to 3 months. Alternately, you may process the jars for 10 minutes in a boiling-water bath to seal, and store in a cool, dry place indefinitely.

Fritz Blank of Philadelphia, Pennsylvania (now in residence on the beaches of Thailand)

Grape-Leaf Pickles

For grape-leaf pickles, layer cucumbers with grapes and grape leaves, cover with brine, and allow to sour. The grapes contribute an earthy taste as well as an enzyme-inhibiting substance that prevents pickles from softening. These pickles are a specialty around Winston-Salem, North Carolina, where they can be found at farmers' markets and church suppers. LaRue Shouse learned this recipe, which has been passed down word-of-mouth for generations, from her mother-in-law.

Makes about 2 gallons

1 cup pickling salt
2 gallons water
25 grape leaves

50 to 60 green grapes
1½ gallons small pickling
   cucumbers

Dissolve the salt in the water in a large bowl. Lightly crush the grapes to split the skins enough to let the brine seep in. Line the bottom of a 2- to 3-gallon pickling crock with a third of the grape leaves. Add half of the grapes and half of the cucumbers. Cover with another third of the grape leaves. Add the rest of the grapes and cucumbers to the crock. Cover with the rest of the grape leaves. Pour in the salt brine. Cover the grape leaves with a plate or large plastic lid that is less than the diameter of the crock. Press down the plate to submerge everything under the brine. Weight the plate with a sterilized river rock. Cover the crock with a lid or cloth tied on tightly and let sit undisturbed in a cool place.

After 2 to 3 days, scrape off the scum that forms on top of the pickles and taste the brine. If it's not salty enough, add a little more pickling salt. The scum is not harmful but should be removed every few days. It takes 8 to 10 days for the pickles to sour. Taste them, and when they are soured to your liking, pack them in jars and store them in the refrigerator. As long as the pickles are kept completely submerged in their brine and refrigerated, they will last for many months. For longer storage, pack the pickles into 8-quart jars, being sure to include a few grapes and grape leaves in each jar. Process in a hot-water bath for 15 minutes.

LaRue Shouse of Winston-Salem, North Carolina

LEATHER BRITCHES, by Bill Best of Berea, Kentucky

Long before canning and refrigeration became commonplace, beans were a vital part of the diet of people living in the Americas. They were eaten fresh and preserved for later as dried beans. The drying did not just involve the seeds themselves; often the entire bean, including hull, was dried.

Dried beans have had several names throughout the centuries, with the most common in the United States being shuck beans, shucky beans, leather britches, and, at one time in the Cumberland Plateau area of Kentucky and Tennessee, fodder beans. In the Haywood County area of North Carolina, where I grew up, they are still called leather britches.

Because dried beans provided what many families considered to be superior flavor, bean-drying traditions have continued. Some families reserve their pots of leather britches for special occasions, such as family reunions and holidays, such as Christmas and New Year's Day.

When preparing dried beans, great care must be taken with the choice of beans. Modern commercial beans, with their tough hulls, are typically not suitable. This also applies to commercial half-runner beans. Modern plant breeding has toughened them up too much as well. If you start with tough beans, no amount of cooking time will make them tender.

This essentially leaves heirloom cornfield beans, which include greasy beans, cutshorts, and most any other heirloom running bean. Colors range from white to black with many in between.

Most people today prefer full beans, by which they mean that the beans within the hull are fully mature but the hull hasn't started losing its green color. Timing is important. The beans need to be strung and broken while the hulls still snap readily. If the hulls are too mature, seeds tend to pop out of the snapped hulls.

Piccalilli

Piccalilli is a spiced mixed vegetable relish. It's also popular in England, from whence it came via India. Piccalilli and its sister chowchow are similar in ingredients and in application, though piccalilli almost always contains green tomatoes and chowchow often doesn't.

The spicy, sweet, and sour flavor of piccalilli is a taste of the days when the whole family gathered around an old plank table filled with simple, honest homegrown food—the perfect palate for condiments.

Makes about 4 pints

3 pounds medium green tomatoes, cut into ¼-inch dice
1 small onion, cut into ¼-inch dice
3 green bell peppers, cut into ¼-inch dice
3 red bell peppers, cut into ¼-inch dice
1½ yellow bell peppers, cut into ¼-inch dice
3 cups apple cider vinegar, divided

1¾ cups sugar
2 tablespoons salt
1 teaspoon ground allspice
2 cinnamon sticks
1 tablespoon celery seed
¼ cup mustard seed
1 spray fresh bay leaves (optional)

Place the tomatoes, onion, and bell peppers in a 4-quart nonreactive Dutch oven or kettle. Stir in 2 cups of the vinegar and bring to a boil. Boil for 30 minutes, uncovered, stirring frequently. Drain and discard the liquid. Return the vegetables to the kettle. Add the remaining 1 cup of vinegar, the sugar, salt, allspice, cinnamon, celery seed, mustard seed, and bay leaves, if using. Bring to a boil and cook for 3 minutes. Discard the cinnamon sticks and bay leaves. Ladle into hot, sterilized pint jars. Refrigerate for up to 6 months or process the jars in a hot-water bath for 5 minutes to seal and store indefinitely.

Ben Barker of Durham, North Carolina

Pickled Eggs

Often tinted fluorescent pink and sold in gallon jars at convenience store checkout counters, pickled eggs are an ideal way to make use of Easter Monday leftovers. Traditionally paired with nothing more than ice-cold beer, homemade versions are worthy of a white tablecloth.

You may add red pickled beet juice to your pickling liquid for magenta eggs or turmeric for golden ones. Add slices to salads. Halve them and top with homemade mayonnaise and trout caviar. Use them to make avant-garde deviled eggs. Or just scarf them out of hand.

Makes 1 dozen

12 hard-cooked medium eggs, peeled
3 cups apple cider vinegar or enough to
    cover the eggs
1 tablespoon salt
3 small dried hot peppers
10 whole allspice berries

6 whole cloves
2 blades mace
12 coriander seeds
2 bay leaves
1 tablespoon sugar

Pack the eggs in a sterilized quart jar. In a medium saucepan, stir together the vinegar, salt, hot peppers, allspice, cloves, mace, coriander, bay leaves, and sugar. Bring to a boil over high heat. Reduce the heat to medium and simmer for 5 minutes. Pour the unstrained hot brine over the eggs, submerging them completely, and tightly close the jar. Refrigerate the eggs for at least a week before serving.

VARIATIONS

Pink eggs: Add 1 cup of pickled beet juice to the vinegar brine. For the brightest color, substitute distilled white vinegar for the apple cider vinegar.

Golden eggs: Add ½ teaspoon ground turmeric to the brine.

Hot and spicy eggs: Omit the allspice, cloves, and mace. Add 4 to 6 fresh jalapeño chiles slit lengthwise and 2 garlic cloves, chopped.

Craig Claiborne of Indianola, Mississippi

Sauerkraut

Translated from German, *sauerkraut* literally means "sour or fermented cabbage." A traditional and important food in the cold countries of Europe and Asia, sauerkraut was a source of vitamins through the winter and an aid to digestive health. Sauerkraut as we know it was likely brought to this country by Germans.

Sauerkraut was once such a common food in the South that, although some families made a fifty-gallon barrel of it from the fall cabbage harvest, it was gone before summer. They chopped the cabbage in the barrel with a sharp hoe on which the blade had been straightened. They sipped kraut juice for its medicinal properties and as a bracing treat. These traditions have all but been left by the wayside. Traditional sauerkraut is long overdue a resurrection.

Makes 4 quarts

5 pounds fresh green cabbage (about 2 heads), shredded or chopped

3 tablespoons sea salt, divided
Dried juniper berries

Put about one-third of the cabbage in the bottom of a 1- or 2-gallon pickling crock. Sprinkle with 1 tablespoon of the salt. Add another third of the cabbage, topped with 1 tablespoon of the salt. Add the rest of the cabbage and sprinkle with the remaining 1 tablespoon of salt.

Fit a heavy 1-gallon plastic freezer bag inside another. Fill the inner bag with water and tightly close both bags to prevent leaks. Place on top of the cabbage, making sure the bags fit tightly around the inner edge of the crock. (This acts as an airtight weight on top of the cabbage, which will discourage the growth of yeast and scum.) Store the crock in a cool place (around 60° to 65°F). Liquid will seep from the cabbage as it ferments, so place the crock on a tray or inside another container to contain any overflow.

Check the cabbage after 24 hours to make sure that the cabbage is completely submerged in brine. If not, dissolve 1½ tablespoons of sea salt in 1 quart of water and pour in enough to cover the cabbage. Let the cabbage ferment for 4 weeks for mild kraut or 5 weeks for sour kraut. Check the kraut every week and remove any scum that has formed on the surface.

When the kraut is ready, it will be a light golden color and smell tart and refreshing. When soured to your liking, remove any scum from the surface and pack the kraut into sterilized quart jars. Add 2 or 3 juniper berries to each jar. Store the jars of kraut in the refrigerator for many months or process the jars in a hot-water bath for 20 minutes to seal for shelf storage. Be aware, however, that cooking the kraut kills its live bacteria and beneficial enzymes for which it is highly regarded.

John Folse of Donaldsonville, Louisiana

Sauerkraut-Stuffed Smoked Turkey

Sauerkraut has many culinary applications, but here is one in need of a larger audience. It comes from the family of Ray Robinson, longtime pit master at Cozy Corner in Memphis, Tennessee. As a barbecue man, Ray knew ribs. But he was also proficient in poultry.

Here, Ray takes on the turkey and illustrates sauerkraut's transformative powers. "Although the main seasoning in this recipe is sauerkraut," he once said, "the turkey somehow doesn't end up tasting like sauerkraut."

Makes 10 to 12 servings

1 ten- to twelve-pound turkey
Drained sauerkraut, to fill the cavity of
   the turkey

Salt or seasoned salt and ground black
   pepper

Wash the turkey inside and out. Fill the cavity loosely with sauerkraut and sew up the cavity, front and back. Season the outside of the turkey with salt and pepper. Roast the turkey over a pit for 8 hours, turning it every 20 to 30 minutes.

Ray Robinson of Memphis, Tennessee

Yellow Squash Pickles

This recipe is a fine response to a bumper squash crop. The recipe originally came from Ora Lee Butler. It leverages a classic sweet-and-sour flavor profile.

Makes about 4 pints

6 cups ½-inch-thick slices of yellow
   squash
½ teaspoon salt
1¼ cups white vinegar
2 cups sugar
1 bell pepper, chopped (about 1 cup)

2 medium white onions, thinly sliced
   (about 3 cups)
¼ cup chopped pimentos, drained
1 teaspoon celery seed
1 teaspoon turmeric

Toss the squash and salt together in a bowl. Let stand at least 2 hours and up to overnight. Drain, rinse, and drain again. Stir together the vinegar and sugar in a large saucepan. Bring to a boil, stirring to dissolve the sugar. Stir in the drained squash, bell pepper, onions, pimentos, celery seed, and turmeric. Just as soon as it returns to a boil, remove from the heat. Pack into hot, sterilized pint jars and close with sterilized rings and lids. Process the jars in a hot-water bath for 5 minutes to seal. Store indefinitely and eat with everything.

Ora Lee Butler of West Monroe, Louisiana, by way of Thomas Head of Washington, D.C.

Dilly Beans

No one can resist a beautiful, fresh-picked batch of green beans, and this is one of their finest applications. Farmers' markets continue to offer both new and rediscovered varieties, so feel free to experiment.

Makes 8 pints

4 pounds green snap beans, stem ends
    trimmed
2 teaspoons crushed red pepper flakes,
    divided
4 teaspoons whole mustard seeds,
    divided

4 teaspoons dill seed, divided
8 garlic cloves, divided
5 cups vinegar
5 cups water
½ cup pickling salt

Working quickly, pack the beans upright into hot sterilized pint jars. Add ¼ teaspoon of the pepper flakes, ½ teaspoon of the mustard seeds, ½ teaspoon of the dill seed, and 1 garlic clove to each jar.

Bring the vinegar, water, and pickling salt to a boil in a saucepan, stirring to dissolve the salt. Pour the boiling liquid over the beans, filling to within ½ inch of the top of the jars. Put the caps and rings on the jars and close tightly. Process the jars in a hot-water bath for 5 minutes.

Rick McDaniel of Asheville, North Carolina

Spicy Okra Refrigerator Pickles

This pickle does double duty, introducing the canning-shy and okra-phobic alike to the glories of pickling and okra. Despite its pervasiveness, pickled okra is not an old Southern recipe. Although many nineteenth-century Southern cookbooks contained a plethora of recipes for various relishes, chutneys, and pickles, pickled okra recipes did not show up with frequency until the middle part of the twentieth century.

Makes 6 pints

3 pounds small (2- to 3-inch) okra pods, stem ends trimmed
3 cups apple cider vinegar or white wine vinegar
6 cups water
½ cup kosher salt

12 garlic cloves, minced
3 small Thai chiles, halved lengthwise
1 teaspoon coriander seed
1 teaspoon celery seed
1 tablespoon yellow mustard seed
2 teaspoons black peppercorns

Place the okra in a large jar, glass bowl, or pickling crock. Set aside. Bring the vinegar, water, and salt to a boil in a large saucepan over high heat, stirring to dissolve the salt. Remove from the heat and stir in the garlic, chiles, coriander seed, celery seed, mustard seed, and peppercorns. Pour the hot vinegar solution over the okra. Place a bowl or plate over the okra to keep it submerged in the liquid. Cool to room temperature, cover, and refrigerate. The longer the okra sits, the better the flavor. The pickles should be ready to eat in 3 to 4 days but are best after at least a week.

Lynne Sawicki of Decatur, Georgia

Pickled Okra

"As a child growing up in Tennessee, we had huge amounts of okra to consume each summer," says Eliza Brown. "Okra seemed to be able to survive any blight or pest that took everything else in the garden. The slimy boiled stuff was very unpopular with me and my siblings. We relished the times my father would slice okra, coat it in cornmeal, and fry it slowly in the iron skillet. The next best was our mother's pickled okra, which we all developed a real affection for as we got older."

Makes 4 pints

2 pounds medium (3- to 4-inch) okra
   pods, stem ends trimmed
4 sprigs fresh dill, divided
4 garlic cloves, divided
1 hot red pepper, quartered lengthwise,
   divided

3 cups water
1 cup white vinegar
¼ cup pickling salt
Tiny pinch of powdered alum

Soak the okra in a large bowl of ice water for 24 hours, then drain well. Pack the okra into sterilized pint jars. Add 1 sprig dill, one garlic clove, and one pepper strip to each jar. Bring the water, vinegar, pickling salt, and alum to a boil in a saucepan over high heat, stirring to dissolve the salt. Boil for 15 minutes. Pour this hot brine into the jars, leaving ½ inch of headspace. Let sit until the brine stops bubbling, about one hour, then top off the jars with more brine. Close the jars with sterilized lids and rings and process in a hot-water bath for 5 minutes to seal.

Eliza Brown of San Francisco, California

Pepper Jelly Vinaigrette

Southerners know that pepper jelly is the basis for any number of last-minute hors d'oeuvres. Start with store-bought crackers. Trowel on grocery-store cream cheese. Or maybe ricotta. Or goat cheese. Then top with a dollop of pepper jelly.

So satisfied are we with the use of pepper jelly as a gilding for cheese that we rarely ask it to do anything more. But its culinary applications are numerous, as Chuck Subra Jr. proves. Here, he uses pepper jelly to add sweet heat to a simple vinaigrette. We love it on a spinach salad.

Makes about 1½ cups

¼ cup pepper jelly
1 tablespoon minced garlic
1 tablespoon minced shallot
¼ cup champagne vinegar

¼ cup extra-virgin olive oil
½ cup vegetable oil
Salt and ground black pepper

Whisk together the pepper jelly, garlic, shallot, and vinegar in a small bowl. While whisking vigorously, slowly add the olive oil and vegetable oil. Season with salt and pepper.

Chuck Subra Jr. of New Orleans, Louisiana

Peach Leather

This great-great-great-granddaddy of the modern fruit roll-up represents an early preservation method. After Spanish explorers introduced peaches into the South in the sixteenth century, residents of the American South learned to puree and cook peaches and then spread the mixture out thinly to dry in the sun for days. While it dried they kept vigil, protecting the spread from predators: birds, bees, rain, and eager children.

This recipe comes from the Dowdney family of Charleston, where peach leather has been produced since the early eighteenth century.

Makes about 24 rolls

Nonstick cooking spray
2 pounds peaches, peeled, pitted, and
    pureed

3 cups sugar, plus more for dusting
2 tablespoons lemon juice

Preheat the oven to the lowest setting (150°F). Lightly coat an 11-by-17-inch rimmed baking sheet with nonstick spray and set aside.

Stir together the peach puree, sugar, and lemon juice in a large saucepan. Bring to a boil, stirring often, over medium heat. Pour into the prepared pan. Tilt the pan to spread the mixture into a thin, even layer that is about ⅛-inch thick. Place in the oven to dry until it is no longer wet to the touch but not crisp. The mixture should feel like pliable leather. This might take as long as 24 hours. Peel the leather off the pan. Use a pizza cutter to cut it into 2½-by-3-inch rectangles. While the leather is still warm, roll each piece into a cylinder, starting with the short side. Dust the rolls with sugar. Store in a candy jar or in plastic wrap.

Stephen Palmer Dowdney of Charleston, South Carolina

Strawberry Jam

"When May approaches, my canning buddies start asking when we're going to make the strawberry jam," says Debbie Moose. "We never use the first or the last berries of the season, but try to hit the peak, when the strawberries are at their best. And I always go looking for 'the fat man' at the Raleigh farmers' market—his berries are the finest and usually come with an entertaining story or two. Use a potato masher to crush the strawberries, and be sure to get the no-sugar-needed version of the pectin."

Makes about 6 half-pints

5 cups crushed strawberries (about 2 quarts)
1 cup water

1 (1.75-ounce) package no-sugar-needed powdered pectin
1½ cups sugar

Stir together the crushed berries and water in a large saucepan. Stir in the pectin. Bring to a boil over high heat, stirring constantly. Stir in the sugar and return to a boil. Boil, stirring constantly, until the mixture falls from a cold spoon in sheets (about 220°F on a candy thermometer), about 1 minute. Remove from the heat. Ladle into hot, sterilized half-pint or pint jars. Process the jars in a hot-water bath for 5 minutes to seal. Let the jam sit for at least 2 weeks to fully jell.

Debbie Moose of Raleigh, North Carolina

12 CANE
SWEET STUFF FROM THE BANANA PUDDING REPUBLIC

I opened the safe, took a biscuit off a plate, and punched a hole in it with my finger. Then, with a jar of cane syrup, I poured the hole full, waited for it to soak in good, and then poured again.
—Harry Crews, *A Childhood: The Biography of a Place*

LEARNING to make good caramel cake icing is a life's work. Attaining the perfect consistency—neither grainy nor runny—is no easy task. Ann Cashion, a Mississippi native, knows the import of icing. She wraps her caramel cakes in warm, sugary shawls. Cashion's recipe follows. Recipes for plenty of pies and cakes follow too: familiar dishes that are pan-Southern in their appeal and desserts that are highly regarded beyond our cultural and geographical borders. Pound cake gets its due. So does coconut.

But we celebrate sweets that are far more localized too. Like bread pudding from the Gulf South. And Sazerac tassies inspired by New Orleans's beloved cocktail. And apple stack cake from Appalachia. And pecan pralines from the onetime Republic of Texas.

Desserts conjure memories of the groaning boards in church and synagogue basements stacked with the bounty of skilled bakers and those other, more lopsided efforts we all learned to politely and subtly avoid. But in our mind's eye, we picture an idealized spread of coconut and burned-sugar cakes perched on cut-glass pedestals beneath cloche tops. Of red-velvet jewel-tone cakes. And jiggly gelatin salads bracketed by crockery bowls brimming with ambrosia. Of a bounty so tempting that there could never be enough forks to go around.

Sweet goods serve as a pleasant close to time at the table. They symbolize plenty. And loving indulgence. But they also remind us of aspects of the history of our region about which we are ashamed. These sugary treats are subtle markers of a day, thankfully past, when men and women of African descent planted and worked cane fields, first for no money, later for very little.

Sugar, these days, is also fraught with concerns about health and well-being. For the past several decades, sugar consumption has been on the wane. As a result, some of our best-loved sweets have been in retreat. Take chess pie, well-known to most. Search for an old-line bakery in your town that makes it regularly and makes it well, and, chances are, you'll be on an endless quest. If you do find one, hold on tight. Better yet, start making these things yourself and teach your children to make them and appreciate them. Passing on that legacy is the sweet stuff.

Revelatory Caramel Cake

Ann Cashion's parents were transplants from Texas to the Mississippi Delta, where she grew up; they had no caramel cake tradition themselves. She borrowed that from the Robert N. Stockett family of Jackson—or, more accurately, the family's cook, Demetrie McLorn.

"Her icing had the consistency of caramel fudge, and when the Stocketts would send me a caramel cake on my birthday every year during college, the icing doubled as the packing material," Cashion remembers. "Demetrie would just pour vast amounts of icing over the top of the cake while it was already in the foil-lined box and let it run into the corners to make a solid slab of caramel, which held the cake in place during shipping."

Makes 1 eight-inch layer cake

WHITE CAKE LAYERS

4 large egg whites, at room temperature
1 cup whole milk, divided
2¼ teaspoons vanilla extract
3 cups sifted cake flour
1½ cups sugar

4 teaspoons baking powder
¾ teaspoon salt
¼ pound plus 4 tablespoons (1½ sticks)
    unsalted butter, cut into 1-tablespoon
    pieces, at room temperature

CARAMEL ICING

3 cups sugar, divided
3 tablespoons light corn syrup
1½ cups whole milk

4 tablespoons (½ stick) unsalted
    butter
1 teaspoon vanilla extract

To make the cake layers: Preheat the oven to 350°F. Grease 3 eight-inch cake pans. Line the bottoms with rounds of parchment and grease the parchment. Lightly coat the inside of the pans with flour, tapping out the excess. Set the pans aside.

Stir together the egg whites, ¼ cup of the milk, and the vanilla in a small bowl; set aside. In a large bowl, whisk together the flour, sugar, baking powder, and salt. Scatter the pieces of butter over the top and pour in the remaining ¾ cup of milk. Use an electric mixer set to low speed to mix the batter until the dry ingredients are moistened. Increase the mixer to medium speed and beat the batter for 90 seconds. Scrape down the sides of the bowl with a rubber spatula. With the mixer set to medium speed, add the egg mixture in 3 additions, beating the batter for 20 seconds after each addition.

Divide the batter evenly among the 3 prepared pans and smooth the tops with the spatula. Bake until a tester inserted into the center of the cakes comes out clean and the cakes are just beginning to pull away from the sides of the pan, about 20 minutes. The layers will be light golden on top, not browned. Cool the layers in the pans on a wire rack for 10 minutes. Turn out the layers onto the rack to cool to room temperature before making the icing.

To make the caramel icing: In a small saucepan, stir together 2½ cups of the sugar, the corn syrup, and the milk; cook over medium heat, stirring until the sugar dissolves. Keep warm over low heat. In a deep, heavy saucepan, sprinkle the remaining ½ cup of sugar evenly over the bottom. Cook over medium heat without stirring until the sugar dissolves, caramelizes, and turns the color of amber. Carefully pour the warm milk mixture into the caramel; the mixture will bubble vigorously and hiss, and the caramel will harden. Cook over medium-high heat, stirring constantly with a wooden spoon, until the caramel loosens from the bottom of the pan and dissolves into the liquid. Cook without stirring until the mixture reaches soft-ball stage (235°F) on a candy thermometer. Remove from the heat and stir in the butter and vanilla. Set aside to cool for 15 minutes. Beat vigorously with a wooden spoon or an electric mixer set to medium speed until the icing is no longer shiny and is thick and creamy enough to spread, about 15 minutes.

To assemble the cake: Place a cake layer on a serving plate. Pour enough icing over the layer to cover the top. Add the next cake layer and cover the top with icing. Add the final cake layer and slowly pour the rest of the icing over the top, letting it run down the sides. Use an offset spatula to gently spread the icing evenly around the sides of the cake, taking care to not rip the cake. Let the cake rest at room temperature at least 2 hours or until the icing is set before serving.

Note: You can also bake the cake in 2 nine-inch pans. Increase the baking time to about 30 minutes.

Ann Cashion of Washington, D.C.

Applesauce Cake with Black Walnuts

Erin Caricofe makes this cake each year, usually around Christmas. The recipe is from her great-grandmother. "My mom remembers picking the fallen black walnuts off the ground at her grandparents' farm in the Shenandoah Valley of Virginia," Erin says, "and taking them inside, where she and other siblings smashed the hulls with some manner of ten-pound blocks of metal. She doesn't remember getting her hands dirty pulling the nuts from their hulls, however, so that task must have been taken over by an adult cook in the house." Although this cake is also delicious when made with run-of-the-mill walnuts, black walnuts add an exotic, sweet dimension.

Makes 1 ten-inch cake, or 12 to 16 servings

2½ cups all-purpose flour
1½ teaspoons baking soda
1½ teaspoons baking powder
1½ teaspoons salt
¾ teaspoon cinnamon
½ teaspoon ground cloves

½ teaspoon ground allspice
¼ pound (1 stick) butter, melted
2 cups sugar
1 large egg
1½ cups applesauce
1 cup chopped black walnuts

Preheat the oven to 350°F. Grease and flour a 10-inch tube pan.

Sift together the flour, baking soda, baking powder, salt, cinnamon, cloves, and all-spice into a medium bowl. In a large bowl, beat the butter and sugar until light and fluffy. Beat in the egg. Beat in the applesauce. Add the flour mixture to the applesauce mixture in 3 equal additions, adding ¼ cup of water after the first and second addition of the flour mixture, beating only until the batter is smooth after each addition. Fold in the walnuts with a rubber spatula. Scrape the batter into the prepared pan and bake until a tester inserted into the center comes out clean, about 1 hour and 15 minutes. Cool for 10 minutes in the pan, then invert onto a wire rack to cool to room temperature.

Erin Caricofe of Columbus, Ohio

Apple Stack Cake

Dried-apple stack cake is a humble treat. Scott County, Virginia, native Jill Sauceman learned the following recipe from her grandmother, Nevada Parker Derting, who was, as you might expect, a humble but talented baker.

"The recipe is very basic," says Jill. "It doesn't use spices in the cake or in the dried-apple sauce. Most recipes call for spices, but during the Depression, spices weren't readily available. My grandmother just let the apple and sorghum flavors come through. My family likes it this way."

Makes 1 eight- or nine-inch cake

1 pound dried tart apples
½ cup sugar, plus 1 to 2 tablespoons for
sprinkling
4½ cups all-purpose flour, plus more for
rolling
1 teaspoon baking powder

1 teaspoon baking soda
½ teaspoon salt
1 egg, lightly beaten
½ cup sorghum
½ cup buttermilk
⅓ cup shortening

Place the apples in a medium saucepan and cover with water. Cook over medium-low heat until most of the water is absorbed and the apples break up when stirred. If the apples are not soft enough to break up, add more water and keep cooking. If desired, add a tablespoon or so of sugar to taste. Cool and run the apples through a sieve or food mill to produce smooth, thick sauce. Set aside to cool.

Preheat the oven to 400°F. Lightly grease as many cookie sheets as you have. You might have to cook the cake layers in batches.

Stir together ½ cup of the sugar, the flour, baking powder, baking soda, salt, egg, sorghum, buttermilk, and shortening to make dough the consistency of stiff cookie dough. Divide the dough into 5 to 7 equal pieces. On a very lightly floured surface, use a very lightly floured pin to roll each piece of dough into an 8- or 9-inch round that is between ⅛- and ¼-inch thick. Use a plate as a template so that the layers are the same size and perfectly round. (Sauceman's grandmother used a pie pan with a scalloped edge to cut out rounds with a decorative edge.) Transfer the rounds to the prepared cookie sheets, making sure there is a little space between the rounds. Prick the top of each round with a fork, making a nice design. Sprinkle with sugar. Bake until the dough is golden brown and dry to the touch, 5 to 8 minutes, depending on the thickness. Cool the layers to room temperature on a wire rack.

To stack the cake, place the first layer on a cake plate. Spread a coating of the cooked applesauce over the layer to within a half inch of the edge. Continue stacking, alternating cake and applesauce, ending with the prettiest cake layer on top. Store covered in a cool place for at least 2 days before serving.

Jill Sauceman of Johnson City, Tennessee

Classic Pound Cake

Pound cake is our bedrock cake, although it's a lot more tender than that sounds. In times past, it seemed that every Southern woman had one on hand in case unexpected company dropped by.

Damon Lee Fowler explains that while recipes for pound cake have evolved a bit, there is merit in baking them the old-fashioned way. "This is the original formula—made up with a pound of everything. Some of the old recipes were so specific about equal weights that they went so far as to recommend weighing a dozen eggs and using this weight to proportion the butter, sugar, and flour. It isn't as sweet as most modern cakes, but its richness and body are more satisfying."

Makes 1 round tube cake or 2 loaf cakes, 12 to 16 servings

1 pound (4 sticks) unsalted butter, at
   room temperature
1 pound (2 cups) sugar
1 teaspoon salt
8 large eggs

1 pound (about 3½ cups) Southern
   soft-wheat flour or unbleached
   all-purpose flour
½ cup heavy cream
1 tablespoon vanilla extract

Preheat the oven to 325°F. Grease and flour a pan and set it aside.

Cream the butter until it is light and fluffy in a medium bowl. Beat in the sugar and salt until very light and fluffy. Beat in the eggs, one at a time, alternating with the flour, a little at a time, until both are incorporated. Be careful not to overbeat the batter. Stir in the heavy cream and vanilla. Scrape the batter into the prepared pan. Bake until a toothpick inserted into the center comes out clean, 1½ to 2 hours. Don't open the oven door for the first 1 hour and 15 minutes. Cool the cake for 15 minutes in the pan, then turn it out onto a cake plate or wire rack to cool completely.

Damon Lee Fowler of Savannah, Georgia

Coconut Layer Cake

When Angie Mosier was growing up in Atlanta, Georgia, a trip downtown meant a visit to the Rich's bakeshop and a purchase of its famous coconut cake. Angie loved the pomp of the bakeshop. She loved how a counterwoman pulled the cake from the glass case, placed it in a box with the Rich's logo, and tied it with twine to make it easy to carry. "When I opened my own small bakery just south of Atlanta, I tried my best to re-create that cake," says Angie. "From the flavor all the way down to the box and the twine. One day an elderly man came into my bakery and told me, 'I ran the Rich's bakeshop for thirty years.' Carl Dendy and I became friends. He even shared the formula for his huge batch of cake batter and icing, which I have adapted here."

Makes 1 eight- or nine-inch layer cake, 12 servings

BASIC YELLOW CAKE

2 cups all-purpose flour
1 tablespoon baking powder
1 teaspoon salt
¼ pound (1 stick) unsalted butter, at
　　room temperature

1¼ cups granulated sugar
2 large eggs
¾ cup whole milk
1 teaspoon pure vanilla extract

EASY BUTTERCREAM ICING

½ pound (2 sticks) unsalted butter, at
　　room temperature
1 teaspoon pure vanilla extract

1 pound 10x confectioners' sugar
1 to 3 tablespoons whole milk, half-and-
　　half, or cream

COCONUT FILLING

2 (14-ounce) bags sweetened, shredded
　　coconut, divided

1 cup heavy cream
1 cup easy buttercream icing

To make the cake layers: Preheat the oven to 350°F. Grease and flour 2 eight- or nine-inch cake pans; set aside. Whisk together the flour, baking powder, and salt in a bowl; set aside. Cream the butter and sugar in a large bowl with an electric mixer until light and fluffy, about 3 minutes. Beat in the eggs, 1 at a time, beating well after each addition. Add the flour mixture in 3 equal additions, alternating with half of the milk, beating only until the batter is smooth after each addition. Scrape down the sides of the bowl with a rubber spatula as you go. Beat in the vanilla. Scrape the batter into the prepared cake pans.

Bake until the center of the cakes springs back when pressed lightly with your finger, about 25 minutes. Cool in the pans for 10 minutes, then turn out onto wire racks to cool completely. Meanwhile, make the icing and then the filling.

To make the icing: Beat the butter and vanilla in a bowl with an electric mixer until smooth. Gradually beat in the sugar, letting each addition blend into the butter before adding more. Scrape down the sides of the bowl with a rubber spatula as you go. The mixture should look a little dry at this point. Add the milk 1 tablespoon at a time, beating on high speed until you get the right texture. The icing should be smooth but not so creamy that it won't hold onto the cake.

To make the filling: Stir 1 bag of the coconut and the cream together in a bowl. Let sit and soak for 10 minutes. Stir in 1 cup of the easy buttercream icing.

To assemble the cake: Place 1 of the cooled cake layers on a serving plate or cake stand. Tuck pieces of wax paper or plastic wrap under the edges to catch the excess coconut. Spread the filling over the top of the cake. Stack the second cake layer on top. Spread the remaining icing over the top and sides of the cake. Cover the icing with the coconut in the remaining bag, gently pressing to adhere. When all of the coconut is on the cake, gently ease the wax paper strips out from under the cake.

Angie Mosier of Atlanta, Georgia

Red Velvet Cake

According to Nancie McDermott, the flavor of a red velvet cake is as important as the color. Everyone knows about the red food coloring, Nancie says, but that distinctive flavor owes to "the unusual combination of vinegar, buttermilk, and cocoa."

Some folks argue that the original recipe was developed at the Waldorf Astoria in New York. And they may be right. But by way of our penchant for velvet—think Scarlett's green dress, think black-velvet Elvis—and our heavy hand with food coloring, we Southerners have made this recipe our own.

Makes 1 nine-inch layer cake

CAKE

2½ cups all-purpose flour
½ teaspoon salt
1 teaspoon vanilla extract
1 cup buttermilk
2 tablespoons cocoa
1 (1-ounce) bottle (2 tablespoons) red food coloring

½ pound (2 sticks) butter, at room temperature
2 cups granulated sugar
2 large eggs
1½ teaspoons baking soda
1 tablespoon apple cider vinegar or white vinegar

CREAM-CHEESE FROSTING

8 ounces cream cheese, at room temperature
4 tablespoons (½ stick) butter, at room temperature

1 pound (3⅔ cups) confectioners' sugar, sifted
1 teaspoon vanilla extract

To make the cake layers: Preheat the oven to 350°F. Grease 2 nine-inch round cake pans generously and line them with parchment circles. Grease the parchment and flour the pans, tapping out the excess.

Stir together the flour and salt in a medium bowl with a fork; set aside. In a separate small bowl, stir the vanilla into the buttermilk. In another small bowl, combine the cocoa and the red food coloring and mash them together with a fork to make a thick, smooth paste.

Beat the butter in a large bowl with a mixer at low speed until creamy and soft, about 1 minute. Add the sugar and beat well for 3 to 4 minutes, stopping to scrape down the bowl now and then. Add the eggs, 1 at a time, beating after each one, until the mixture is creamy, fluffy, and smooth. Scrape the cocoa paste into the batter and beat to mix it in evenly.

Add about a third of the flour mixture and then about half of the buttermilk, beating the batter with a mixer at low speed and mixing only enough to make the flour or liquid disappear into the batter. Mix in another third of the flour, the rest of the buttermilk, and then the last of the flour in the same way.

In a separate small bowl, combine the baking soda and vinegar and stir well. Use a rubber spatula or wooden spoon to quickly mix this last mixture into the red batter, folding it in gently by hand.

Scrape the batter into the prepared pans. Bake until the layers spring back when touched lightly in the center and are just beginning to pull away from the sides of the pan, about 20 to 25 minutes.

Cool the cakes in the pans on wire racks or folded kitchen towels for 15 minutes. Then turn them out onto the racks, remove the parchment circles, and turn the top sides up to cool completely.

To make the frosting: Beat the cream cheese and butter in a bowl with a mixer on medium speed. Add the confectioners' sugar and vanilla and beat at high speed until the frosting is fluffy and smooth, stopping once or twice to scrape down the bowl and mix everything well. Use at once, or cover and refrigerate for up to 3 days.

To assemble the cake: Place 1 layer, top side down, on a cake stand or a serving plate. Spread frosting on the layer. Place the second layer, top side up, on top. Frost the sides and then the top of the cake. Refrigerate for 30 minutes or more to help the frosting set.

Nancie McDermott of Chapel Hill, North Carolina

Brown Sugar Shortcakes with Strawberries and Cream

In warmer climes, strawberries overwinter and bear their fruit early, in April and May, before the bugs mature, the ones that would devour them. As far south as Louisiana, they peak in February and March. Strawberries seem to hang in wait for cane lovers to pick them and lay them atop a sweet biscuit with a whipped-cream pillow. Virginia Willis embellished this strawberry shortcake, flavoring it with orange zest and sprinkling the cakes with raw sugar.

Makes 8 servings

SHORTCAKES

3½ cups all-purpose flour, plus more for rolling

⅓ cup granulated sugar

4 teaspoons baking powder

1 teaspoon fine sea salt

¼ pound plus 4 tablespoons (1½ sticks) unsalted butter, cut into small pieces and chilled

Grated zest of 1 orange or 2 tablespoons orange liqueur, such as Grand Marnier

1 cup heavy cream, plus more for brushing

½ cup whole milk

Turbinado, demerara, or raw brown sugar, for sprinkling

BERRIES AND CREAM

2 pints strawberries, hulled and quartered lengthwise

Juice of 1 orange

1 tablespoon granulated sugar

Whipped cream

To make the shortcakes: Preheat the oven to 400°F. Line a baking sheet with a silicone baking mat or parchment paper.

Combine the flour, sugar, baking powder, and salt in the bowl of a heavy-duty mixer fitted with the paddle attachment. Mix on low speed. Add the butter and zest or liqueur; mix on low until the mixture resembles coarse meal, about 2 minutes. Add the cream and milk and increase the speed to medium; mix until the dough comes together. Remove the dough to a lightly floured surface, lightly knead a few times, and shape into a rectangle about ¾-inch thick. Cut out 8 shortcakes with a 3-inch round cutter. Place on the prepared baking sheet. Brush the tops lightly with cream and sprinkle with turbinado sugar. Bake until the cakes are golden brown, about 20 minutes. Transfer to a wire rack to cool.

To make the berries: Stir together the berries, orange juice, and sugar in a bowl. Set aside.

To serve: Halve the shortcakes horizontally with a serrated knife. Place the bottom halves on individual serving plates, top each with a dollop of whipped cream, then some berries, and another dollop of whipped cream. Cover with the tops of the shortcakes and serve.

Virginia Willis of Atlanta, Georgia

Bread Pudding with Bourbon Crème Anglaise

Respect for bread—this recipe begins there. Just like the French, who brought us their baguette, New Orleanians have a deep relationship with the crusty loaf. No day-old remnant is safe in a city that relishes baptizing pretty much anything in cream, eggs, and bourbon.

This bread pudding, from Diana Cottier, a New Orleans cook and caterer, is classic. No white chocolate. No lemon curd. No froufrou. This recipe allows the bread and the bourbon to speak.

Makes 12 to 16 servings

1 loaf day-old New Orleans French bread
   (about 1½ standard French baguettes)
½ cup raisins
½ cup chopped pecans
6 large eggs
1¾ cups sugar, divided

4 tablespoons vanilla extract
1 tablespoon cinnamon
½ teaspoon nutmeg
1 tablespoon vegetable oil
4 cups whole milk
Bourbon crème anglaise (recipe follows)

Cut the bread on a slight diagonal into ¼-inch-thick slices to yield 8 to 9 cups of bread. Arrange the slices in a 9-by-13-inch baking dish or shallow 4-quart casserole, overlapping the slices and sprinkling raisins and pecans between each layer. Don't worry if the top of the bread is a little higher than the top of the dish.

Whisk together the eggs and 1½ cups of the sugar in a large bowl. Whisk in the vanilla, cinnamon, nutmeg, oil, and milk and mix well. Slowly pour or ladle the egg mixture over the bread, being sure to coat every piece, even the edges. Stop pouring intermittently to gently press down the bread. Cover with aluminum foil and place in the refrigerator to soak overnight.

When ready to bake, preheat the oven to 375°F. Remove the aluminum foil and sprinkle the remaining sugar over the top. Cover again and bake for 40 minutes. Remove the foil and continue baking until the top is browned and the custard is set, another 20 to 30 minutes. Test by inserting a thin knife into the center; it should come out moist but not wet and eggy. Serve warm, topped with cold bourbon crème anglaise.

BOURBON CRÈME ANGLAISE

Makes about 3 cups

2 cups heavy cream
6 tablespoons sugar, divided
8 egg yolks

¼ cup bourbon (or to taste) or ½
    teaspoon vanilla extract

Prepare an ice bath by placing 3 cups of ice and about ½ cup of water in a large mixing bowl. Place a smaller bowl in the ice water. The hot crème anglaise will cool in this chilled smaller bowl, so make sure that it sits securely down in the ice water.

Stir together the cream and 2 tablespoons of the sugar in a medium saucepan. Bring to just below a simmer on medium-low heat, stirring to dissolve the sugar. Keep warm on low heat.

Meanwhile, in a large mixing bowl, beat the egg yolks and the remaining 4 tablespoons of sugar until the mixture is thick and pale yellow. (You may do this by hand with a balloon whisk or use an electric mixer.) Ladle half of the warm cream mixture into the eggs to temper, whisking constantly until smooth.

Slowly whisk the egg mixture into the warm cream mixture. Cook over medium-low heat, stirring constantly with a wooden spoon, until the sauce is thick enough to coat the back of the spoon. Carefully run your finger through the sauce that coats the spoon. If the sauce doesn't run into the bare space cleared by your finger, the sauce is ready. Strain through a fine sieve into the chilled bowl sitting in the ice bath and stir until the sauce cools to room temperature. Stir in the bourbon or vanilla. Transfer the sauce into a glass or metal bowl and chill. Serve cold.

Diana Cottier of Covington, Louisiana

Persimmon Pudding

Wild, native persimmons are plum-sized fruits that ripen around December. Unripe persimmons are too tart to eat. But if you're patient enough to wait until a russet color blushes through the fruit, and you're lucky enough to catch the windfall, the reward is sweet. The real trick is getting to them before the raccoons and possums do, which you must do for this recipe to reach its potential. If wild persimmons aren't an option, buy the Hachiya variety.

Makes 10 servings

1¼ cups all-purpose flour
¾ teaspoon baking soda
¾ teaspoon baking powder
½ teaspoon ginger
½ teaspoon cinnamon
⅛ teaspoon nutmeg
⅛ teaspoon ground cloves
½ teaspoon kosher salt

7 tablespoons butter, at room
    temperature
¾ cup plus 1½ tablespoons sugar
3 large eggs
1½ cups half-and-half
1½ cups strained persimmon puree
    (see note)
2 tablespoons apricot jam

Preheat the oven to 350°F. Butter a 10-inch round cake pan or a 9-by-9-inch baking pan. Line the bottom of the pan with parchment paper and butter the paper.

Sift together the flour, baking soda, baking powder, ginger, cinnamon, nutmeg, cloves, and salt into a bowl. Cream the butter and sugar in the bowl of a stand mixer fitted with the paddle. Add the eggs 1 at a time, scraping the bowl several times. Alternately add the sifted flour mixture and the half-and-half. Add the persimmon puree and the apricot jam. Mix to blend.

Pour the mixture into the prepared pan and place the pan in a water bath. Bake until the pudding is firm and golden brown, about 70 minutes. When tested with a toothpick, the pudding should be moist, but not wet. Remove from the oven and cool for 30 minutes. Turn out onto a parchment paper–lined baking sheet and invert onto a service platter. Serve warm. This can be made 1 day ahead and reheated.

Note: To extract the persimmon pulp, discard the caps and stems from the fruit. Cut the fruit in halves or quarters and run them through a food mill or press them through a mesh sieve with your fingers or a rubber spatula, letting the smooth pulp fall into a bowl. Discard the skins and large seeds.

Karen Barker of Chapel Hill, North Carolina

Fancy-pants Banana Pudding

When, in the wake of Hurricane Katrina, the SFA asked Dana Logsdon to make dessert for a lunch at the annual Southern Foodways Symposium, she was displaced in Baton Rouge. "My eight housemates were complaining that I was getting them fat by baking too much," Logsdon recalls. "But this was the perfect opportunity for me to bake for a crowd. After throwing out several ideas, I tried my hand at banana pudding. I had never made it the conventional way, which is why I dared to make it so luxe."

Makes 12 servings

BANANA CARAMEL

2 cups granulated sugar
1 cup water

2 cups pureed, very ripe bananas (about 6 medium bananas)

PASTRY CREAM

1¾ cups (7 ounces) cornstarch
1¾ cups (14 ounces) sugar
1 teaspoon salt
6 cups whole milk
2 cups heavy whipping cream

8 eggs, lightly beaten
4 tablespoons (½ stick) unsalted butter, cut into pieces and chilled
1 teaspoon vanilla extract

PUDDING

1 tablespoon butter
1 (12-ounce) box gingersnaps (about 80 cookies)
6 firm (almost green) bananas, peeled and sliced

2 cups chilled whipping cream
Fresh mint and gingersnaps, to garnish

For the banana caramel: Cook the sugar and water in a saucepan over medium-high heat until the color of amber. Remove from the heat to stop the cooking. Stir in the banana puree and mix well. Set aside.

For the pastry cream: Stir together the cornstarch, sugar, and salt in a large saucepan; set aside. In another large saucepan, bring the milk and cream to a boil over medium-high heat. Slowly whisk the hot milk mixture into the cornstarch mixture, stirring until dissolved and thickened. Slowly whisk in the eggs. Cook, stirring slowly, over medium heat until the pastry cream is thick enough to coat the back of a spoon. Add the butter, one piece at a time, stirring constantly. Reduce the heat to low and cook for 1 minute, stirring constantly. Remove from the heat and stir in the banana caramel and vanilla. Press plastic wrap directly onto the surface of the pastry cream and cool completely.

To assemble the pudding: Butter a 9-by-13-inch baking dish. Line the bottom and sides with gingersnaps. Pour in half of the cooled pastry cream. Layer the bananas over the cream. Cover with a layer of gingersnaps. Top with the rest of the pastry cream, smoothing the top. Press plastic wrap directly onto the surface and refrigerate until well chilled, at least 4 hours. Just before serving, whip the cream in a chilled bowl and spread over the top of the pudding. Garnish each serving with fresh mint and a gingersnap.

Dana Logsdon of New Orleans, Louisiana

Pecan Sorghum Tarts

People love to fiddle with pecan pie. Chocolate pecan pie. Bourbon pecan pie. Sweet potato pecan pie. But fresh pecans and good sugar don't need to play dress up. One belief is that the Karo corn syrup company invented this dessert, and some of us still call it "Karo pie." What seems more probable is that some smart cook in Texas or Georgia took stock of her larder and heated up some molasses or sorghum, added egg yolks and butter, and tossed in some pecans. With such a concoction staring you down, your only logical next step is a pie crust.

John Fleer's tart is a quadruple threat to your sweet tooth, sweetened as it is with white sugar, brown sugar, honey, *and* sorghum.

Makes 2 ten-inch tarts

SWEET PASTRY DOUGH

1½ cups all-purpose flour, plus more for rolling
1½ cups cake flour
¾ cup sugar
½ teaspoon salt

¾ teaspoon baking powder
¼ pound plus 4 tablespoons (1½ sticks) unsalted butter, cut into cubes and chilled
3 large eggs, lightly beaten

FILLING

¾ pound (3 sticks) unsalted butter, at
    room temperature
2½ cups packed light brown sugar
4 large eggs
2 tablespoons pure vanilla extract
¼ cup honey
1 cup sorghum, divided

1½ teaspoons ground cinnamon
¾ cup plus 2 tablespoons all-purpose
    flour
2 cups (8 ounces) pecans, finely ground
1¼ cups (5 ounces) pecan halves
½ cup bourbon

To make the dough: Whisk together the flour, cake flour, sugar, salt, and baking powder in a large bowl. Use a pastry blender or your fingertips to cut in the butter until the mixture resembles coarse meal with some pea size lumps of butter. Stir in the eggs. Gently knead with floured hands just until dough forms. Turn out onto a lightly floured surface and knead gently 4 or 5 times more. Divide the dough in half. Press each piece over the bottom and up the sides of a 10-inch-diameter tart pan with removable bottom. Cover and freeze for 30 minutes.

Preheat the oven to 350°F. Line the crusts with parchment paper and pie weights. Bake until the dough sets, 15 to 20 minutes. Carefully remove the weights and paper and bake until light golden, about another 10 minutes. Cool completely on wire racks before filling.

To make the filling: Beat the butter and sugar in a bowl until creamy and fluffy. Add the eggs, vanilla, honey, and ½ cup of the sorghum and mix well. Stir in the cinnamon, flour, ground pecans, and pecan halves. Divide the filling between the two cooled tart crusts. Bake until the filling is set and browned, 15 to 20 minutes. Meanwhile, stir together the remaining ½ cup of sorghum and the bourbon in a small bowl. As soon as the tarts come out of the oven, brush the tops with the bourbon mixture. They should sizzle! Cool to room temperature on wire racks before slicing and serving.

John Fleer of Maryville, Tennessee

Scuppernong Sweet-Potato Pie

Richard Bunn is the product of a long line of cooks who were self-taught and who cooked, as circumstances often dictated, from the land. Richard found this recipe buried deep in the recipe files of his mother, Edna Brooks Bunn of Griffin, Georgia.

While the combination of scuppernong hulls and sweet potatoes is unusual, the preparation is worth the effort. For the uninitiated, the scuppernong, a type of muscadine, is a super-sweet grape native to the southeastern United States. It has a greenish or bronze color (sometimes both at once) and is double the size of your average grape.

Makes 1 nine-inch deep-dish pie

4 cups scuppernong grapes
1 cup water
½ teaspoon baking soda
2 large eggs, separated
½ cup sugar
1 cup cooked, mashed, and strained
   sweet-potato puree

4 tablespoons (½ stick) butter, at room
   temperature
¼ cup heavy cream
1 teaspoon vanilla extract
1 nine-inch deep-dish pie shell

Gently squeeze the grapes over a saucepan so that the pulp slips out of the hulls. Set the hulls aside. Cook the pulp over medium heat until it releases the seeds, about 10 minutes. Run the pulp through a food mill or press through a mesh sieve to remove the seeds. Return the strained pulp to the pan and stir in the hulls, water, and baking soda. Bring to a simmer over medium-high heat and cook, stirring occasionally, until the hulls are completely soft and the mixture is thick and jammy, about 20 minutes. Drain and reserve the cooking liquid. Puree the grape mixture by running it through a food mill or in a food processor fitted with a metal blade. The puree should be the texture of thick preserves, similar to the texture of the sweet-potato puree. If the mixture is dry, add a little of the cooking liquid. If the mixture is too soupy, drain in a fine sieve and discard the excess liquid. There should be at least 1 cup of finished scuppernong puree. Set aside.

Preheat the oven to 350°F.

Whip the egg whites to soft peaks in a medium bowl and set it aside. Beat the yolks and sugar until creamy in a large bowl with an electric mixer. Add the sweet-potato puree, butter, cream, and vanilla and beat until smooth. Fold the egg whites into the sweet-potato mixture with a rubber spatula.

Spread 1 cup of the scuppernong puree in the bottom of the pie shell. (Use any remaining puree in another recipe.) Spoon the sweet-potato mixture over the scuppernong puree, gently smoothing the top. Bake until the filling is set and lightly browned in spots on top, 35 to 45 minutes. Cool to room temperature on a wire rack. Serve at room temperature or refrigerate until chilled.

Edna Brooks Bunn of Griffin, Georgia, by way of Richard Bunn of Atlanta, Georgia

Muscadine Meringue Pie

Muscadines and scuppernongs grow wild and have very thick skins. April McGreger developed this recipe one September while up to her ears preserving muscadines and scuppernongs. She took inspiration from her great-aunt Margaret's muscadine-hull pie, adding her own marshmallow meringue. And who doesn't adore a gal whose inspirations lead to marshmallow meringue?

Makes 1 nine-inch pie

PIE

2½ pounds muscadine grapes, at least half of them of the purple variety
½ cup sugar
⅓ cup all-purpose flour or minute tapioca
Zest and juice of 1 lemon

Pinch of salt
¼ pound plus 2 tablespoons (1¼ sticks) unsalted butter, cut into 1-tablespoon pieces and chilled
1 nine-inch pie shell, baked and cooled

SWISS MERINGUE

Scant ½ cup egg whites (about 3 large eggs)
¾ cup plus 2 tablespoons sugar

Pinch of salt
1 vanilla bean

To make the pie: Use your fingers to squeeze the insides of the grapes into a large saucepan. Put the hulls in a bowl. Bring the skinned grapes to a boil over high heat and cook until they soften and give up their seeds, about 10 minutes. Push the cooked grapes through a fine or medium sieve back into the saucepan. Discard the seeds. Stir in the grape hulls, sugar, flour, lemon zest and juice, and salt. Cover the pan and simmer over low heat, stirring often, until the filling thickens and no longer tastes of flour. Be careful not to scorch the mixture; add cold water 1 tablespoon at a time if the mixture seems too thick or wants to stick to the bottom of the pan. Remove from the heat and let cool to 140°F on a candy thermometer or until the mixture is just cool enough that you can stick your finger in without burning it.

Puree the filling in a food processor, blender, or with an immersion blender. With the machine running, add the butter one piece at a time, waiting until each piece mixes in before adding the next. Use the filling at once or transfer to a stainless steel or glass bowl, cover, and refrigerate for up to 5 days. (If refrigerated, gently reheat by placing the bowl of filling over a saucepan of simmering water, stirring until it softens.) Scrape the filling into the pie shell.

To make the meringue: Pour water into a large saucepan to a depth of 2 inches and bring to a simmer over medium-low heat. Place the egg whites, sugar, and salt together in a large metal or glass bowl that fits snugly into the saucepan without the bottom touching the water. Split the vanilla bean in half lengthwise and scrape out the seeds with the point of a paring knife and add them to the egg-white mixture. (Save the vanilla bean pod for another use.) Position the bowl over the simmering water and whip with an electric mixer until the meringue reaches 120°F on a candy thermometer. Remove the bowl from above the hot water and continue whipping until the meringue is glossy and holds stiff peaks.

Spread the meringue over the filling, making sure it lightly touches the inside edge of the crust. Brown the tips of the meringue under a broiler or with a torch.

Variation: Top the pie with whipped cream instead of meringue for muscadine cream pie.

April McGreger of Carrboro, North Carolina

Sweet Tea Lemon Chess Pie

Chess pie is a classic. It includes ingredients that any honest Southern cook ought to have on hand: eggs, butter, sugar, cream, and cornmeal.

Martha Foose knows those basics. She knows them so well that she knows she can toss the basics out the door. Ask Martha how she came to bake a sweet tea chess pie, and she'll answer with an offhand comment that suggests anyone with a pitcher of tea in the refrigerator might have done the same thing.

Makes 1 nine-inch pie

CRUST

3 ounces cream cheese, at room
  temperature

¼ pound (1 stick) unsalted butter, at
  room temperature
1¼ cups unbleached all-purpose flour

FILLING

½ pound (2 sticks) unsalted butter, at
  room temperature
2 cups granulated sugar
Zest of 1 lemon
8 large egg yolks
¾ cup warm, freshly brewed strong
  orange pekoe tea

1 tablespoon vanilla extract
1 teaspoon apple cider vinegar
1 tablespoon fresh lemon juice
2 tablespoons unbleached all-purpose
  flour
2 teaspoons cornmeal

For the crust: Beat the cream cheese and butter in a bowl with an electric mixer until well-combined. Add the flour and mix at low speed until the dough comes together into a ball. Pat the dough evenly and thinly into a 9-inch pie pan, building up a thicker top edge. Place the pie shell in the freezer while preparing the filling.

For the filling: Beat the butter in a bowl with an electric mixer until light and fluffy. Gradually beat in the sugar. Beat in the zest. Add the egg yolks 1 at a time, mixing well after each addition and scraping the bowl often. Slowly add the tea, vanilla, vinegar, and lemon juice. Add the flour and cornmeal. Scrape the bowl and mix well. Don't be alarmed if the mixture looks slightly curdled.

To assemble: Preheat the oven to 350°F. Remove the pie shell from the freezer and pour in the filling. Bake until only a quarter-sized area in the center jiggles slightly when the pie is shaken gently, about 50 minutes. Cool to room temperature on a wire rack and then chill at least 2 hours before serving.

Martha Foose of Pluto Plantation, Mississippi

Boiled Peanut and Sorghum Swirl Ice Cream

"We love finding innovative uses for sorghum, which is employed on many Southern tables as a condiment for morning biscuits, evening cornbread, and most things in between," say Matt Lee and Ted Lee. "It has a sweet, tangy flavor, like dried fruit mixed with caramel." Peanuts are actually legumes. With that in mind, Matt and Ted take inspiration in the red bean ice creams of Asia as well as American nut-and-fudge swirls. "Like those desserts, the key to this recipe's success is the balance of salty and sweet, cream and bean (or nut, as the case may be)."

Makes about 1 quart

2 large egg yolks	2 teaspoons pure vanilla extract
½ cup sugar	½ cup shelled boiled peanuts, chilled
1 cup whole milk	½ cup pure sorghum
2 cups heavy cream	Benne wafers, for serving (optional)

In a medium bowl, beat the egg yolks lightly with a whisk, then add the sugar and beat until the mixture is a milky lemon-yellow color, about 1½ minutes. In a medium saucepan, warm the milk over medium heat, stirring occasionally, until it reaches 150°F on a candy thermometer, 6 to 8 minutes. (You might see steam rising from the pan, but the milk should not start to boil.) Pour the warm milk into the egg mixture in a slow stream, whisking constantly. The resulting custard will be thin but lustrous and smooth. Return the custard to the saucepan or, preferably, the top of a double boiler and cook slowly over very, very low heat, stirring constantly with a wooden spoon until it reaches 170°F on a candy thermometer and is thick enough to coat the back of a spoon, 8 to 10 minutes. Remove the pan from the heat and let the custard cool to room temperature. Add the cream and vanilla, stir to incorporate thoroughly, transfer to a pitcher or other container, and refrigerate until the custard is very cold, at least 4 hours or overnight.

Pour the chilled custard into an ice-cream maker, add the peanuts, and churn according to the manufacturer's instructions, until the ice cream becomes very thick and holds its shape. It should be the consistency of a very thick milk shake; depending on how cold your custard is and the type of ice-cream maker you have, this will take 15 to 30 minutes. Transfer to a container with a tight-fitting lid and cut several channels through the ice cream with a wooden spoon. Pour the sorghum syrup evenly into the channels, then gently fold the ice cream in swirling patterns until the sorghum is evenly distributed. If there is any space between the surface of the ice cream and the container's lid, press plastic wrap onto the surface.

Freeze the ice cream until it has hardened, at least 2 hours. Remove from the freezer 10 minutes before serving. Serve small scoops of the ice cream in bowls and garnish with benne wafers, if using.

Matt Lee and Ted Lee of Charleston, South Carolina

Peach Ice Cream

"My grandmother grew up in Georgia," says Elizabeth Karmel. "Not surprisingly, she loved peaches, and she loved to eat them year-round. Every summer, she would peel and slice pecks of peaches to freeze for the cold winter ahead. When all the freezing and canning was done, she would make homemade peach ice cream teeming with chunks of juicy sweet-tart peaches." She insisted on using a manual ice-cream maker, saying it made better ice cream than the electric. Plus, she had grandchildren to do the cranking.

Makes about 2 quarts

3 large egg yolks
1½ cups whole milk
¾ cup plus 2 tablespoons sugar, divided
Pinch of salt

1 tablespoon real vanilla extract or
    vanilla paste
2 cups whipping cream
2 or 3 large peaches

Beat the egg yolks in a large bowl and set aside.

Heat the milk to scalding (180°F) in a heavy saucepan over medium heat. Remove from the heat; stir in ¾ cup of the sugar and the pinch of salt. Slowly whisk the hot milk into the egg yolks. Pour the egg mixture into the saucepan and cook slowly, stirring constantly, until the custard thickens enough to coat the back of a silver spoon. Do not overcook the custard or it will curdle. Remove the pan from the heat and stir in the vanilla. Pour the custard into a glass bowl, press plastic wrap directly onto the surface, and refrigerate until well chilled (less than 40°F).

When ready to freeze, stir in the cream. Pour the custard into an ice-cream freezer, filling no more than ⅔ full, and freeze following the manufacturer's instructions. As the ice cream begins to freeze, peel and pit 2 or 3 large peaches (or more if you'd like); slice the fruit and mash gently with a fork. Stir in the remaining 2 tablespoons of sugar and set aside to macerate for up to 30 minutes. When the ice cream is almost frozen, add the peaches and their accumulated juices. At the end of the churning, spoon the soft ice cream into an airtight container and cure in the freezer for several hours until firm. Serve plain or with a favorite topping.

Elizabeth Karmel of New York, New York

Sazerac Tassies

Sonya Jones conceived these fantastic little bites as a takeoff on the famed Sazerac cocktail, a New Orleans concoction, originally made with brandy and absinthe. Over the years, anise liqueur became the common substitute for the absinthe. And rye replaced brandy. Sonya's interpretation is a creative mixture of classic chess pie texture, classic cocktail flavor, and an anise-seed garnish.

Makes 24 tassies

TARTLET SHELLS

1 cup all-purpose flour
½ cup confectioners' sugar
½ teaspoon baking powder

¼ pound plus 4 tablespoons (1½ sticks) unsalted butter, cut into cubes and chilled
Nonstick cooking spray

FILLING

1 cup sugar
2 teaspoons all-purpose flour
¼ teaspoon baking powder
2 eggs, beaten

¼ cup anise liqueur, such as Pernod
1 tablespoon rye whiskey
2 teaspoons honey

3 tablespoons anise seeds, divided

To make the tartlet shells: Stir together the flour, confectioners' sugar, and baking powder in a bowl. Cut in the butter until it resembles coarse meal. (Alternately, combine the dry ingredients in the bowl of a food processor, cut the butter into large pieces and drop on top of the flour, then pulse the mixture until it resembles coarse meal, 20 to 30 seconds.) Press the dough into a ball. (If it won't hold its shape, stir in 1 to 2 tablespoons of water.) Flatten the dough into a disk, wrap tightly in plastic wrap, and chill for 1 hour.

Preheat the oven to 375°F. Spray a 24-cup miniature muffin pan with nonstick cooking spray. Divide the chilled dough into 24 equal pieces and press in the bottom and up the sides of the muffin cups.

To make the filling: Stir together the sugar, flour, and baking powder in a bowl. Stir in the eggs, liqueur, whiskey, and honey and mix well.

To assemble the tassies: Sprinkle 2 tablespoons of the anise seeds into the tartlet shells. Spoon 2 to 3 tablespoons of the filling into each shell. Sprinkle the remaining 1 tablespoon of anise seeds over the filling. Bake until the tassies are lightly browned, 12 to 15 minutes. Place the pan on a wire rack and let the tassies cool to room temperature before serving.

Sonya Jones of Atlanta, Georgia

Peanut Brittle

Fred Fussell obtained this recipe, handwritten on a scrap of newsprint, from the late Evans Mitchell of Columbus, Georgia. His father, Alexander Mitchell, was a Greek immigrant who came to Georgia in 1889. "The elder Mitchell opened the town's first candy shop that same year in downtown Columbus," Fussell says. "Alex Mitchell is supposedly the inventor of peanut brittle. He was also the model for the Greek candy-store owner in Carson McCullers's best-selling novel *The Heart Is a Lonely Hunter.* This is his recipe."

Makes about 5 pounds

2 pounds (5 cups) sugar
2½ cups light corn syrup
2½ cups water
1½ pounds raw shelled Spanish peanuts

2 tablespoons butter
1 teaspoon salt
2 teaspoons baking soda

Grease a slab of marble or baking sheets. Stir together the sugar, corn syrup, and water in a large pot. Cook over medium-high heat, stirring with a wooden spoon until the sugar dissolves completely. Wipe away any sugar crystals clinging to the side of the pan with a wet towel or wet pastry brush. Increase the heat to high, bring to a boil, and cook without stirring until the mixture reaches soft-ball stage (234° to 240°F) on a candy thermometer.

Stir in the peanuts and cook without stirring until the mixture reaches hard-crack stage (300° to 310°F). Remove from the heat and stir in the butter, salt, and baking soda. The candy will foam. Stir quickly until well mixed. Pour onto the prepared slab of marble or baking sheets. Quickly spread into an even layer with a flexible offset spatula. Allow to cool completely and then cut into slabs or break into pieces. Store in airtight containers.

Alexander Mitchell of Columbus, Georgia, by way of Fred Fussell of Columbus, Georgia

Texas Pralines

Pecan pralines are beloved in New Orleans. They are equally beloved in Texas, where they are a staple of Tex-Mex cooking. Along with sugarcane, French and Spanish sweetmeat traditions traveled with explorers and settlers into Louisiana, Texas, and Mexico, where the abundant native pecans replaced European almonds. The pecan candies, sold on the streets of New Orleans by early Creole pralinieres, and the *dulces de nuez*, which spread from Mexico into Texas, share essentially the same ingredients and the same preparation.

"This very typical recipe is adapted from one by my friend, Matt Martinez," says Mary Margaret Pack. "He attributes it to his mother, Janie Martinez."

Makes about 16

1 cup *piloncillo* sugar, broken up (see note)
1 cup whole milk
½ teaspoon baking soda

Pinch of salt
1 tablespoon butter
2 teaspoons vanilla
1½ cups toasted pecan halves or pieces

Line a baking sheet with parchment or wax paper and spray lightly with vegetable oil. Fill a small glass or a measuring cup with cold water.

Mix the sugar, milk, baking soda, and salt in a cast-iron Dutch oven or large heavy saucepan; cook over medium heat, stirring until the sugar dissolves and washing down any sugar crystals clinging to the side with a brush dipped in the cold water. Increase the heat to high and let the mixture boil undisturbed until it reaches soft-ball stage (234° to 240°F on a candy thermometer), at least 15 minutes and up to 30 minutes, depending on the weather. Remove the pan from the heat and let cool to 220°F. Stir in the butter, vanilla, and pecans. Beat vigorously with a large wooden spoon until the mixture starts to thicken and look creamy. Working quickly, drop heaping tablespoons of the batter onto the prepared baking sheet. The pralines will firm up as they cool. Store the pralines in an airtight container between layers of parchment or wax paper. They will keep for several days at room temperature.

Note: Piloncillo is a coarse, brown cane sugar that tastes something like molasses and is molded into small, hard cone shapes. If not available, substitute ½ cup granulated sugar and ½ cup packed light brown sugar.

Janie Martinez, by way of Mary Margaret Pack of Austin, Texas

Creole Cream Cheese

"This popular soft curd cheese (with the consistency of a fine flan), was traditionally made with day-old clabbering milk and hung in cheesecloth by the French Creoles in the early days of New Orleans," says Poppy Tooker. During the latter half of the twentieth century, this indigenous cheese had been abandoned by the large commercial firms posing as local dairies. But in the early years of the twenty-first century, a commercial resurgence began, thanks to a handful of family-owned New Orleans dairies.

Why include a fresh cheese in our cane chapter? Because it's best eaten in the morning, with berries and a couple of spoonfuls of sugar.

Makes about 4 cups

2 quarts skim milk   Small pinch of salt
½ cup buttermilk   3 to 4 drops liquid vegetable rennet

Stir together all of the ingredients in a large stainless steel or glass bowl, mixing well. Cover lightly with plastic wrap and let sit undisturbed at room temperature until the mixture separates into firm curds and liquid whey, 18 to 24 hours. Gently transfer the curds with a slotted spoon into cheese molds or into a flat-bottomed colander lined with several layers of cheesecloth. Place the molds on a wire rack set over a container that is deep enough to collect the whey that will drip from the cheese. Cover lightly with plastic wrap and refrigerate. Let the cheese drain until it no longer drips and is the consistency of very thick yogurt, 6 to 8 hours. Turn the cheese out of the molds. Store covered and refrigerated for up to 2 weeks.

Poppy Tooker of New Orleans, Louisiana

Pawpaw Sauce

The poet James Whitcomb Riley once described pawpaws as "custard pie without a crust." Others compare their taste to a combination of banana, pear, and sweet potato. Pawpaws were dietary standbys of Appalachian folk and American Indians in times past; some sources claim that pawpaws kept Lewis and Clark alive during their explorations. Today pawpaws grow throughout the South but are not often commercially available. A good eye, or a generous neighbor, is key.

This easy, old-fashioned sauce is wonderful spooned over waffles or slices of toasted pound cake.

Makes about 2½ cups

1 quart ripe wild pawpaws	½ cup heavy cream
¼ cup sour cream	Sugar, as needed

Remove the stems and leaves of the pawpaws. Push the pawpaws through a mesh sieve or run them through a food mill to remove the skins and large seeds. There should be about 2 cups of strained pulp.

Mix the pawpaw pulp, sour cream, and heavy cream in a blender until thick and smooth. Fully ripe pawpaw is very sweet and requires no sugar. However, if the pawpaw is underripe, add sugar to taste. Serve at room temperature or chilled.

Patty Schnatter of Louisville, Kentucky

Ambrosia Fruit Salad

In 1989 Susan Puckett's grandmother, known as Dodie, gave Susan's sister a wedding present, a collection of her favorite recipes, written in cursive in a spiral-bound notebook. "Most of the recipes were European classics," says Puckett, "an exception being this take on ambrosia. Though Dodie typically detested such plebeian ingredients, she adored this combo and brought it to many a book club or professors' wives luncheon." Nowadays Susan prefers ambrosia made with fresh, peeled, and sectioned oranges, shredded coconut, a little sugar to taste, and nothing more. But this is what truly takes her back to Mississippi. If you can find it, use Texas-, Louisiana-, or Alabama-grown citrus.

Makes 8 servings

1 (11-ounce) can mandarin oranges, drained	½ cup sweetened, flaked coconut, or to taste
1 (5-ounce) jar maraschino cherries with their juice	1 cup sour cream
1 (20-ounce) can pineapple tidbits, drained	1 cup miniature marshmallows

Stir all the ingredients together in a pretty glass bowl. Cover and refrigerate overnight. Serve chilled.

Susan Puckett of Decatur, Georgia

MORE ABOUT
THE SOUTHERN FOODWAYS ALLIANCE

MISSION STATEMENT

The Southern Foodways Alliance documents, studies, and celebrates the diverse food cultures of the changing American South. We set a common table where black and white, rich and poor—all who gather—may consider our history and our future in a spirit of reconciliation.

We are a member-supported institute of the Center for the Study of Southern Culture at the University of Mississippi in Oxford. Visit our Web site at www.southernfoodways.org.

SFA HISTORY

The Center for the Study of Southern Culture at the University of Mississippi acted as the incubator of the SFA and provided start-up capital, earned from the sale of the center-researched and -written cookbook, *A Gracious Plenty: Recipes and Recollections from the American South*. (In May 1998, the center staged the first Southern Foodways Symposium.)

Two organizations with similar aims preceded the SFA: the Society for the Preservation and Revitalization of Southern Food, spearheaded by Edna Lewis and Scott Peacock, and the American Southern Food Institute, led by, among others, Jeanne Voltz. Soon after the SFA was established, both organizations folded their member rolls and cash reserves into the SFA.

At a July 1999 meeting, the founders elected a board of directors and agreed to hire John T. Edge as director of the SFA. He remained the sole employee until Mary Beth Lasseter was hired as associate director in 2004.

In 2005, Amy Evans became the SFA's oral historian. Soon after, Joe York, who like Edge, Lasseter, and Evans is a graduate of the master's program in Southern studies, came on board as filmmaker. In 2007, Melissa Hall signed on as communications maven, and in 2009 Julie Pickett joined our ranks as office manager. As the SFA has grown, we have honed a mission that leverages oral history and film work through publications and programming.

FOUNDING MEMBERS

Ann Abadie
Kaye Adams
Jim Auchmutey
Marilou Awiakta
Ben Barker
Karen Barker
Ella Brennan
Ann Brewer
Karen Cathey
Leah Chase
Al Clayton
Mary Ann Clayton
Shirley Corriher
Norma Jean Darden
Crescent Dragonwagon
Nathalie Dupree
John T. Edge
John Egerton
Lolis Elie
John Folse
Terry Ford
Damon Lee Fowler
Vertamae Grosvenor
Jessica B. Harris
Cynthia Hizer
Portia James

Martha Johnston
Sally Belk King
Sarah Labensky
Edna Lewis
Rudy Lombard
Ronni Lundy
Louis Osteen
Marlene Osteen
Tim W. Patridge
Paul Prudhomme
Joe Randall
Marie Rudisill
Dori Sanders
Richard Schweid
Ned Shank
Kathy Starr
Frank Stitt
Pardis Stitt
Marion Sullivan
Van Sykes
John Martin Taylor
Toni Tipton-Martin
Jeanne Voltz
Psyche Williams-Forson
Charles Reagan Wilson

CONTRIBUTORS

DALE ABADIE is a retired professor and university administrator in Oxford, Mississippi.

HUGH ACHESON, a Canadian by birth, is the chef at Five and Ten restaurant in Athens, Georgia.

JEAN ANDERSON lives in Chapel Hill, North Carolina. She has written several cookbooks, including *A Love Affair with Southern Cooking*.

BEN AVERITT lives in Oxford, North Carolina. He learned to cook Brunswick stew from Mrs. Sterling Carrington, who presided over a longstanding annual stew at Oxford's Hester Baptist Church.

BEN BARKER owns Magnolia Grill with his wife, Karen, in Durham, North Carolina, and is coauthor of *Not Afraid of Flavor*.

KAREN BARKER does business at Magnolia Grill in Durham, North Carolina, but gathers her persimmons at home in Chapel Hill; she is coauthor of *Not Afraid of Flavor*.

SCOTT BARTON is a chef, educator, and culinary consultant in New York, New York.

BILL BAYLEY is the late proprietor of Bayley's restaurant in Theodore, Alabama.

ALLAN BENTON of Madisonville, Tennessee, is a master ham curer and winner of the SFA's Craig Claiborne Lifetime Achievement Award.

BILL BEST grows heirloom beans in Berea, Kentucky. He is a recipient of the SFA's Ruth Fertel Keeper of the Flame award.

VISHWESH BHATT is the lead chef at Snack Bar in Oxford, Mississippi.

MARCELLE BIENVENU is a chef and writer in St. Martinville, Louisiana, and the author of many cookbooks, including *Who's Your Mama, Are You Catholic, and Can You Make a Roux?*

FRITZ BLANK, the onetime owner of Deux Cheminées in Philadelphia, Pennsylvania, now lives in Thailand.

PAULINE P. BRIDGFORTH of Tupelo, Mississippi, is the grandmother of Georgeanna Milam Chapman.

SEAN BROCK, a native of Wise, Virginia, is the chef of McCrady's Restaurant in Charleston, South Carolina.

GAYLE BROOKS of Brooksville, Florida, is an avid home cook of wild game.

ALTON BROWN, host of *Good Eats* and lead commentator for *Iron Chef America* was educated, in part, at the University of Georgia; he lives and works in Atlanta.

ELIZA BROWN, a native of Tennessee, now lives and gardens in San Francisco, California.

WALTER BUNDY is a chef of the restaurant Lemaire in the Jefferson Hotel in Richmond, Virginia.

EDNA BROOKS BUNN of Griffin, Georgia, is the late mother of Richard Bunn.

RICHARD BUNN is an architect in Atlanta, Georgia.

ORA LEE BUTLER made yellow squash pickles in West Monroe, Louisiana.

ERIN CARICOFE is studying food systems sustainability in Columbus, Ohio.

JOHNNIE CARR, an Alabama civil rights activist, was the longtime president of the Montgomery Improvement Agency.

KATHY CARY is a pioneer in the farm-to-fork movement in Louisville, Kentucky, and the chef-owner of Lilly's.

ANN CASHION, a Mississippi native, is chef and partner at Johnny's Half Shell in Washington, D.C.

Margaret P. Cashion of Jackson, Mississippi, is the mother of Ann Cashion.

Madge Castle of Boone, North Carolina, is Sheri Castle's late grandmother.

Sheri Castle is an author, educator, and recipe tester in Chapel Hill, North Carolina.

Bryan Caswell is the chef and coproprietor of Reef in Houston, Texas.

David Cecelski is a scholar and author living in Durham, North Carolina.

Natalie Chanin is the designer and entrepreneur behind the clothing and furnishings collection Alabama Chanin in Florence, Alabama.

Georgeanna Milam Chapman lives in Lexington, Kentucky, and works part-time for the sfa.

Leah Chase, a winner of the sfa's Craig Claiborne Lifetime Achievement Award, is the chef-proprietor of Dooky Chase Restaurant in New Orleans, Louisiana.

Craig Claiborne, raised in Indianola, Mississippi, was a longtime food writer and editor at the *New York Times*.

Carol Copeland is a crackerjack cook who lives in Athens, Alabama.

Shirley Corriher lives in Atlanta, Georgia, and is the author of *Cookwise*.

Diana Cottier is a caterer of lovely bites in Covington, Louisiana.

Mildred Council is the proprietor of Mama Dip's restaurant in Chapel Hill, North Carolina; she wrote *Mama Dip's Family Cookbook*.

John Coykendall is master gardener and seed saver at Blackberry Farm in Walland, Tennessee.

Amy Crockett is a partner in Volta Taverna in Oxford, Mississippi.

John Currence, a New Orleans native, is a chef, restaurateur, and writer in Oxford, Mississippi.

Carol Darden and Norma Jean Darden of New York, New York, are the authors of the cookbook memoir *Spoonbread and Strawberry Wine*.

Sally Davenport is a Cajun living in Owensboro, Kentucky.

Nan Davis of Oxford, Mississippi, won the sfa's Pimento Cheese Invitational in 2003.

EULA MAE DORÉ lived on Avery Island in Louisiana and cowrote *Eula Mae's Cajun Kitchen*.

STEPHEN PALMER DOWDNEY of Charleston, South Carolina, is the author of *Putting Up*.

CRESCENT DRAGONWAGON, a founding member of the SFA, wrote *Cornbread Gospels*. A longtime resident of Arkansas, she now lives in Vermont.

NATHALIE DUPREE of Charleston, South Carolina, a recipient of the SFA's Craig Claiborne Lifetime Achievement Award, has written several cookbooks, including *New Southern Cooking*.

JOHN T. EDGE, director of the Southern Foodways Alliance, writes about food culture for newspapers and magazines and has published a number of books.

MARY BEVERLY EVANS EDGE of Bowman, South Carolina, is the late mother of John T. Edge.

JASON EDWARDS of Johnson City, Tennessee, knows his wild greens.

LOLIS ELIE, who lives in New Orleans, Louisiana, is an SFA founding member and the author of *Smokestack Lightning*.

BELINDA ELLIS is a baker and the editor of *Edible Piedmont* in Raleigh, North Carolina.

RICK ELLIS is a food stylist based in New York City and a champion deviled-egg maker.

ELIZABETH ENGELHARDT, a North Carolina native, teaches in the University of Texas at Austin and is editor of *The Republic of Barbecue*.

CORBIN EVANS, who now lives in Philadelphia, Pennsylvania, ran several restaurants in New Orleans.

ELI EVANS, a native of Durham, North Carolina, now lives in New York City; the selection "The Secret of Atlanta Brisket" originally appeared in his book *The Provincials*.

PAM EVERSMEYER is a school librarian in Metairie, Louisiana.

JOHN FLEER of Maryville, Tennessee, is a music geek and the chef at Canyon Kitchen at Lonesome Valley in North Carolina.

John Folse of Donaldsonville, Louisiana, wrote *The Encyclopedia of Cajun and Creole Cuisine* and is a recipient of the SFA's Craig Claiborne Lifetime Achievement Award.

Martha Foose of Pluto Plantation, Mississippi, is the author of *Screen Doors and Sweet Tea*.

Kenneth Ford, director of the Institute for Human and Machine Cognition in Pensacola, Florida, is a scientist by vocation and a gardener and eater by avocation.

Sara Foster, author of *The Foster's Market Cookbook*, founded the Foster's Markets in Durham and Chapel Hill, North Carolina.

Damon Lee Fowler of Savannah, Georgia, is an SFA founding member and the author of *Damon Lee Fowler's New Southern Baking*.

Fred Fussell, museum curator in Columbus, Georgia, is the author of *Blue Ridge Music Trails*.

Sara Gibbs is a chef in Taylorsville, Kentucky, and the author of *Southern Thighways*.

Nikki Giovanni is a poet, a resident of Christiansburg, Virginia, and the author of *Acolytes*.

Jim Gossen, a Louisiana native, runs the seafood business Louisiana Foods in Houston, Texas.

Flavius B. Hall Jr. is a retired educator and a writer in New Bern, North Carolina.

Melissa Booth Hall of Oxford, Mississippi, is the SFA's events maven.

Ashley Hansen is the proprietor and head syrup maker at Hansen's Sno-Bliz in New Orleans, Louisiana.

J. C. Hardaway cooked at Hawkins Grill in Memphis, Tennessee, for more than half a century. He was the first recipient of the SFA's Ruth Fertel Keeper of the Flame award.

Jessica Harris, professor at Dillard University and Queens College, author of *The Welcome Table*, is a recipient of the SFA's Craig Claiborne Lifetime Achievement Award.

Chris Hastings is chef at Hot and Hot Fish Club in Birmingham, Alabama, and is author of the *Hot and Hot Fish Club Cookbook*.

Thomas Head is a writer in Washington, D.C. He was the longtime editor of *Gravy*, the SFA's food letter.

EDDIE HERNANDEZ is chef and partner in the Taqueria del Sol restaurants in Atlanta, Decatur, and Athens, Georgia.

BLAIR HOBBS teaches writing, writes poetry, and makes art in Oxford, Mississippi.

LINTON HOPKINS is the chef-proprietor of Restaurant Eugene in Atlanta, Georgia, where he also started a farmers' market.

BECKETT HOWORTH of Oxford, Mississippi, is a retired University of Mississippi administrator and an avid gardener and cook.

DAN HUNTLEY lives in Rock Hill, South Carolina, and is the author of *Extreme Barbecue*.

BRET JENNINGS is the chef at Elaine's on Franklin in Chapel Hill, North Carolina.

SONYA JONES is the chef-owner of Sweet Auburn Bread Company in Atlanta, Georgia.

ELIZABETH KARMEL is chef of the Hill Country restaurants in New York City and author of *Taming the Flame*.

LIONEL KEY carries on his uncle's tradition of hand-grinding filé powder in Baton Rouge, Louisiana.

JOYCE KING of Blytheville, Arkansas, is a grocery store entrepreneur and envy-inducing cook.

JIMMY AND NICKY KOIKOS run the Bright Star Restaurant in Bessemer, Alabama; they wrote *A Centennial Celebration of the Bright Star Restaurant*.

DAVID LASSETER of Valdosta, Georgia, has written postcards to his children every day since they left home; frequently, the postcards feature recipes.

MARY BETH LASSETER is the associate director of the SFA, a feat she accomplishes in Vicksburg, Mississippi.

MIKE LATA is the chef and a partner at FIG (Food Is Good) in Charleston, South Carolina.

PHOEBE LAWLESS operates Scratch Seasonal Artisan Baking in Durham, North Carolina.

EDWARD LEE is the chef and coproprietor of the restaurant 610 Magnolia in Louisville, Kentucky.

Matt Lee and Ted Lee of Charleston, South Carolina, are the authors of *The Lee Bros. Southern Cookbook*.

Austin Leslie of New Orleans, Louisiana, was best known for his dill-pickle-and-garlic-topped fried chicken; he also authored *Creole-Soul: New Orleans' Cooking with a Soulful Twist*.

Donald Link is the chef and owner of Herbsaint and other New Orleans restaurants and the author of *Real Cajun*.

Dana Logsdon is a damn good baker in New Orleans, Louisiana.

Ronni Lundy, a recipient of the SFA's Craig Claiborne Lifetime Achievement Award, authored *Butterbeans to Blackberries: Recipes from the Southern Garden*.

John Malik is a chef who has led a number of kitchens, including 33 Liberty Restaurant in Greenville, South Carolina.

Janie Martinez founded the iconic Austin, Texas, restaurant Matt's El Rancho with her husband in 1952.

Dean McCord is a lawyer and food blogger in Raleigh, North Carolina.

Rick McDaniel is a food historian, chef, and writer in Asheville, North Carolina.

Nancie McDermott of Chapel Hill, North Carolina, is the author of *Southern Cakes*.

April McGreger runs Farmer's Daughter, a farm-driven artisan food business, in Carrboro, North Carolina.

Robby Melvin is the proprietor of Salt Fine Catering in Birmingham, Alabama.

Alexander Mitchell of Columbus, Georgia, is believed to have invented peanut brittle.

Debbie Moose of Raleigh, North Carolina, is the author of *Deviled Eggs*.

Gene and Ouida Morris live in McDonough, Georgia, where they cook in large, festive amounts.

Angie Mosier is a baker, food stylist, and photographer in Atlanta, Georgia.

Jennie Sue Murphree of Batesville, Mississippi, was April McGreger's great-grandmother.

WALTER MURPHREE of Batesville, Mississippi, was April McGreger's grandfather.

BILL NEAL opened Crook's Corner in Chapel Hill, North Carolina, in 1982; he wrote *Bill Neal's Southern Cooking*.

CYNTHIA LEJEUNE NOBLES is a culinary historian in Baton Rouge, Louisiana.

SARAH O'KELLEY is coproprietor of the restaurant Glass Onion in Charleston, South Carolina.

LOUIS OSTEEN, founding SFA member and author of *Louis Osteen's Charleston Cuisine*, is the chef at the Lake Rabun Hotel in Lakemont, Georgia.

MARY MARGARET PACK is a writer in Austin, Texas.

PETER PATOUT is an antiques dealer in New Orleans, Louisiana.

TIM PATRIDGE is a chef and champion barbecue pit master in Atlanta, Georgia, as well as a founding member of the SFA.

SCOTT PEACOCK is a chef living in Decatur, Georgia, and the coauthor of *The Gift of Southern Cooking*.

BOB PERRY of Lancaster, Kentucky, heads the University of Kentucky Food Systems Initiative, working to educate palates about place-based foods.

AUDREY PETTY, a writer, teaches in the English Department at the University of Illinois in Urbana.

FLOYD POCHE is the proprietor of Poche's Market in Breaux Bridge, Louisiana.

MARGARET PROPST was a schoolteacher in Roan Mountain, Tennessee.

PAUL PRUDHOMME, who grew up in Cajun country, owns K-Paul's Louisiana Kitchen in New Orleans, Louisiana, and wrote *Chef Paul Prudhomme's Louisiana Kitchen*.

SUSAN PUCKETT, a writer in Decatur, Georgia, was the architect of the *Atlanta Journal-Constitution*'s Saving Southern Food project.

MARY RANDOLPH of Richmond City, Virginia, wrote *The Virginia House-wife Cookbook*, first published in 1824.

BILLY REID, a native of southern Louisiana, is a clothing designer based in Florence, Alabama.

KAY RENTSCHLER, a onetime *New York Times* writer, works for Anson Mills in Charleston, South Carolina.

TODD RICHARDS is a chef at One Flew South in Atlanta, Georgia.

JARED RICHARDSON is chef at the Cleveland's restaurant in the Woodford Inn in Versailles, Kentucky.

LEE RICHARDSON, a Louisiana native, is the chef at Ashley's in the Capital Hotel in Little Rock, Arkansas.

CAPPY RICKS is a retired physician in Atlanta, Georgia; he's been to every Southern Foodways Symposium since 1998.

ANN GARNER RIDDLE lives in Winston-Salem, North Carolina; her family makes Texas Pete hot sauce.

GRACE RILEY of Decatur, Alabama, was the grandmother of the SFA's oral historian, Amy Evans.

SARA ROAHEN, a writer and oral historian in New Orleans, Louisiana, is the author of *Gumbo Tales*.

GLENN ROBERTS is the founder of Anson Mills in Columbia, South Carolina.

CLINTON ROBINSON of Gray, Georgia, was a childhood friend of John T. Edge.

RAY ROBINSON was the longtime proprietor of Cozy Corner restaurant in Memphis, Tennessee.

TOM SASSER is the president of Harper's Restaurants, Inc., based in Charlotte, North Carolina.

STEVEN SATTERFIELD is the chef and co-owner of the restaurant Miller Union in Atlanta, Georgia.

JILL SAUCEMAN is a museum education specialist in Johnson City, Tennessee.

LYNNE SAWICKI is the proprietor of Sawicki's Meat, Seafood, and More in Decatur, Georgia.

PATTY SCHNATTER works at Lynn's Paradise Café in Louisville, Kentucky.

JAMES SCHROEDER is a chef at the Jefferson Hotel in Richmond, Virginia.

FRANCINE WOLFE SCHWARTZ is a writer in Fort Myers, Florida.

ED SCOTT of Drew, Mississippi, is a recipient of the SFA's Ruth Fertel Keeper of the Flame award.

JAMIE SHANNON was the chef at Commander's Palace in New Orleans, Louisiana; he coauthored *Commander's Kitchen*.

JIM SHIRLEY is the chef at Fish House in Pensacola, Florida, and the author of *Good Grits*.

BETH SHORTT is a North Carolina native living in Oklahoma City, Oklahoma.

LaRUE SHOUSE lives in Winston-Salem, North Carolina, and has won many blue ribbons at fairs for her pickles.

BILL SMITH JR. is the chef at Crook's Corner restaurant in Chapel Hill, North Carolina, and the author of *Seasoned in the South*.

BILL SMITH SR. of New Bern, North Carolina, is the father of that other Bill Smith.

KEN SMITH is the chef at Upperline restaurant in New Orleans, Louisiana.

LEE SMITH of Hillsborough, North Carolina, is the author of *Fair and Tender Ladies*.

GREG SONNIER is the co-chef-proprietor with his wife, Mary, of the Uptowner special events facility in New Orleans, Louisiana.

SUSAN SPICER is the chef at Bayona restaurant in New Orleans, Louisiana, and the author of *Crescent City Cooking*.

MARTHA STAMPS of Nashville, Tennessee, is a chef and the author of *The (New) New Southern Basics*.

KATHY STARR, a founding member of the SFA, grew up in the Mississippi Delta and wrote *The Soul of Southern Cooking*.

ROBERT STEHLING is the chef and proprietor of Hominy Grill in Charleston, South Carolina.

FRANK STITT, a winner of the SFA's Craig Claiborne Lifetime Achievement Award, is a chef and restaurant owner in Birmingham, Alabama, and author of *Frank Stitt's Southern Table*.

AMY EVANS STREETER of Oxford, Mississippi, is the SFA's staff oral historian. She learned to make Delta hot tamales while working on the Tamale Trail oral history project.

CHUCK SUBRA JR. is the chef at La Cote Brasserie in New Orleans, Louisiana.

John Martin Taylor, a founder of the SFA, lives in Washington, D.C., and wrote *Hoppin' John's Lowcountry Cooking*.

Katherine Forbes Taylor, late of Maple, North Carolina, was a whiz-bang game cook.

Sarah Thomas is a poet in Black Mountain, North Carolina.

Poppy Tooker, a native of New Orleans, Louisiana, wrote the *Crescent City Farmers Market Cookbook*.

Miguel Torres is a sous chef at Lantern Restaurant in Durham, North Carolina.

Celeste Uzee lives in Luling, Louisiana, and works at Tulane University in New Orleans.

Vance and Julie Vaucresson run Vaucresson's Sausage Company in New Orleans, Louisiana.

Robb Walsh lives in Houston, Texas, and has authored several books, including *Legends of Texas Barbecue*.

Ari Weinzweig is a founding partner of the Zingerman's Community of Businesses in Ann Arbor, Michigan, and the author of *Zingerman's Guide to Good Eating*.

Hal White, along with his brother Malcolm White, runs Hal and Mal's in Jackson, Mississippi.

Liz Williams is the founding director of the Southern Food and Beverage Museum in New Orleans, Louisiana.

Randall Williams is a civil rights veteran and book editor in Montgomery, Alabama.

Virginia Willis of Atlanta, Georgia, is the author of *Bon Appetit Y'all*.

Joe York is the SFA's filmmaker. He's the author of *With Signs Following: Photographs from the Southern Religious Roadside*.

Alex Young is chef at Zingerman's Roadhouse in Ann Arbor, Michigan, and a fervent believer in oysterman Tommy Ward's Apalachicola catch.

INDEX OF NAMES

Italicized page numbers refer to recipes.

Abadie, Ann, xvii, 260
Abadie, Dale, *179–80*
Acheson, Hugh, *174*
Adams, Kaye, 260
Adams, Roady, 165
Anderson, Brett, xv
Anderson, Jean, *104*
Auchmutey, Jim, 260
Averitt, Amy, 152
Averitt, Ben, *152*
Awiakta, Marilou, 260

Barber, Robert, xviii
Barker, Ben, *217*, 260
Barker, Karen, *243*, 260
Barton, Scott, *90*
Bayley, Bill, *189–90*
Benedict, Jennie, 6
Benjamin, Ethel, 165
Benton, Allan, *20–21*
Best, Bill, *216*
Beverly, Frankie, 159
Bhatt, Vishwesh, *21*
Bienvenu, Marcelle, *148*
Blank, Fritz, *213–14*
Blount, Roy, Jr., 15–16, 27
Brennan, Ella, 260
Brewer, Ann, 260

Bridgforth, Pauline P., *199–200*
Brock, Sean, 3, *11*
Brooks, Gayle, *206*
Brown, Alton, xi, xiii, xvii
Brown, Eliza, *223*
Brown, Francis (Frankie/Tankie), *110–11*
Bundy, Walter, *48*
Bunn, Edna Brooks, *247–48*
Bunn, Richard, *247–48*
Butler, Ora Lee, *220–21*

Caricofe, Erin, *232–33*
Carr, Arlam, Sr., 182
Carr, Johnnie, *182*
Cary, Kathy, *62*, *135–36*
Cash, Johnny, 120
Cashion, Ann, *197*, 207, 229, *231–32*
Cashion, Margaret P., *197*
Castle, Madge, *74–75*, *211–12*
Castle, Sheri, xv, *49*, *106*
Caswell, Bryan, *137*
Cathey, Karen, 260
Cecelski, David, *152*
Chanin, Natalie, *105*
Chapman, Georgeanna Milam, xvii, *199–200*
Chase, Leah, *72–74*, 88, 260
Claiborne, Craig, *217–18*
Clayton, Al, 260
Clayton, Mary Ann, 260
Clevenger, JoAnn, 41

Clower, Jerry, 193
Copeland, Carol, *183*
Corriher, Shirley, *136–37*, 260
Cosby, Bill, 62
Cottier, Diana, *241–42*
Council, Mildred, *154–55*
Cox, Devin, iv, xvii
Coykendall, John, *39–40*
Crews, Harry, 227
Crockett, Amy, *212–13*
Currence, John, *115–16*

Darden, Carol, *118–19*
Darden, Norma Jean, *118–19*, 260
Davenport, Sally, *91*
Davis, Nan, *5–6*
Davis, Timothy C., xv
Dendy, Carl, 236
Derting, Nevada Parker, *233–34*
Doré, Eula Mae, *78, 92–93*
Dowdney, Stephen Palmer, *224–25*
Dragonwagon, Crescent, *113*, 260
Dupree, Nathalie, *56*, 260

Edge, John T., xiii–xv, *58*, 259, 260
Edge, Mary Beverly Evans, *17*
Edwards, Jason, *72*
Egerton, John 85, 183, 260
Elie, Lolis, 142, *150–51, 159*, 260
Ellis, Belinda, *101*
Ellis, Rick, *134–35*
Engelhardt, Elizabeth, *103*
Evans, Amy. *See* Streeter, Amy Evans
Evans, Corbin, *88–89*
Evans, Eli, 164, *165*
Eversmeyer, Pam, *180*

Ferris, Marcie, xvii, 139
Fishburne, Emily (Whaley), 17
Fleer, John, *245–46*
Folse, John, *204, 219*, 260
Foose, Martha, *190, 249–50*
Ford, Kenneth, *71*
Ford, Terry, 260
Foster, Sara, *31*
Fowler, Damon Lee, *8, 235*, 260
Fussell, Fred, *254*

Gibbs, Sara, *126–27*
Giovanni, Nikki, *59*
Gossen, Diane, 160
Gossen, Jim, *160*
Graybeal, Florence, 23
Green, Al, 159
Grosvenor, Vertamae, 81, 260

Hall, Flavius B., Jr., 33, *112*
Hall, Melissa Booth, xvii, *162–63*, 260
Hamaker, Brooks, xvii
Hansen, Ashley, *109*
Hardaway, J. C., 142, *159*
Hargrave, Zola, 165
Harris, Jessica, *10, 36*, 260
Harris, Joel Chandler, 68
Harris, Julian, 68
Hastings, Chris, *56–57, 69*
Head, Thomas, *220–21*
Hernandez, Eddie, *34, 76*
Hess, Karen, 85, 131
Hilliard, Sam Bowers, 141
Hizer, Cynthia, 260
Hobbs, Blair, *7, 61*
Hopkins, Linton, *70–71*
Howorth, Beckett, *108*
Huntley, Dan, *175*

Jackson, Andrew, 20
James, Portia, 260
Jefferson, Thomas, 41
Jennings, Bret, *188–89*
Johnston, Martha, 260
Jones, Booker T., 53
Jones, Sonya, *253–54*

Karmel, Elizabeth, *252*
Key, Lionel, *158*
King, Albert, 159
King, Joyce, 164, *167–68*
King, Martin Luther, Jr., 182
King, Sally Belk, 260
Koikos, Jimmy and Nicky, *94–95*

Labensky, Sarah, 260
Lasseter, David, *161*
Lasseter, Mary Beth, xvii, *115, 161*, 259, 260

Lata, Mike, *75*
Lawless, Phoebe, *128–30*
LeBoeuf, Camille Roussel, 179
Lee, Edward, *45–46*
Lee, Matt and Ted, *251–52*
Leigh, Archibald, *67–68*
Leslie, Austin, *37*, 124, *125*
Lewis, Edna, 99, *259*, 260
Link, Donald, 141, *146–47*
Logsdon, Dana, *244–45*
Lombard, Rudy, 260
Long, Huey, 68
Loudin, Nancy, 202
Lundy, Ronni, *19–20, 32–33*, 260

Malik, John, *203*
Mama Dip, *154–55*
Martinez, Janie, *255*
Martinez, Matt, *255*
McCord, Dean, *201*
McCullers, Carson, 1, 254
McDaniel, Rick, *176*, 221
McDermott, Nancie, *238–39*
McGill, Ralph, 123–24
McGreger, April, xv, *185–86, 248–49*
McIlhenny, Paul, 92
McLorn, Demetrie, 231
Melvin, Robby, *63*
Memphis Minnie, 15
Miller, Zell, 65, 68
Mitchell, Alexander, *254*
Mitchell, Evans, *254*
Mitchell, Nicole, xviii
Monk, Thelonious, 67
Moose, Debbie, *225*
Morris, Gene and Ouida, *149*
Mosier, Angie, xv, *236–37*
Murphree, Jennie Sue, *32*
Murphree, Walter, *45*

Neal, Bill, 127, *183–84*
Nobles, Cynthia LeJeune, *178–79*

O'Kelley, Sarah, *181*
Osteen, Louis, *131*, 260
Osteen, Marlene, 260

Pack, Mary Margaret, *255*
Parks, Rosa, 182
Patout, Peter, *177–78*
Patridge, Tim, *205*, 260
Peacock, Scott, *132–33*, 259
Perry, Bob, *89*
Petty, Audrey, *144*
Petty, Naomi, *144*
Pickett, Julie, xviii, 260
Poche, Floyd, *145*
Prewitt, Wiley, 196
Propst, Margaret, *23*
Prudhomme, Paul, 141, *155–56*, 260
Puckett, Susan, *257*

Randall, Joe, 260
Randolph, Mary, *41*
Rawlings, Marjorie Kinnan, 100
Reid, Billy, *44*
Rentschler, Kay, *102*
Rhett, Blanche S., 97
Ricard, Joseph William, 158
Richards, Todd, *55*
Richardson, Jared, *134*
Richardson, Lee, *191*
Ricks, Betty, 127
Ricks, Cappy, *127–28*
Riddle, Ann Garner, *176–77*
Riley, Grace, *38*
Riley, James Whitcomb, 256
Roahen, Sara, xiv, xv, *72–74*
Roane, Carolyn, 177
Roberts, Glenn, *93–94*
Robinson, Clinton, 24
Robinson, Ray, *220*
Roosevelt, Franklin D., 15
Rose, Marilyn, 188
Rudisill, Marie, 260

Sanders, Dori, 260
Sasser, Tom, *79*
Satterfield, Steven, *9*
Sauceman, Fred, xv
Sauceman, Jill, *233–34*
Sawicki, Lynne, *222*
Schnatter, Patty, *256–57*
Schroeder, James, *48*

Schwartz, Francine Wolfe, *188*
Schweid, Richard, 260
Scott, Ed, *114*
Scott, Edna, 114
Shank, Ned, 260
Shannon, Jamie, 141, *153–54*
Shirley, Jim, *18*
Shortt, Beth, *173*
Shouse, LaRue, *215*
Smith, Bill, Jr., *43, 60, 198*
Smith, Bill, Sr., *198*
Smith, John, 195
Smith, Ken, *41–43*, 199
Smith, Lee, *120*
Smith, Lurlene Brown, *110–11*
Snyder, Gary, 51
Sonnier, Greg, *186–87*
Spicer, Susan, *35–36*
Stamps, Martha, *95*
Starr, Kathy, *33, 150*, 260
Stehling, Robert, *85–86*
Stevens, Erika, xviii
Stitt, Frank, *77*, 260
Stitt, Pardis, 260
Stockett, Robert N., 231
Streeter, Amy Evans, xviii, *38, 116–18*, 260
Subra, Chuck, Jr., *223–24*
Sullivan, Marion, 260
Sykes, Van, 260

Taylor, Emest, 201
Taylor, Joel Gray, 99, 169
Taylor, John Martin, *10–11*, 260

Taylor, Katherine Forbes, *201*
Thomas, Sarah, *202*
Timura, Catherine, 157
Tipton-Martin, Toni, 260
Tooker, Poppy, *96, 256*
Torres, Miguel, *143*
Trout, Allan M., 13

Uzee, Celeste, *87*
Uzee, Donald, 87

Vaucresson, Sonny, 12
Vaucresson, Vance and Julie, 3, *12*
Voltz, Jeanne, 259, 260

Walsh, Robb, *157–58, 164, 166–67*
Walter, Eugene, 185
Waltman, Zeldo Kroll, 180
Watson, Vernon Scott, 180
Weinzweig, Ari, *6–7, 40–41*
Welty, Eudora, v
Whaley, Mrs. Ben Scott (née Emily Fishburne), 17
White, Hal, *46–47*
Williams, Liz, *18–19*
Williams, Randall, *182*
Williams-Forson, Psyche, 123, 260
Willis, Virginia, *240–41*
Wilson, Charles Reagan, 260
Wilson, Justin, 3

York, Joe, *110–11*, 260
Young, Alex, *22*
Young, Kevin, 142

INDEX OF FOOD

Ambrosia Fruit Salad, 257
andouille sausage
    Duck and Andouille Étouffée, 199
    Gumbo z'Herbes, 72–74
Angel Biscuits, 101
anise liqueur, 253–54
Appalachian Pickle Beans and Corn, 211–12
apples
    Apple Stack Cake, 233–34
    Stuffed Pork Chops, 155–56
Applesauce Cake with Black Walnuts, 232–33
Atlanta Brisket, 165
Avery Island Jambalaya, 92–93
Awendaw Spoonbread, 102

bacon
    Bacon Forest, 162–63
    Breakfast Shrimp Gravy, 17
    Brown Butter Creamed Winter Greens,
        70–71
    Deep-Fried Bacon, 161
    Dirty Rice, 87
    Killed Lettuce, 74–75
    Sopping Chocolate, 25
    Tomato Gravy, 19–20
    Tomato Pie, 44
Baked Eggs, 136–37
Baked Wild Duck, 197
banana pudding, 244–45
barbecue sauce, 159

Barbecue Shrimp and Sweet-Potato Tarts, 186–87
Basic Grits, 107
beans
    Appalachian Pickle Beans and Corn, 211–12
    Butterbean Gravy, 18
    Collard Green and White Bean Gratin, 77
    Country Cooked Green Beans with New
        Potatoes, 32–33
    Dilly Beans, 221
    dried, 216
    Leather Britches, 216
    North Carolina Brunswick Stew, 152
    Okra and Butterbean Succotash, 36
    Red Beans and Rice, 153–54
Beaten Biscuits, 103
béchamel sauce, 70
beef
    brisket, 165
    Chicken-Fried Steak with Cream Gravy,
        166–67
    chuck roast, 116–18
    Grits and Grillades, 109
    ground, 179–80
    Gumbo z'Herbes, 72–74
    North Carolina Brunswick Stew, 152
    Parsons Vegetable Beef Stew, 167–68
    round steak, 109, 166–67
    stew meat, 72–74, 167–68
Benedictine: The Spread, 6–7
Benne Seed Biscuits, 104

biscuits
Angel Biscuits, 101
Beaten Biscuits, 103
Benne Seed Biscuits, 104
Buttermilk Biscuits, 105
Miracle Drop Biscuits, 106
spoonbread, 102
black-eyed peas
Kentucky Hoppin' John, 89
Refried Black-Eyed Peas, 34
Blue Cheese Straws, 9
Blue Ribbon Pimento Cheese, 5–6
Boiled Peanut and Sorghum Swirl
Ice Cream, 251–52
Boiled Peanuts, 10–11
Boiled-Peanut Beurre Blanc, 174
Boudin Blanc, 146–47
bourbon
Bourbon Crème Anglaise, 242
Carrot Soup with Bourbon and Ginger, 55
Molasses-Brined Wild Turkey Breast with
Bourbon Pan Sauce, 203
Braised Collard Greens with Ham-Hock
Broth, 69
Braised Coon or Possum with
Sweet Potatoes, 198
bread
cornbread, 110–11
rolls, refrigerator, 118–19
White Loaf Bread, 120
Bread Pudding with Bourbon Crème Anglaise,
241–42
Breakfast Shrimp Gravy, 17
brisket, beef, 165
Broiled Flounder, 173
broth, ham hock, 69
Brown Butter Creamed Winter Greens, 70–71
Brown Sugar Shortcakes with Strawberries
and Cream, 240–41
Brunswick Stew, North Carolina, 152
butterbeans
Butterbean Gravy, 18
North Carolina Brunswick Stew, 152
Okra and Butterbean Succotash, 36
buttermilk
Angel Biscuits, 101
Buttermilk Biscuits, 105
Hush Puppies, 114

Red Velvet Cake, 238–39
Tankie's Cornbread, 110–11

cabbage
Carolina Coleslaw, 79
Gumbo z'Herbes, 72–74
Sauerkraut, 219
Smothered Cabbage, 78
cakes
Apple Stack Cake, 233–34
Applesauce Cake with Black Walnuts, 232–33
Brown Sugar Shortcakes with Strawberries
and Cream, 240–41
Classic Pound Cake, 235
Coconut Layer Cake, 236–37
Red Velvet Cake, 238–39
Revelatory Caramel Cake, 231–32
Calas, 96
candy
Peanut Brittle, 254
Texas Pralines, 255
Caramelized Onion Pudding, 62
Carnitas, 143
Carolina Coleslaw, 79
Carolina Fish Muddle, 175
carrots
Carrot Soup with Bourbon and Ginger, 55
Chicken and Root Vegetable Hot Pot, 59
Drippings-Cooked Potatoes, Onions,
Turnips, and Carrots, 56
catfish
Fried Catfish, 190
Rice-Fried Catfish, 191
Chaudin, 148
Cheerwine Barbecue Chicken, 126–27
cheese. *See also* cream cheese
Blue Cheese Straws, 9
Blue Ribbon Pimento Cheese, 5–6
Cheese Boxes, 7
Cheese Grits Casserole, 108
Cheese Straws, 8
Macaroni and Cheese, 40–41
Pimento Cheese Hush Puppies, 115–16
chicken
Cheerwine Barbecue Chicken, 126 27
Chicken and Dumplings, 127–28
Chicken and Roasted Root Vegetable
Pot Pie, 128–30

Chicken and Root Vegetable Hot Pot, 59
Chicken Bog, 131
Chicken Purloo, 85–86
Country Captain, 132–33
Fried Chicken with New Orleans Confetti,
    125
giblets, 88–89
Gumbo z'Herbes, 72–74
livers, 87, 88, 134
Mississippi Delta Hot Tamales, 116–18
Mushroom Dirty Rice, 88–89
North Carolina Brunswick Stew, 152
Red Jambalaya, 91
Chicken-Fried Steak with Cream Gravy, 166–67
Chitlins, 144
Chocolate Gravy, 25
chuck roast, 116–18
Classic Pound Cake, 235
Coca-Cola
    Atlanta Brisket, 165
    Carnitas, 143
    Vegetable Soup, 47
Coconut Layer Cake, 236–37
coleslaw, 79
collard greens
    Braised Collard Greens with Ham-Hock
        Broth, 69
    Collard Green and White Bean Gratin, 77
    Gumbo z'Herbes, 72–74
Comeback Sauce, 212–13
corn
    Appalachian Pickle Beans and Corn, 211–12
    Corn Dumplings, 112
    Creamed Corn, 32
    Creamy Corn Pudding, 31
    Fresh Corn Fritters, 113
    Limpin' Susan, 90
    Okra and Butterbean Succotash, 36
    Roan Mountain Corn Gravy, 23
cornbread, 110–11
Country Breakfast Sausage, 149
Country Captain, 132–33
Country Cooked Green Beans with New Potatoes,
    32–33
country ham
    Country Ham with Redeye Gravy, 20–21
    Oyster Gravy, 22
Country-Fried Chicken Livers, 134

crab
    Crab Stew, 177–78
    Pan-Fried Soft-Shell Crabs, 188–89
    Seafood Gumbo, 183
    Slow-Cooker Crab Dip, 176–77
    Stuffed Mirliton, 37
    West Indies Salad, 189–90
cracklings, 150
Cranberry Congealed Salad with Poppy
    Seed Dressing, 49
Crawfish Étouffée, 178–79
cream cheese
    Benedictine: The Spread, 6–7
    Creole Cream Cheese, 256
    frosting, 238
    pie crust, 250
Cream Gravy, 166–67
Cream of Sorrell Soup, 71
Creamed Corn, 32
Creamy Corn Pudding, 31
cremini mushrooms, 88–89
Creole Cream Cheese, 256
Creole Red Gravy, 18–19
Crowder Peas with Potlikker, 33
cucumbers
    Benedictine: The Spread, 6–7
    Grape-Leaf Pickles, 215
curry powder, homemade, 133
Cushaw Griddle Cakes, 39–40

Deep Fried Peanuts, 11
Deep-Fried Bacon, 161
desserts. See also cakes; pies; puddings
    Ambrosia Fruit Salad, 257
    Boiled Peanut and Sorghum Swirl
        Ice Cream, 251–52
    Creole Cream Cheese, 256
    Pawpaw Sauce, 256–57
    Peach Ice Cream, 252
    Peanut Brittle, 254
    shortcakes, 240–41
    Texas Pralines, 255
Deviled Eggs, 134–35
Dilly Beans, 221
dips
    Slow-Cooker Crab Dip, 176–77
    Smoked Mullet Dip, 188
Dirty Rice, 87

Drippings-Cooked Potatoes, Onions, Turnips, and Carrots, 56
duck
    Baked Wild Duck, 197
    Duck and Andouille Étouffée, 199
    Duck Gumbo, 199–200
dumplings
    Chicken and Dumplings, 127–28
    Corn Dumplings, 112
    Indian dumplings, 112

eggplant
    Chicken Purloo, 85–86
    Eggplant, Oyster, and Tasso Gratin, 35–36
eggs
    Baked Eggs, 136–37
    Deviled Eggs, 134–35
    Eggs Derby, 135–36
    Pickled Eggs, 217–18
    Sriracha and Citrus Rémoulade, 137
Everlasting Refrigerator Rolls, 118–19

Fancy-pants Banana Pudding, 244–45
Filé Marinade, 158
fish. See also specific fish
    Boiled-Peanut Beurre Blanc, 174
    Carolina Fish Muddle, 175
    Pine-Bark Stew, 176
flounder, broiled, 173
Fresh Corn Fritters, 113
Fried Catfish, 190
Fried Chicken with New Orleans Confetti, 125
Fried Dill Pickles with Comeback Sauce, 212–13
Fried Green Tomatoes and Shrimp Rémoulade, 41–43
Fried Rabbit, 201
Fried Squirrel with Gravy, 202
fritters, corn, 113
fritters, rice, 96
frog legs, 204

giblets, chicken, 88–89
Ginger Ale-Spiked Sweet Potatoes, 58
Gingery Crisp Watermelon-Rind Pickles, 213–14
grapes
    Grape-Leaf Pickles, 215
    Muscadine Meringue Pie, 248–49
    Scuppernong Sweet-Potato Pie, 247–48

gravy
    Breakfast Shrimp Gravy, 17
    Butterbean Gravy, 18
    Country Ham with Redeye Gravy, 20–21
    Cream Gravy, 166–67
    Creole Red Gravy, 18–19
    Mississippi Madras Okra Gravy, 21
    Oyster Gravy, 22
    Roan Mountain Corn Gravy, 23
    Sawmill Gravy, 24
    Sopping Chocolate, 25
    Tomato Gravy, 19–20
green beans
    Country Cooked Green Beans with New Potatoes, 32–33
    Dilly Beans, 221
green tomatoes
    Fried Green Tomatoes and Shrimp Rémoulade, 41–43
    Piccalilli, 217
greens. See also specific greens
    Brown Butter Creamed Winter Greens, 70–71
    Gumbo z'Herbes, 72–74
    Skillet Greens, 75
Griddle Cakes, Cushaw, 39–40
grillades, 109
grits
    Awendaw Spoonbread, 102
    Basic Grits, 107
    Cheese Grits Casserole, 108
    Grits and Grillades, 109
    Limpin' Susan, 90
    Slow-Cooker Grits, 107
    Smothered Quail and Stone-Ground Grits, 205
gumbo
    Duck Gumbo, 199–200
    Gumbo z'Herbes, 72–74
    Seafood Gumbo, 183

ham
    Country Ham with Redeye Gravy, 20–21
    Gumbo z'Herbes, 72–74
    Ham Hock Broth, 69
    Oyster Gravy, 22
    Root Beer Glazed Ham, 160
Herbed Salt, 57
hominy, 183–84

Hot Sausage Balls, 12
hush puppies, 114–16

ice cream
    Boiled Peanut and Sorghum Swirl
        Ice Cream, 251–52
    Peach Ice Cream, 252
Indian dumplings, 112

jambalaya
    Avery Island Jambalaya, 92–93
    Red Jambalaya, 91
jams and jellies
    Pepper Jelly Vinaigrette, 223–24
    Strawberry Jam, 225
Jell-O, 49
Jerusalem Artichoke Relish, 60

kale
    Brown Butter Creamed Winter Greens, 70–71
    Gumbo z'Herbes, 72–74
    Skillet Greens, 75
Kentucky Hoppin' John, 89
kidney beans, 153–54
Killed Lettuce, 74–75

Leather Britches, 216
Lella's mayonnaise, 5–6
lettuce
    Gumbo z'Herbes, 72–74
    Killed Lettuce, 74–75
Limpin' Susan, 90
livers, chicken
    Country-Fried Chicken Livers, 134
    Dirty Rice, 87
    Mushroom Dirty Rice, 88
livers, pork, 146–47

Macaroni and Cheese, 40–41
Macaroni Pudding, 41
Madras curry powder, 21
mayonnaise, 5–6
meats. *See also specific meats*
    Grits and Grillades, 109
    Mississippi Delta Hot Tamales, 116–18
    organ meats, 87
    Souse Meat, 154–55
Miracle Drop Biscuits, 106

mirlitons, 37
Mississippi Delta Hot Tamales, 116–18
Mississippi Madras Okra Gravy, 21
Molasses-Brined Wild Turkey Breast with
    Bourbon Pan Sauce, 203
mullet, smoked, 188
Muscadine Meringue Pie, 248–49
Mushroom Dirty Rice, 88–89
mustard greens
    Brown Butter Creamed Winter Greens, 70–71
    Gumbo z'Herbes, 72–74
    Skillet Greens, 75

noodles
    Macaroni and Cheese, 40–41
    Macaroni Pudding, 41
    Venison and Noodles, 206
North Carolina Brunswick Stew, 152

okra
    Chicken Purloo, 85–86
    Crowder Peas with Potlikker, 33
    Limpin' Susan, 90
    Mississippi Madras Okra Gravy, 21
    Okra and Butterbean Succotash, 36
    Okra Tempura, 45–46
    Pickled Okra, 223
    Skillet-Fried Okra, 45
    Spicy Okra Refrigerator Pickles, 222
onions
    Caramelized Onion Pudding, 62
    Drippings-Cooked Potatoes, Onions,
        Turnips, and Carrots, 56
    Spring Onion Puree, 63
organ meats, 87
Osso Buco of Frog Legs, 204
oysters
    Eggplant, Oyster, and Tasso Gratin, 35–36
    Oyster Dressing, 179–80
    Oyster Gravy, 22
    Oyster Patties, 180
    Oyster Stew, 181
    Seafood Gumbo, 183

Pan-Fried Soft-Shell Crabs, 188–89
parsnips
    Chicken and Root Vegetable Hot Pot, 59
    Root Cellar Gratin, 57

Parsons Vegetable Beef Stew, 167–68
pastry
    cream cheese crust, 250
    pie crust, 129–30, 245–46, 250
    Sweet Pastry Dough, 245–46
Pawpaw Sauce, 256–57
peaches
    Peach Ice Cream, 252
    Peach Leather, 224–25
peanuts
    Boiled Peanut and Sorghum Swirl Ice
       Cream, 251–52
    Boiled Peanuts, 10–11
    Boiled-Peanut Beurre Blanc, 174
    Deep Fried Peanuts, 11
    Peanut Brittle, 254
    Peanut Soup, 48
peas, crowder, 33
pecans
    Pecan Sorghum Tarts, 245–46
    Spiced Pecans, 10
    Texas Pralines, 255
Pepper Jelly Vinaigrette, 223–24
Persimmon Pudding, 243
Piccalilli, 217
pickles
    Appalachian Pickle Beans and Corn, 211–12
    Dilly Beans, 221
    Fried Dill Pickles with Comeback Sauce,
       212–13
    Gingery Crisp Watermelon-Rind Pickles,
       213–14
    Grape-Leaf Pickles, 215
    Pickled Eggs, 217–18
    Pickled Okra, 223
    Spicy Okra Refrigerator Pickles, 222
    Yellow Squash Pickles, 220–21
pie crust, 129–30, 245–46, 250
pies
    Muscadine Meringue Pie, 248–49
    Pecan Sorghum Tarts, 245–46
    Scuppernong Sweet-Potato Pie, 247–48
    Sweet Tea Lemon Chess Pie, 249–50
    Tomato Pie, 44
pimento cheese
    Blue Ribbon Pimento Cheese, 5–6
    Pimento Cheese Hush Puppies, 115–16

pimentos, 5, 61, 115, 220
Pine-Bark Stew, 176
Poke Sallet, 72
pork. See also sausage
    backbones, 145
    Boudin Blanc, 146–47
    Carnitas, 143, 145
    Chaudin, 148
    chitlins, 144
    chops, 91, 155–56
    cracklings, 150
    ears, 154–55
    feet, 154–55
    ground, 148, 179–80
    ham, 20–21, 22, 72–74, 160
    livers, 146–47
    Mississippi Delta Hot Tamales, 116–18
    North Carolina Brunswick Stew, 152
    Pork and Sauerkraut, 157–58
    Pork Backbone Stew, 145
    Pork Roast, 150–51
    Pork Shoulder and Sauce, 159
    Red Beans and Rice, 153–54
    Red Jambalaya, 91
    ribs, 143, 157–58
    roast, 150–51
    Root Beer Glazed Ham, 160
    shoulder, 116–18, 143, 146–47, 150–51, 159
    stomach, 148
    Stuffed Pork Chops, 155–56
possum, 198
potatoes
    Carolina Fish Muddle, 175
    Chicken and Root Vegetable Hot Pot, 59
    Country Cooked Green Beans with New
       Potatoes, 32–33
    Drippings-Cooked Potatoes, Onions,
       Turnips, and Carrots, 56
    Everlasting Refrigerator Rolls, 118–19
    Root Cellar Gratin, 57
    Shout Hallelujah Potato Salad, 61
pralines, 255
puddings
    Bread Pudding with Bourbon Crème
       Anglaise, 241–42
    Caramelized Onion Pudding, 62
    Creamy Corn Pudding, 31

Fancy-pants Banana Pudding, 244–45
Macaroni Pudding, 41
Persimmon Pudding, 243
Rice Pudding, 95

quail
Avery Island Jambalaya, 92–93
Smothered Quail and Stone-Ground Grits, 205

rabbit, 201
raccoon, 198
Red Beans and Rice, 153–54
Red Jambalaya, 91
Red Velvet Cake, 238–39
Refried Black-Eyed Peas, 34
relish, Jerusalem artichoke, 60
rémoulade, 42, 137
Revelatory Caramel Cake, 231–32
rice
Avery Island Jambalaya, 92–93
Calas, 96
Chicken Bog, 131
Chicken Purloo, 85–86
Dirty Rice, 87
fritters, 96
grits, 90
Kentucky Hoppin' John, 89
Mushroom Dirty Rice, 88–89
Red Beans and Rice, 153–54
Red Jambalaya, 91
Rice Pudding, 95
Rice-Fried Catfish, 191
Savannah Red Rice, 93–94
Spinach and Rice Casserole, 94–95
Roan Mountain Corn Gravy, 23
rolls, refrigerator, 118–19
Root Beer Glazed Ham, 160
Root Cellar Gratin, 56–57
root vegetables. *See also specific root vegetables*
Brown Butter Creamed Winter Greens, 70
Chicken and Roasted Root Vegetable Pot
Pie, 128–30
Chicken and Root Vegetable Hot Pot, 59
Drippings-Cooked Potatoes, Onions,
Turnips, and Carrots, 56
Parsons Vegetable Beef Stew, 167–68
Root Cellar Gratin, 56

round steak, 109, 166–67
roux, 145
rutabaga, 57

salad dressings
Pepper Jelly Vinaigrette, 223–24
Poppy Seed Dressing, 49
salads
Ambrosia Fruit Salad, 257
Carolina Coleslaw, 79
Cranberry Congealed Salad with Poppy Seed
Dressing, 49
Shout Hallelujah Potato Salad, 61
Tomato and Watermelon Salad, 43
West Indies Salad, 189–90
Salmon Croquettes, 182
salt, herbed, 57
sauces
barbecue sauce, 159
béchamel sauce, 70
Bourbon Crème Anglaise, 203
bourbon pan sauce, 203
Comeback Sauce, 212–13
Pawpaw Sauce, 256–57
sauerkraut
Pork and Sauerkraut, 157–58
Sauerkraut, 219
Sauerkraut-Stuffed Smoked Turkey, 220
sausage
Avery Island Jambalaya, 92–93
Boudin Blanc, 146–47
Country Breakfast Sausage, 149
Dirty Rice, 87
Duck and Andouille Étouffée, 199
Gumbo z'Herbes, 72–74
Hot Sausage Balls, 12
Kentucky Hoppin' John, 89
Red Jambalaya, 91
Sawmill Gravy, 24
Savannah Red Rice, 93–94
Sawmill Gravy, 24
Sazerac Tassies, 253–54
Scuppernong Sweet-Potato Pie, 247–48
seafood. *See* fish; *and specific fish and shellfish*
Seafood Gumbo, 183
Shad Roe with Hominy, 183–84
shellfish. *See specific shellfish*

shortcakes, 240–41
Shout Hallelujah Potato Salad, 61
shrimp
    Barbecue Shrimp and Sweet-Potato Tarts,
      186–87
    Breakfast Shrimp Gravy, 17
    Fried Green Tomatoes and Shrimp
      Rémoulade, 41–43
    Limpin' Susan, 90
    Seafood Gumbo, 183
    Shrimp Paste, 185–86
    Stuffed Mirliton, 37
Skillet Greens, 75
Skillet-Fried Okra, 45
Slow-Cooker Crab Dip, 176 77
Slow-Cooker Grits, 107
Smoked Mullet Dip, 188
Smothered Cabbage, 78
Smothered Quail and Stone-Ground Grits, 205
snapper, red, 176
soft-shell crabs, 188–89
Sopping Chocolate, 25
sorrell, 71
soups
    Carrot Soup with Bourbon and Ginger, 55
    Cream of Sorrell Soup, 71
    Peanut Soup, 48
    Vegetable Soup, 46–47
Souse Meat, 154–55
Spiced Pecans, 10
Spicy Okra Refrigerator Pickles, 222
Spicy Turnip Greens, 76
spinach
    Gumbo z'Herbes, 72–74
    Spinach and Rice Casserole, 94–95
spoonbread, 102
spreads, 6–7
Spring Onion Puree, 63
squash, yellow
    Summer Squash Soufflé, 38
    Yellow Squash Pickles, 220–21
squirrel
    Fried Squirrel with Gravy, 202
    North Carolina Brunswick Stew, 152
Sriracha and Citrus Rémoulade, 137

stew meat, beef, 72–74, 167–68
stews
    North Carolina Brunswick Stew, 152
    Oyster Stew, 181
    Parsons Vegetable Beef Stew, 167–68
    Pine-Bark Stew, 176
    Pork Backbone Stew, 145
strawberries
    Brown Sugar Shortcakes with Strawberries
      and Cream, 240–41
    Strawberry Jam, 225
Stuffed Mirliton, 37
Stuffed Pork Chops, 155–56
succotash, 36
Summer Squash Soufflé, 38
sunchokes, 60
Sweet Pastry Dough, 245–46
sweet potatoes
    Barbecue Shrimp and Sweet-Potato Tarts,
      186–87
    Braised Coon or Possum with Sweet
      Potatoes, 198
    Chicken and Root Vegetable Hot Pot, 59
    Ginger Ale-Spiked Sweet Potatoes, 58
    Scuppernong Sweet-Potato Pie,
      247–48
Sweet Tea Lemon Chess Pie, 249–50
sweetbreads, 135–36

tamales, 116–18
Tankie's Cornbread, 110–11
tarts, 245–46
tassies, 253–54
tasso, 35–36
tea, 249–50
Texas Pralines, 255
tomatoes
    Chicken Bog, 131
    Fried Green Tomatoes and Shrimp
      Rémoulade, 41–43
    Okra and Butterbean Succotash, 36
    Piccalilli, 217
    Tomato and Watermelon Salad, 43
    Tomato Gravy, 19–20
    Tomato Pie, 11

turkey
    Molasses-Brined Wild Turkey Breast with
        Bourbon Pan Sauce, 203
    Sauerkraut-Stuffed Smoked Turkey, 220
turnip greens
    Gumbo z'Herbes, 72–74
    Spicy Turnip Greens, 76
turnips
    Drippings-Cooked Potatoes, Onions,
        Turnips, and Carrots, 56
    Root Cellar Gratin, 57

veal, 109
Vegetable Soup, 46–47

Venison and Noodles, 206
Vidalia onions, 63

walnuts, black, 232–33
watermelon
    Gingery Crisp Watermelon-Rind Pickles,
        213–14
    Tomato and Watermelon Salad, 43
West Indies Salad, 189–90
white beans, 77
White Loaf Bread, 120

Yellow Squash Pickles, 220–21

CREDITS

In the spirit of the community cookbook genre, we have attempted to present all recipe contributors, whether they be book authors or home cooks, as equals. In a few cases, publishers required formalized credits. Those follow.

"Creamy Corn Pudding" (p. 31) from *The Foster's Market Cookbook: Favorite Recipes for Morning, Noon, and Night* by Sara Foster, copyright © 2002 by Sara Foster. Used by permission of Random House, Inc.

"Eggplant, Oyster, and Tasso Gratin" (pp. 35–36) from *Crescent City Cooking: Unforgettable Recipes from Susan Spicer's New Orleans* by Susan Spicer with Paula Disbrowe, copyright © 2007 by Susan Spicer. Used by permission of Alfred A. Knopf, a division of Random House, Inc.

"Stuffed Mirliton" (p. 37) from *Creole Soul: New Orleans Cooking with a Soulful Twist* by Austin Leslie and Marie Rudd Posey. Published in 2000 by De Simonin Publications.

"Roots" (p. 51) by Gary Snyder, from *Regarding Wave*, copyright © 1970 by Gary Snyder. Reprinted by permission of New Directions Publishing Company.

"Benne Seed Biscuits" (p. 104) from *A Love Affair with Southern Cooking*, by Jean Anderson. Copyright 2007. Reprinted with permission by William Morrow / An Imprint of HarperCollins.

"Boudin Blanc" (pp. 146–47) from *Real Cajun: Rustic Home Cooking from Donald Link's Louisiana* by Donald Link with Paula Disbrowe. Copyright 2009 by Donald Link. Used by permission of Clarkson Potter/Publishers, an imprint of the Crown Publishing Group, a division of Random House, Inc.

"Pickled Eggs" (pp. 217–18) from *Craig Claiborne's Southern Cooking* by Craig Claiborne, foreword by John T. Edge and Georgeanna Milam. Copyright 2007. Used by permission of the University of Georgia Press by arrangement of Crown Publishers, a division of Random House, Inc.

"Brown Sugar Shortcakes with Strawberries and Cream" (pp. 240–41) from Virginia Willis's *Bon Appetit, Y'all: Recipes and Stories from Three Generations of Southern Cooking* (Berkeley: Ten Speed Press, 2008)